Genocide and Rescue

Genocide and Rescue

The Holocaust in Hungary 1944

Edited by
David Cesarani

Oxford • New York

First published in 1997 by
Berg
Editorial offices:
150 Cowley Road, Oxford, OX4 1JJ, UK
70 Washington Square South, New York, NY 10012, USA

Berg is an imprint of Oxford International Publishers Ltd.

Library of Congress Cataloging-in-Publication Data

A catalogue record for this book is available from the Library of Congress.

British Library Cataloguing-in-Publication Data

A catalogue record for this book is available from the British Library.

ISBN 1 85973 121 X (Cloth)
1 85973 126 0 (Paper)

Typeset by JS Typesetting, Wellingborough, Northants.
Printed in the United Kingdom by WBC Book Manufacturers, Bridgend, Mid Glamorgan.

Contents

Acknowledgements

This volume grew out of a gathering of historians in London on 17–18 April 1994, organized by the Institute of Contemporary History and Wiener Library, to mark the fiftieth anniversary of the Nazi occupation of Hungary and the implementation of the 'Final Solution' on Hungarian territory. Not all the papers could be adapted for publication and presented here and I would like to thank Dr Avihu Rosen of 'Moreshet' at Givat Haviva and Dr Meir Sompolinsky of 'Mikve Israel' High School in Israel, Dr Andras Ban, Teleki Laszlo Foundation at the Institute for Central Europe, Budapest, and Dr Maria Schmidt of Budapest for their contributions. I would also like to thank Mrs Anne Beale, Miss Gerta Regensburger and the staff of the Wiener Library for their essential administrative assistance.

The conference was generously supported by The Lord Ashdown Charitable Settlement; The Paul Balint Charitable Trust; The R. M. Burton Charitable Trust; CP Holdings Ltd; The Sue Hammerson Foundation; The Jack Goldhill Charitable Trust; The Rena and Robert Lewin Charitable Trust; The Sir Sigmund Sternberg Charitable Foundation.

I would also like to thank Kathryn Earle of Berg Publishers who has been a patient midwife to this book. Professor Braham helped to secure additional material from Hungarian scholars. Since the conference took place the number of those involved has been sadly diminished. Professor Asher Cohen of Haifa University died at a tragically young age in 1996. Rabbi Hugo Gryn, a survivor of the deportations to Auschwitz-Birkenau in the summer of 1944, closed the conference with reflections that were characteristically illuminating, wise and sensitive. He was a great friend of the Wiener Library and I was personally privileged to learn much from him. Hugo Gryn died in August 1996 and it is to his memory that this book is dedicated.

David Cesarani

—1—

Introduction

David Cesarani

I

One man's experiences may serve as a point of entry into one of the most appalling human tragedies of this century. On 22 March 1944, the Jewish Hungarian-born writer Arthur Koestler wrote in his diary 'What a misery to be in a minority'. At the time he was living in London and had achieved success as a novelist and journalist. But he had drunk from the bitter cup of exile and was well acquainted with Nazi barbarity. Three days earlier the Germans had occupied the country of his birth, where his mother and most of his family still lived. He knew what they could expect.[1]

As a member of the Communist Party in Berlin in 1931–2 Koestler had fought against the politically ascending Nazis. He had been imprisoned in Franco's Spain in 1937 and was nearly shot for his anti-Fascist work. In 1940 he escaped from France to Britain having been twice interned by the French in camps for 'aliens', mainly Spanish Republican exiles and Jewish refugees from Nazism, which subsequently became antechambers for the Nazi *Konzentrationslager*. While in the British Pioneer Corps in 1941–2, Koestler tried desperately to interest British politicians in schemes to rescue anti-Fascists and Jews from the French internment camps. He was simultaneously struggling to extract his estranged wife, a German Jew, from Marseilles. The Germans occupied Vichy France in November 1942, just before she could take advantage of the ship's passage and visa to Cuba that he had arranged for her.[2]

Koestler became one of the small band of people in Britain who sought to alert public opinion to the nature of the catastrophe engulfing the Jews across the English Channel.[3] In November 1942, he had met Jan Karski, a courier for the Polish underground, who brought the West an authoritative eye-witness account of conditions in the Warsaw Ghetto and the operation of the death camps in Poland. On the strength of Karski's testimony Koestler wrote an account of the gassings for the BBC Radio European Service. It was broadcast in June 1943.[4]

Koestler also incorporated into his current novel, *Arrival and Departure*, what he had heard from the envoy. Part of the novel describes the murder in gas vans of Jews taken from a 'mixed transport'. This section was published in *Horizon*, the leading British literary magazine of the war years, in October 1943. It aroused controversy and was condemned by several British writers as propaganda. Koestler was outraged. In a letter replying to his critics he asked why intellectuals who would never dream of questioning facts about literature, for example, insisted on querying something as grave as the mass murder of Jews.

> There is no excuse for you – for it is your duty to know and to be haunted by your knowledge. As long as you don't feel, against reason and independently of reason, ashamed to be alive while others are put to death; not guilty, sick, humiliated because you were spared, you will remain what you are, an accomplice by omission.[5]

Still incensed Koestler wrote 'On Disbelieving Atrocities', an essay that was published in the *New York Times Magazine* in January 1944. It was a perceptive explanation of how people can deny or evade information which is too unsettling or horrible to contemplate. In it he commented famously, 'Statistics don't bleed.' The number of Jews being murdered was so vast it was incomprehensible; and it was happening a long way away. Distance and the sheer scale of the disaster conspired with dullness of imagination.[6]

Just a few weeks before the German onslaught against the Jews of Hungary, Koestler had thus experienced the frustration attending efforts to awaken the public to the Jewish fate. Once the Hungarian Jews were tipped into the maw of the 'Final Solution', Koestler experienced the far more nauseating frustration of seeing attempts to save them come to nothing.

In September 1943 Koestler had been introduced to Chaim Weizmann, the president of the World Zionist Organization. He saw him almost monthly until the end of 1944. He also met Moshe Shertok (later Sharret), Weizmann's right-hand man, and served as a member of the Anglo-Palestine Committee which met under the chairmanship of the wealthy British Zionist Israel Sieff. This group included Sieff's brother-in-law Simon Marks, Guy de Rothschild, Kingsley Martin, editor of the *New Statesman*, Michael Foot, Labour Party activist and left-wing journalist, David Astor, editor of the *Observer*, and Frank Packenham, then a rising Labour politician.[7]

The German occupation of Hungary diverted the energies of the committee from its pro-Zionist work. In May and June Koestler continued to see Weizmann, but all business was overwhelmed by the crisis in Hungary where the Germans had begun to deport Jews to the concentration camp and extermination centre at Auschwitz.[8] Thanks to his involvement with Weizmann and Shertok, Koestler became privy to an extraordinary offer by the Nazis to exchange Hungarian Jews for trucks and goods. On 10 June he reported in his diary that Weizmann 'says that Hungarian Zionist leader Brand arrived Istanbul in Gestapo plane with Nazi offer to let 800,000 Hungarian Jews go to Iberian peninsula [*sic*] if allies deliver 10,000 lorries, tea, coffee etc. Shertok went to negotiate – i.e. to temporise'. Koestler was even vouchsafed a copy of the top-secret notes of the conversation between Joel Brand and Shertok in Aleppo, where Brand, one of the emissaries selected by Adolf Eichmann to convey the deal, had been detained by the British.[9]

Koestler was personally affected in a dramatic way. He wrote in his diary, 'First batch 2,000 Jews gassed in Osswetchian [*sic*] Mother . . .' Koestler had last heard of his mother, via relatives in Switzerland, in February 1944. After that there was a ghastly silence. In desperation he tried to get her a Palestine immigration certificate which offered a slender chance that the Nazis would not deport her to a death camp but hold her as a hostage. Several of his friends and acquaintances in political circles assumed the worst: Koestler received condolence letters from Fenner Brockway, MP, and Harold Laski, chairman of the Labour Party.[10]

Koestler also played an active role in the development of a plan for bombing Auschwitz-Birkenau. He recorded on 11 July that he had 'Lunch with Shertock [*sic*] and John [Strachey]. Worked out the case for bombing the death camps, made drafts sent it to John . . .' The proposal was taken to the Allied governments, but it failed to carry weight with the British or US bomber force commanders in spite of receiving Churchill's personal endorsement.[11]

As the contributions to this volume show, Eichmann's offer was treated with extreme caution by the Allies who suspected correctly that it was a device to lure them into negotiations that would alarm the Russians. The British also feared that if the offer were genuine any Jews allowed to leave Hungary would want to enter Palestine. They consequently did their best to frustrate the rescue scheme.

Koestler was embittered by the apparent lack of official or public concern while Hungarian Jews were slaughtered. 'One more funereal lunch with Weizmann', he wrote on 8 July. 'So far 400,000 Jews deported from Hungary, 100,000 killed. Eden charmingly indignant. Not one paper-headline for 5 million Jews. But for 50 British Officers – what a ballyhoo.' Meanwhile, the Brand negotiations were leaked to the press and the rescue scheme collapsed amidst recriminations between the Foreign Office and the Jewish Agency for Palestine.[12]

Shortly afterwards Koestler suffered a breakdown and retreated to the country. In solitude he reflected on the Europe-wide disaster, against which he had warned, that had now swallowed up his family, mocking his puny efforts to avert it.

> According to JTA [Jewish Telegraphic Agency] report Jews deported to Oswiecim die by new gas manufactured in Hamburg, thrown into death-chamber by SS-men wearing gas-masks; the victims (c. 1,000 at a time) are stripped naked under the pretext of having shower – it takes approximately 3 minutes. Or if sick, phenol injections over heart. – So that is how mama died, or is dying, in this minute, or shall die, – I have tried, all day, to analyse what's going on now.[13]

Later in July the Anglo-Palestine group heard Michael Foot address the implications of the massacre of Hungarian Jewry. Shertok provided details of the Brand negotiations which Koestler described as 'grand guignol – horrifying beyond words'. The group decided that the Allies must be asked to protect the Jews still alive in Hungary. They also came up with the bizarre idea that Koestler should himself go to Budapest with George Kuhlman, from the League of Nations High Commission for Refugees. Needless to say this suicidal proposal was dropped but it says a lot about Koestler's state of mind. Until the deportations were suspended he, Victor Gollancz, Foot and Shertok continued to lobby the government to act.[14]

Around 25 August 1944, Koestler received a telegram informing him that his mother was miraculously still alive. But after the war he would learn that in the weeks between 15 May and 7 July 1944 almost every other member of his family had been murdered in Auschwitz-Birkenau, along with over 325,000 Hungarian Jews.[15]

Koestler's story encapsulates much of the tragedy of Hungary's Jews. He and his family epitomized the peculiar trajectory which Hungarian Jewry followed into modernity and the singularity of Jewish assimilation in Hungary. Arthur Koestler, born in 1905, was raised as a proud Hungarian. Despite experiencing local anti-Semitism from the 1900s onwards, and more viciously after 1919, his parents remained in Budapest. Koestler was sent to school and university in Austria to avoid the *numerus clausus* enforced against Jews seeking higher education in his own country, but his parents saw no difficulty in staying in Hungary.[16]

By 1940, Koestler had gained first-hand knowledge of the evils of Fascism and Nazism. Yet he found it hard to convince people in Britain of the danger faced by Jews and anti-Nazis. He reacted with commendable alacrity to the German occupation of Hungary, but even working in the company of influential Jewish leaders and British political figures he could make little impression on official circles. In London he could follow the course of the genocide, but could do little to stop it. There was no problem of information or hard evidence: his analysis of the insensate observer was horribly vindicated.

II

In the unremittingly grim record of the Holocaust no single chapter is quite so awful as the fate which befell Hungary's Jewish population. At the beginning of 1944 about 750,000 Jews lived on Hungarian territory even though all around them Jewish communities had been uprooted and destroyed. On 19 March 1944 the German army crossed the border of its former ally to forestall diplomatic initiatives by the Hungarian government to take their country out of the war. Adolf Eichmann, the SS Colonel who ran Office IVb4 of the Gestapo, which dealt with 'Jewish affairs', and a small cohort of SS men followed. Eichmann had by this time amassed years of experience in deporting Jews from all over Europe to the death camps in Poland. With the full cooperation of the local administration the Eichmann *Kommando* quickly set about enumerating, plundering, concentrating and deporting the country's Jewish population. Between 15 May and 7 July, 437,000 Jews were rounded up and sent to the concentration and extermination camp complex at Auschwitz-Birkenau in Upper Silesia. Only a fraction were selected for work, and of them but a few thousand survived.[17]

This whirlwind of destruction, resembling a genocide within the genocide, was unique in terms of the speed and intensity with which it was executed and the conditions under which it occurred. German military power and diplomatic influence were on the wane. For nearly three years the Jews of Hungary had been able to monitor Nazi policy towards Europe's Jewish inhabitants. From the first hours of the occupation the Western Allies were able to follow the anti-Jewish measures being implemented there. Jews in the free world, now better placed than earlier to intervene with their governments or to act independently in aid of the Jews in Europe, watched the onslaught progress. Most crucially, the Nazi leadership seemed willing to trade Jewish lives for military material or diplomatic advantage.

Yet to all appearances the Jews of Hungary meekly surrendered their rights, their wealth, their property and finally their lives. Instances of resistance were few and late. Until nearly the end, rescue schemes seemed to benefit a tiny minority of Jews. Meanwhile there was less of an outcry in the West than there had been following the initial disclosure of the 'Final Solution' in late 1942. There were no mass protests by Jews or non-Jews in London or Washington. Although Allied air power now stretched to Auschwitz-Birkenau there was no military intervention on behalf of the doomed Jews. Rescue plans conveyed to the outside world became mired in doubts about Nazi intentions and were fatally compromised by diplomatic entanglements in the Middle East and Stalin's adverse reaction.[18]

The dilemmas and questions surrounding the downfall of Hungarian Jewry resonate to this day in every country touched by the disaster. In post-Communist Hungary scholars are now free to delve into their country's past. Between 1945 and the early 1980s, Hungarian historiography was warped by the domination of the Soviet Union. For fear of validating Zionism, a form of 'bourgeois nationalism', the specific fate of the Jews under the Nazis was played down. German Fascists and a few local collaborators who shared their malign ideology were held responsible for the destruction of the country's Jews and its more general devastation. Even when official anti-Zionism, which was in reality a conduit for old-fashioned Jew-hatred, was relaxed so that the Holocaust could be more openly discussed the targets for obloquy were typically the discredited aristocratic conservatives or the Catholic Church. From 1989, however, with the disjunction of the Eastern Bloc, scholarship and politics were both freed from Soviet mind-control.

As Randolph Braham has pointed out, this had contradictory results. The 'nationalist-populist reaction to 45 years of Soviet-guided Communism in some cases acquired a xenophobic, anti-Jewish coloration'. The 'Jewish Question' resurfaced after decades of being repressed or displaced onto 'anti-Zionism'. For almost the first time the Holocaust could be discussed honestly. Research was at last published which showed that the deportations had been carried out by Hungarian policemen and soldiers with the cooperation of the entire civil administration and with the passive support of the population. Yet this version of history threatened the nationalist and populist veneration of the pre-Soviet and anti-Communist leaders who had allied Hungary with Nazi Germany. Consequently, politics soon led to attempts to whitewash the conservative wartime leaders. The 'Jewish Question' and the Holocaust were widely debated in the free Hungarian elections in 1990 and in the controversy surrounding the decision in 1993 to repatriate and reinter in Hungary the remains of the wartime leader Admiral Horthy. The Jews were accused of placing selfish interests before those of their country: the myth of the Jews as 'alien' was resurrected in reply to the attempt by historians (not necessarily Jewish) to document their deracination from their native soil and subsequent destruction under the guise of action against 'alien Jews'.[19]

Several of the historical questions addressed in this volume are thus of burning contemporary importance. How significant was indigenous anti-Semitism in Hungary before 1944 and what role did it play in the fate of the Jews? How much did Admiral Horthy, the head of state throughout this period, know of the fate that was in store for the Jews following the German occupation and the installation of a puppet regime over which he continued to preside and to which he gave the mantle of legitimacy?

Inevitably, the Holocaust dominates much of the present agenda of Jews in the Diaspora and Israel. Bernard Wasserstein has gone so far as to argue that 'The central position that the Holocaust has come to occupy in contemporary Jewish self-understanding threatens to become an almost necrophiliac obsession.'[20] Such strictures are unfair because, as is shown by the examples given above, the Holocaust is far from dead yet. Jews may be obsessed with it because many survivors and perpetrators are still alive, as are the issues. This is nowhere truer than in Israel where interpretations of the Holocaust are important for understanding (and influencing) Jewish policy and behaviour. As Michael Marrus and others have pointed out, the Holocaust has been used and abused by successive Jewish leaders and Israeli politicians to justify various lines of policy.[21]

In Israeli society it has also acted as a means by which the young state has defined itself. By chance, the Holocaust in Hungary became one of the first, and remains one of the most important, points of definition. In 1947, Rudolf Kasztner, one of the leaders of the Budapest Relief and Rescue Committee and a veteran Zionist, settled in Palestine. He twice stood for election to the Knesset (Parliament) of Israel on the ticket of the Mapai (Labour) Party. In 1952, while he held a minor government post, he was attacked in a pamphlet which claimed he had collaborated with the Nazis in the annihilation of Hungarian Jewry. The attack was written by an elderly Hungarian Jewish survivor called Malkiel Grunwald. The government prosecuted Grunwald for slandering a government official, but Grunwald's lawyer, Shmuel Tamir, ended up putting Kasztner and Mapai on trial. Tamir was a member of the opposition Herut Party. He saw the story of Brand's thwarted rescue mission and the role of Kasztner as a way to blacken Shertok, the Israeli Foreign Minister, and Mapai, for whom Kasztner had worked before 1944. He convinced the judge that Kasztner had known the fate of deported Jews, but concealed the truth from the mass of his Hungarian co-religionists as a service to the Nazis. In return, Grunwald alleged, Kasztner was allowed to save one trainload of Jews which he packed with members of his family and political cronies.[22]

In the course of the hearings before the Jerusalem District Court, which began in January 1954, and the verdict in June 1955, Grunwald and Tamir seemed to answer the troubling question of why the Jewish community in Hungary had failed to heed the warnings from all around them in 1941–4, and why the Zionists, always a more militant element, achieved so little in the way of rescue or resistance. The government, acting on behalf of Kasztner, lost the libel suit. An appeal was launched, but Kasztner was assassinated in Tel Aviv in March 1957 before the Israeli Supreme Court reversed the verdict of the lower court and essentially exonerated him. As well as correcting important facts in the case, the ultimate judgment exposed the simplifications in which Tamir had indulged. Yet Tamir had articulated the views of a substantial segment of Israeli opinion and it took many more years for the revised verdict to gain wide acceptance.

In the late 1940s and for most of the 1950s, Jews who had arrived in Palestine before 1940 or been born there tended to see Diaspora Jews as deserving their fate. They had chosen to ignore the Zionist message and remained in the vulnerable Diaspora, guided by leaders who eschewed energetic, independent action in favour of obedience to the law and reliance on the national authorities. Kasztner's 'betrayal' and the 'passivity' of Hungarian Jews were explained by the axioms of Zionist ideology. However, to right-wing Zionists like Tamir, the Mapai activists in the Diaspora and the Zionist leaders in London who failed to save Hungarian Jews had reappeared as the establishment in Israel. In a vivid apophthegm that yoked history to politics, the radical editor Uri Avneri wrote in June 1955 that 'The "who's who" of the Kasztner Trial is the "who's who" of the state of Israel.'[23]

It was not until the 1960s that Israeli attitudes towards the Holocaust and Diaspora Jews began to change. Through the Eichmann trial Israelis learned more about the machinery of mass destruction and, conversely, the extent of and limits to resistance to the Nazis. The Six Day War was a lesson in vulnerability, as well as Jewish solidarity. Identification with the victims of the Holocaust was deepened by the Yom Yippur War in 1973 and the prolonged period of diplomatic isolation, sharpened by anti-Semitism on the world stage, which followed it. By this time, the agonising dilemmas of Hungarian Jews were more sensitively appreciated. The research presented in this volume gives evidence of this nuanced approach and seems light-years from the harsh, judgemental statements of the 1950s.[24]

A fair evaluation of the behaviour of Jewish leaders in 1944 rests on understanding the context in which they acted and, hence, the stance taken by the Allies. Until the late 1960s the role played by the British and the Americans in the fate of Europe's Jews had largely escaped critical scrutiny. During the 1970s a number of landmark studies appeared that used newly released official documents to record the treatment of Jewish refugees from 1933 to 1940 and the paucity of rescue efforts in the 1940s. These studies by Walter Laqueur, Martin Gilbert, Bernard Wasserstein and David Wyman buried forever the notion that Western leaders did not know about the 'Final Solution', but opened a controversy about just how much they could have done even given accurate data about the genocide.[25]

The debate was not merely academic. It was initiated and is still taking place against a background of war, war crimes, mass murder and genocide in different parts of the world. The linkage of history to politics was made explicit in the most dramatic fashion when Elie Wiesel, a survivor of the Holocaust in Hungary, turned to President Clinton at the opening of the US National Holocaust Memorial Museum in Washington in 1993, and berated him for not committing the United States to intervention to prevent mass murder and ethnic cleansing in the war then raging in Bosnia-Herzegovina.

Wiesel gave voice to the predominant view, the one enshrined in the US National Holocaust Museum, that the West had indeed failed the Jews in 1940–5 and that it was now at risk of failing the people of Bosnia. Yet his perception was and is not uncontested. There is a serious debate about what was technically feasible in 1944 by way of rescue measures, including the bombing of Auschwitz.[26] There is also a growing sense of the complexity of Nazi intentions which, in turn, influenced Allied responses. It is relatively straightforward to work out whether it was possible effectively to bomb Auschwitz or the rail lines leading to it, although the moral dimension is far more complicated and may never be unequivocally resolved. By contrast, the lack of documents and the deep contradictions inherent to human behaviour render it more testing to determine what the Nazi leaders intended and, consequently, what was an appropriate response by the Allies.[27]

Were genuine possibilities for rescue opened up by despondent Nazi chieftains looking for a deal with the West? Or were promises of negotiations a feint intended to embarrass the Allies while Jews continued to pour into Auschwitz-Birkenau? Even if negotiations with the Nazis were out of the question, could more have been done by way of rescue work? These questions raise several more concerning the actions of Jews in the free world. Could they have done more to help or were they prisoners of myopic civil servants and politicians in Whitehall and the State Department who could see no further than winning the war? Jews in the West and in Palestine could not have physically rescued Jews from Birkenau or stopped the deportations, but should they have protested more strenuously and thereby persuaded the Allies to do more to help, perhaps by egging neutral powers into extending diplomatic protection to the Jews? Were Jews the victims of powerlessness or of an ideology that rendered them impotent? Instead of shifting the critical gaze onto the ideology of the bureaucrats and the leaders of the Allied powers, is it an example of blaming the victims to criticize Jewish responses when only Allied weapons or diplomacy could have had any effect?[28]

These questions can only be approached on the basis of painstaking research of the sort that is presented here. Some of it is based on new sources from the former Soviet archives or is the work of Hungarian historians whose voices, until now, have not been heard widely in the West.

III

Randolph Braham, the doyen of studies of the Holocaust in Hungary, roots the events of 1944 in the evolution of Hungarian Jewry and the Hungarian matrix over the preceding century. Although there is evidence of a Jewish presence in Hungary before even the arrival of the Magyar tribes and throughout the centuries of Magyar independence, the number of Jews declined precipitously after Hungary was conquered by the Turks in the sixteenth century. The Jews returned to Hungary in the modern era after the region was wrested back for Christendom by the Habsburgs. The first Jewish settlers came from Moravia, Bohemia and Austria. They were followed by an influx of Polish Jews drawn by the favourable conditions created by Joseph II's patent of toleration in 1780. The mass immigration of Jews to Hungary began in the 1830s and 1840s, stemming mainly from Galicia. These Jews quickly became the most energetic, mobile and talented sector of the Hungarian population.[29]

In 1800 Jews had formed 1.5 per cent of the population of Greater Hungary. By 1910 they had expanded to 5 per cent of the Hungarian population. In Budapest they grew from 16 per cent of the capital's population in 1876, to 21.5 per cent in 1900 and 23 per cent in 1910, earning the city the label 'Judapest' in the slang of Viennese anti-Semites. The Jews comprised over 40 per cent of all journalists, 52 per cent of all industrial employers, 59 per cent of medical personnel, 61 per cent of all lawyers, and 64 per cent of those engaged in trade and finance.[30] The Magyar ruling classes, the nobility and lesser gentry, embraced the Jews in the first decades of 'dualism', the era of Hungarian autonomy within the Habsburg Empire that commenced in 1867. The Jews were a ready-made middle class with no inhibitions about entering zealously into finance, trade and industry. In gratitude for the opportunities offered to them the Jews enthusiastically Magyarized, dispensing with Yiddish, dropping their traditional orientation towards Vienna and Berlin, and softening the contours of their Judaism. In the Jewish congresses of 1868–9, the lay leadership of Hungarian Jews opted for Reform Judaism, known locally as the Neolog variety. Although Orthodoxy never disappeared, it, along with the adherents of the 'Status Quo' tendency, were a minority within the Jewish population.[31]

From the 1890s, however, this happy 'community of interest' became increasingly troubled. Magyar nationalism had always been romantic, employing windy rhetoric to obscure the fissures permeating a multinational empire. The gentry who were once the backbone of liberal nationalism became increasingly conservative, anti-urban and chauvinistic as free trade and the depression in agricultural prices led them to financial ruin. A vicious cycle was set in motion as heightened Magyar assertiveness provoked nationalist unrest at the fringes of the Empire, especially in the Balkans. For the first time right-wing and anti-Jewish movements espousing the modern 'anti-Semitism' pioneered in Germany and Austria found a home in Hungary.[32]

All of these trends were felt to an extreme degree in the hothouse environment of Budapest, home to both the Hungarian ruling elite and the Jews.[33] By 1900, anti-Jewish feeling in the Hungarian capital was a well-remarked fact of life. In 1883 the metropolitan press had reported a blood-libel trial in the provincial town of Tisza-Elsar. The following year the first anti-Semitic deputies were elected to Parliament. In 1899 the respected Catholic Party politician Ottokár Prohászka proclaimed a 'Christian awakening' in Hungary. Although the anti-Semitic parties faded away, the effect of their propaganda did not. Social and athletic clubs, including the famous casinos, began to refuse Jewish applicants. Jewish and non-Jewish students brawled in the university. Budapest became increasingly segregated at an informal level, with Jewish and non-Jewish residential zones and streets for shopping or promenading that were patronized either by Jews or gentiles, but not both.[34]

Randolph Braham (chapter 2) stresses that the disastrous consequences of Hungary's participation in World War I radicalized and magnified anti-Jewish tendencies in Magyar nationalism. Hungary lost huge swathes of territory to the 'successor states' to the Habsburg Empire, but with them went the turbulent national minorities against whom the enthusiastically

Magyarized Jews had provided useful ballast. Since the Hungarian economy shrank too, the Jews also lost their economic value. From being indispensable adjuncts to the ruling class, they were turned into a precariously poised minority which was both resented and envied. Thanks to the role of so many Jews in the shortlived Hungarian Soviet Republic, or commune, they were feared and hated too. The Hungarian commune lasted for about 130 days under the leadership of Béla Kun, a Jewish intellectual. A high proportion of the Communists who filled the ranks of this brief regime were Jews, like Georg Lukács, a fact which provoked a savage anti-Jewish backlash after a Romanian army crushed the Communists and installed a conservative clique led by Admiral Horthy. Relations between Jews and Christians in Hungary never recovered from the events of 1919–20.[35]

A *numerus clausus* established by the government in 1920 to fix the percentage of Jews allowed to enter higher education symbolized the fallen status of the Jewish population. However, Hungarian Jews, like the Koestler family, failed to acknowledge the changing mood. Instead, they redoubled their protestations of loyalty to the Hungarian nation and state. They rejected any thought of appealing to the League of Nations for protection under the minority rights clauses of the peace treaty which Hungary had concluded with the Allies in 1919. Neither the leadership nor the mass of Hungarian Jews were inclined to perceive itself or to act as a threatened minority. Braham attributes this to self-deception, but in an interesting variation Asher Cohen argues that it resulted from a failure to see themselves as anything other than Hungarians of the Mosaic persuasion.[36] Their assimilationist ideology disarmed them since it forestalled collective political action: 'they refrained from taking any significant steps in the areas of vital importance to their existence, such as the legal status and the freedom to engage in all occupations. Jews in Hungary had no leaders because the Jews did not want leaders with either real or perceived political powers.'[37]

For this reason the Jews did nothing to oppose the anti-Jewish legislation passed in 1938, 1939 and 1941. Anti-Semitism was a staple element of Hungarian politics in the 1920s and 1930s, but Jews became habituated to it.[38] When it worsened under the premierships of Gyula Gombos (1932–6), Kálmán Darányi (1936–9) and László Bárdossy (1939–42), Jews attributed this to a natural consequence of Hungary's closer relations with the Third Reich. Anti-Jewish measures were shocking and damaging, but they could be rationalised as pragmatically rather than ideologically motivated acts.[39]

Whatever their cause Yehuda Don (chapter 3) shows that the anti-

Jewish laws gravely weakened Hungarian Jewry. Don emphasizes that the laws were rooted in indigenous Hungarian anti-Semitism and reflected a resentment of Jewish 'domination' of the economy. They rested on the 1935 Budapest census which was manipulated by 'rational' anti-Semites who claimed to be defending Hungary's national interest. Stereotypes of Jewish power and wealth, which had been benign before 1914, now became malignant. Wealthy Jews managed to evade the full effect of the legislation, but middle-class Jews, small traders and artisans were badly hit.

If the Hungarian regime had dealt harshly with its Jewish subjects since 1938, it stopped short of lethal measures. The Hungarian military were complicit in the deportation and murder of 16,000–18,000 'alien' Jews (from territories annexed since 1938) at Kamenets Podolsk in the Ukraine in the summer of 1941, but further deportations were stopped once the Interior Ministry in Budapest found out about the atrocity. The government of Bárdossy actually fell after an outcry against the role of the Hungarian government and military in the massacre of 2,500 Serbs, including 700 Jews, at Novi Sad (Ujvidek) in January 1942.[40]

On the strength of these actions by the Hungarian state, as contrasted with the fact that Jews in Slovakia and elsewhere were being slaughtered with the connivance of their own governments, Hungarian Jews felt shielded from the worst depredations. From his assumption of office in March 1942 until his removal two years later, the new prime minister, Miklós Kálláy, successfully fended off German demands for tougher action against Hungary's Jews. The official attitude towards the Jews in Hungary was perceptibly relaxed. It was reasonable for the Jews there to think that their patriotism was paying dividends.[41]

Even the imposition of labour service on Jewish males of military age (generously defined) was shot through with contradictions. The first wave of conscripts was issued with khaki uniforms. They were commanded by Hungarian officers and NCOs who were tough and often brutal, but who rarely shared the genocidal outlook of Germans in the SS, the police and frequently in the Wehrmacht. Hungarian Jews sent into the Soviet Union in June 1941 with Hungarian military units were in the strange position of witnessing the mass murder of local Jews while being protected by their para-military status in the Hungarian armed services. Others, like Miklós Hammer, were assigned to parts of annexed Transylvania where they had a very quiet time. Hammer, whose memoirs have been written up by a British journalist, even recalls being sent home on leave to Budapest over the New Year holidays in 1941–2.[42]

Hammer was lucky to escape posting to the Don Bend where the

Hungarian 4th Army was annihilated in the Soviet offensive to encircle the German forces in the Stalingrad region in late 1942. Of 50,000 Jewish labour servicemen only 6,000–7,000 returned home. Most of these fortunate ones were captured by the Russians. But those who perished were more the victims of a military disaster than of the 'Final Solution'. Jewish men who remained in labour battalions or who were called up after Stalingrad were actually protected from the deportations in 1944.[43]

At the start of 1944 the Germans were retreating on every front and the Jews of Hungary confidently expected the war to be over soon. It is understandable that precisely because the 'Final Solution' had lapped all about them from mid-1941 to early 1944, while they remained invulnerable, they were lulled into trusting their government to defend them from any future Nazi attacks. By another, tragic paradox the very efforts of the Hungarian government under Admiral Horthy to get out of the war without falling prey to either German or Soviet hegemony provoked the invasion of 19 March 1944.

But what were Nazi intentions towards the Jews? Was the extension of the 'Final Solution' to Hungary inevitable or were there opportunities to delay or minimize the blow? Richard Breitman and Shlomo Aronson (chapters 4 and 5) utilize dramatic new evidence to demonstrate that the Nazi leadership, up to and including Hitler, was willing to bargain Jewish lives with the Allies. Notwithstanding the ease with which millions of Jews had been robbed and murdered, Hitler and Himmler remained convinced that Jewry was a global power which controlled decision-making in London and Washington. They believed that Jews could provide a channel of communication to the Allied leaders and would prevail on them to trade Jews for military resources to use against the Red Army. If such an approach sowed discord between the Western Allies and Stalin, so much the better.

However, according to Breitman, Himmler was working behind the Führer's back and using Jewish intermediaries sent on a 'rescue' mission to explore a still more far-reaching avenue. He wanted to test the receptivity of the Western Allies to a separate peace. It was knowledge of these ulterior motives that, in Allied eyes, compromised the rescue plans. Since the Jews in the free world and in Palestine depended on the Allies to execute any large-scale rescue efforts, their naive and false hopes were dashed.

Aronson's archival discoveries help to clarify several contentious issues in the rancorous dispute over the Brand mission and the role of the Zionists in Hungary, a saga of recriminations which as we have seen has echoed into the post-war Jewish world. Eichmann listened carefully when members of the Zionist Relief and Rescue Committee in Budapest, which included Ottó Komoly, Rudolf Kasztner and Joel Brand, proposed a deal whereby money or goods to be obtained from the West would be exchanged for Jews marked out for deportation. Eichmann transmitted this interesting idea up the SS hierarchy and after due consideration by his superiors, sent Brand to Istanbul with the offer of a deal. He was accompanied by Bandi Grosz, a Gestapo agent whose covert task was to sound out the Allies on a separate peace agreement on behalf of Himmler.

It is clear from Aronson's research that the Allies saw through the Grosz mission. His presence alongside Brand fatally jeopardized the rescue bid. The Allies, wary of offending Stalin, declined the bait of negotiations and imprisoned Brand. Leaders of the Jewish Agency protested at Allied prevarications in the belief that Brand's mission offered a real possibility of rescue. Back in Budapest Kasztner persuaded Eichmann to make a 'goodwill gesture' and allow a trainload of Jews to be sent to a safe location pending the hoped-for wider agreement. Breitman shows that Hitler and Himmler were willing to use Jews as bargaining counters, keeping some alive while at the same time allowing the transportations to Birkenau to roll on. Himmler, unlike Hitler, may have been willing to spare even larger numbers of Jews but the opportunity never arose. Aronson demonstrates that the Nazis tried to use the Jews to extract concessions from the Allies which the Allies could not possibly make. The Jews were pawns in a game not of their making or one which they even grasped. They were like flies to wanton boys, and like flies, not human beings, they died in their hundreds of thousands.

After the war survivors suspected that the so-called 'Kasztner train' was at best a one-off opportunity that the Zionists had engineered to save their own skins or, at worst, a kind of down-payment on their complicity in the deportations. In return for the trainload it was alleged that they declined to warn Jews in the provinces, allowing them to be rounded up and deported with the minimum of resistance.[44] This calumny can now be finally laid to rest. The record shows that the Relief and Rescue Committee initiated a bold rescue plan for Hungarian Jewry and even had ambitions to save the remnant of Jews in the whole of Europe. But they were misled by false assumptions about the outcome of earlier negotiations with the SS in Slovakia and were cunningly led on by Eichmann.[45]

Asher Cohen modifies Randolf Braham's conclusion that the Jewish leadership participated in a 'conspiracy of silence'. Attempts were made to alert Jews about the impending danger, but the Jewish leaders in Budapest held little sway beyond the capital and, in any case, the already available information about Auschwitz was simply not believed. He maintains that ordinary Jews in the capital and the provinces had as much chance as the leadership to learn what was happening in Russia and Poland. All strata of the Jewish population had access to radios during 1941–3 and could have listened to BBC European Service broadcasts. About 15,000 Jewish refugees from Slovakia and Poland percolated into Hungary during 1941–3 bringing with them first-hand reports of mass shootings and murder using gas. However, Hungarian Jews had good reason to believe that such things could not happen to them. Under Kállay they had been shielded from the genocide. They could see that in Bulgaria and Romania, countries that were in a comparable situation to Hungary, the relative autonomy of the client regimes with respect to the Third Reich had enabled them to preserve most of their long-established Jewish citizens. Above all, they could not have foreseen the German occupation. Nor could they have reckoned that the civil administration would fall in line with Eichmann's murderous project and do so while Admiral Horthy remained in office, projecting a sense of continuity and normalcy to the bulk of the population.[46]

Ultimately, the Hungarian government and Admiral Horthy bear a dreadful responsibility for the fate of their Jewish subjects. At several stormy meetings with Hitler at Klessheim on 18–19 March 1944, Horthy seems to have approved the transfer into German hands of 100,000 Jews for 'forced labour'. A few days later he appointed Döme Sztójay, a notorious Jew-hater and pro-Nazi, as prime minister. The Jews were deprived of their rights, forced to wear the Yellow Star, plundered and then forced into ghettos and holding camps with bewildering speed. The country was divided into six districts, matching the regional organisation of the gendarmerie, and the Jews were systematically removed area by area. The gendarmerie rounded them up, guarded the camps and escorted the columns of Jews to the trains. Hungarian police or troops sat watch on the transports until they crossed the border into Slovakia.[47]

Some Hungarian historians, including Andras Ban, have argued that Horthy was an old-style 'rational' anti-Semite who would never have considered allowing the mass murder of his country's Jews. When he learned that the deportations were leading to mass murder he intervened to stop them on 7 July 1944. Yet as Maria Schmidt has shown, the Hungarian government was well-informed about the murderous policies of the Nazi regime. During 1942–3, its own gendarmes had reported on the deportation of Jews from Slovakia.[48] Horthy was in receipt of appeals from the Vatican and the neutral powers well before he acted to stop the deportations from Hungary. That he finally did so seems to have been a consequence of American bombing raids on Budapest, which he saw as a reprisal for the deportations, and the success of the Allied landings in Normandy, which tolled the death knell for the Third Reich.

Regardless of Horthy's own dilemmas, the Hungarian civil authority, gendarmerie, police and military carried out the deportations efficiently and without any resistance. While it may be true that without a German occupation there would have been no Holocaust in Hungary, the Hungarian historian Attila Pók (chapter 8) notes that once the Germans were in control they did not lack helpers. Hungarians had been prepared for this moment by decades of xenophobic nationalism, anti-Semitism and anti-Jewish measures. Because the Jews had long been made the scapegoat for all Hungary's ills they were isolated and vulnerable by the time the Nazis arrived. Hungarians must consequently take a national responsibility for the catastrophe which overtook their Jewish fellow-citizens.

Hungary's Jews were ill-equipped to react to the German occupation. They were already weakened by the economic effects of the anti-Jewish legislation, documented here by Yehuda Don, while tens of thousands of able-bodied men had been conscripted into labour battalions and lost on the Russian Front. The response to the Nazis was formulated by ageing communal leaders and young people, mainly those active in the Zionist youth movements.

Between 1940 and early 1944 Jewish organisations in Hungary, spear-headed by Zionist groups, had rescued thousands of Polish and Slovakian Jews. Many had reached Hungary as illegal immigrants under their own steam, but others were smuggled over the border by Zionist youth groups. These refugees brought with them information about the 'Final Solution', but seen through the 'global optic' described by Asher Cohen (chapter 6) this news could convey a quite different message. Trude Levi, a survivor from the Hungarian town of Szombathely who many years later settled in London, recalled in her autobiography: 'As Hungary was the last country to be occupied by the Germans, we had already heard stories of German oppression. Refugees from all over Europe . . . had sought asylum in Hungary.'[49] But Hungarian Jews refused to believe that such a disaster could befall them and the longer it was staved off, the safer they felt. Trude Levi remembers that, 'In 1941 and 1942 we had expected Hungary to be occupied by the Germans but not in 1944. We all thought with relief that we had escaped the German yoke.'[50] The information about atrocities had reached them, but it was of no avail.

Events moved so rapidly when the disaster struck that no amount of forewarning would have saved the Jews. The traditional communal leadership was shattered, to be succeeded at an improvised level by Zionist activists who had links with international bodies and Jews abroad. The

Zionist youth were the first to realise the need for urgent action, but initially could not prevail over their more cautious elders. Even so, they pioneered an escape route to Romania which was subsequently taken by thousands of Hungarian Jews.

While Zionist leaders engaged in frantic negotiations with the duplicitous SS representatives, Zionist youth with the knowledge and support of the leadership organised the mass forging of diplomatic papers to protect Jews in Budapest. They also helped to establish 'safe houses' under the flags of neutral powers.[51] By autumn 1944 international agencies and neutral countries finally joined relief and rescue work. The Vatican, the Red Cross and the diplomatic representatives of Portugal, Spain, Sweden and Switzerland began to take active measures to shield Jews from the Germans and the Arrow Cross, the local Fascist party. The Arrow Cross took power in Budapest on 15 October 1944, under the leadership of Ferenc Szálasi, and remained in anarchic control until most of the besieged city was liberated by the Red Army on 18–19 January 1945.

Carl Lutz, the Swiss consul, persuaded his government to sanction the distribution of 7,000 permits for emigration to Switzerland, permits that offered the holders a modicum of protection. The Swedish attaché Raoul Wallenberg, who arrived in Budapest in July 1944, saved thousands of Jews by issuing them with Swedish diplomatic papers and setting up 'safe houses' where Jews could gather safely under the protection of neutral powers. Over 30,000 Jews eventually found refuge in these houses.

On 17 October 1944, the Germans decreed that all able bodied Jewish men had to perform forced labour building anti-tank ditches. Several days later 50,000 Jews, most of them elderly men, were marched out of the city towards the frontline. This episode is vividly captured in the recently translated memoir by Ernö Szép, *The Smell of Humans*. Szep was a Jewish intellectual in his sixties when he was forced to carry a shovel and march out of Budapest. He and many more like him would have perished had it not been for Wallenberg's energetic counter-measures. Hundreds were recalled to the capital after they were given Swedish diplomatic certificates. Wallenberg also organized aid to 25,000 Jewish men, women and children marched out of Budapest towards Austria on a death march in early November.[52]

Despite the speed of the catastrophe and the isolation of the Jewish population, the Zionist youth groups performed heroic feats. Asher Cohen outlines the three strategies they had elaborated months earlier in the light of events in neighbouring territories and the experience of refugees who had reached them. One group tried to reach the Slovak partisans: few succeeded. A second group blazed a trail into Romania, a country which offered fugitives a fragile security. The third, and largest, group set about constructing hiding places in Budapest and producing forged passes.

Youthful Zionists also helped to rescue some of the 50,000 Jews force-marched out of Budapest in November 1944. Inside the besieged city they barred the safe-houses against marauding bands of the Arrow Cross militia. Uniquely for the annals of Jewish resistance, this was an urban conflict which the Jews won: although crudely armed and with few allies in the weak Hungarian underground, they fought off repeated assaults by Fascist groups until the Russians liberated Pest, the part of the city that included the Jewish quarter. Yehuda Don, who contributes chapter 3 of this volume, was one of those young Zionists.

Robert Rozett (chapter 7) observes that such resistance would not have been possible except for the singular conditions prevailing in late 1944. In Poland, Lithuania and White Russia Jewish armed resistance first occurred in 1943, when the outcome of the war was in the balance. Uprisings such as those in the Warsaw, Bialystok and Vilna ghettos were more of a defiant gesture against the Nazis than a strategy to save Jewish lives. In Hungary, in spring 1944, young Zionists knew that the Red Army was advancing steadily in their direction, while the attitude of neutral powers and international agencies was hardening against the Nazis.

Even so, the possibilities of armed resistance were pitifully limited. There was no national resistance movement in Hungary which Jews could join or to which they could link up. Most Jews of military age were in the labour battalions or dead. Jewish resistance therefore focused on measures that would keep Jews alive until the Soviets arrived, a realistic possibility that had been denied to Jews elsewhere in Eastern Europe. Heroic though it was, the activity of armed Jews in defence of the Budapest ghetto in the winter of 1944–5 was unrepresentative of the community's dominant survival strategy.

Just as Cohen insists on using a 'global optic' to understand Jewish responses inside Hungary, Tony Kushner (chapter 9) applies a similar approach to the analysis of reactions in Britain, a key player in any rescue or relief missions. In late 1942 there had been widespread outrage at the genocide against the Jews, but by late 1943 it had faded out. This was not because of any lack of information about the massacre of Europe's Jewish population. Nor was it the result of 'compassion fatigue'. As Koestler noted angrily the British public was still capable of horror at the news of Japanese atrocities against British POWs. However, British officials consistently rejected 'particularistic' measures in favour of the Jews and subordinated rescue work to winning the war. In the absence of any government lead to help the Jews, their case seemed hopeless and left all but the most hardy activists in a state of demoralization.

Nevertheless, the uproar in Britain in 1942–3 helped to trigger a governmental response in the United States. In January 1944, President Roosevelt ordered the establishment of the War Refugee Board (WRB), charged with assisting Jewish and other victims of Nazi persecution. The British government regarded the WRB with a dubious eye. It gave more financial aid to the WRB than did the US administration, but it flinched from mass rescue measures. When in the summer of 1944 Horthy dramatically offered to release 7,500 Jews and the WRB wanted to take up the offer, the British prevaricated. They feared a 'flood of refugees' destined for Palestine. Such an influx would embarrass them in the eyes of the Arabs whose wartime support they had underpinned with restrictions on Jewish immigration to the Jewish National Home in Palestine. British officials frustrated the eagerness of the WRB until the opportunity for rescue was lost.

If Palestine was a key to British policy towards mass rescue, what was the behaviour of Palestinian Jews in the Yishuv, the modern Jewish community in Palestine? Dina Porat (chapter 10) reveals that the fate of Hungarian Jewry was peripheral to the main concerns of Palestinian Jews during the war years. The Hungarian Zionist movement was insignificant before 1939. There were few immigrants from Hungary in the Yishuv and fewer still in the Zionist establishment. Public anguish focused on the treatment of the Jews in Russia, Poland and Romania which had supplied the bulk of the population of the Yishuv.

Although Palestinian Jews knew all about the 'Final Solution' by 1943 and understood that where the German army went the killing squads followed, the response to the occupation of Hungary was muted. Before 1944 the Hebrew press in Palestine treated Hungary sarcastically as an 'oasis' for the Jews in Europe. The German occupation of its former ally came as a shock. Coverage of the crisis soon increased and demands were raised for the Zionist leadership to do something to aid the Hungarian Jews. But there was no official response. The Zionist leaders were engaged in rescue efforts surrounding the Brand mission, but for obvious reasons they could not disclose this.

Contrary to claims that the Zionist leadership in Palestine put the interests of Zionism above those of rescue, the Jewish Agency fought for a successful outcome to Brand's mission even though it was premised on the saved Jews not going to Palestine. These negotiations were an example of the Yishuv's authorities putting rescue before narrow Zionist goals. Unfortunately, Ben-Gurion, the leader of the Yishuv, was not interested in telling this to anyone. He disparaged public opinion and saw no point in mobilising people *en masse*. While the press railed, the leadership remained silent and inadvertently fostered the notion, which persists until today, that they sat on their hands while Hungarian Jewry was destroyed. Yet Porat notes that there is no record that the leadership discussed the disaster as it unfolded, even *in camera*, which remains a disturbing lacuna for which she can find no explanation.

Yehuda Bauer (chapter 11) concludes that, contrary to popular belief in Israel and the Diaspora, the Zionists inside Hungary and in the free world achieved a great deal by way of negotiations.[53] They were not caught in a trap: there were options to pursue and a few courageous leaders explored them. Ben Gurion in Tel Aviv wanted to keep the Brand negotiations going to stall for time. Kasztner in Budapest succeeded in rescuing one trainload of Jews with the little bargaining power at his disposal, and managed to save even more Jews in Budapest. It is wrong, Bauer argues, to accuse the Zionists of betraying the Jews of Hungary.

First of all, the Zionists had little influence in the population before 1944. Second, Hungarian Jews had many opportunities to learn the truth about the 'Final Solution'. After the war they claimed they had been misled by their leaders, but this was an alibi for their own short-sightedness. They did not want to face the truth that they had been 'easy prey' for German tactics. It is also easier to lacerate those within reach, even though they may be innocent, than an unattainable culprit. It was the German occupation that allowed the SS to operate in Hungary. The Hungarians permitted and facilitated the implementation of the 'Final Solution' on their soil. Prior Hungarian policy had impoverished the Jews and sapped the strength of their communities. Anyway, there was little they could have done given the suddenness of the onslaught, the terrain or the attitude of the Hungarians. Their reaction and their fate were, in Yehuda Bauer's words, 'tragically understandable, almost inevitable' (p. 197).

It is only by accepting these facts that Jews will be able to reconcile themselves to the catastrophe that overwhelmed the last intact, relatively unscathed community of Jews in Nazi Europe. Only then will it be possible to assess where the responsibility for the calamity lay and to guard against such conditions ever repeating themselves.

IV

In spite of repeated instances of mass murder and genocide since 1945 the world has never witnessed anything like the Hungarian disaster. Without intending to belittle by one iota the scale and depth of human suffering which they involved, the similarities between 'ethnic cleansing' in the former Yugoslavia or the genocide in Rwanda and the events in Hungary are superficial. What surface parallels do exist only highlight the profound differences. Yet it is useful and potentially important to understand the differences since, in spite of everything, these recent disasters still happened.

The events in Hungary were unique because they were part of a global enterprise to exterminate an entire people. The object was not simply to displace a particular population group or wreck the basis for its organised communal and cultural life, but to render it biologically null. Although the deportations from Hungary occurred with the broad knowledge of foreign powers, there were few individuals *in situ* who could report on the unfolding tragedy in any detail, let alone record it and transmit the evidence instantaneously around the world.

Paradoxically, the instantaneity of news coverage of events in Bosnia and Rwanda partially frustrated the very expectations and rescue possibilities which they created. Public outrage followed news footage of massacres or forced removals of population. There was a clamour for 'something to be done'. Politicians who depended on votes and the publicity which generated them felt compelled to act. But they faced many constraints and were often paralysed. Under scrutiny and pressure to be seen 'to do something', Western governments and the people's representatives devised spectacular gestures to disguise their inactivity.

By another paradox, thanks to the effects of television, the most useful measures were often the least popular with electorates. Because TV has graphically recorded the fate of 'our boys' suffering in other people's wars there is widespread resistance to sending troops abroad for peace-keeping duties. In this sense, media scrutiny actually frustrated potential acts of benevolence.

When the Jews of Hungary went to their deaths in 1944 information was available, but the governments in the United States and Britain did not want to raise expectations concerning rescue measures or face a clamour to divert resources away from the war effort. The low level of publicity and the secrecy of government conduct may actually have facilitated a certain level of assistance. British and US officials did approach neutral countries and the Vatican, imploring them to intervene in Budapest. They did warn Horthy that his actions would be called to account after the war. This was not much, but it was something. Meanwhile, the Allies went about the task of defeating Nazi Germany. However inappropriate such a response may have been in the short term, it was surely superior to the empty threats, posturing and shifting around of puny military forces that characterised the Western response to the mayhem in ex-Yugoslavia.[54]

Although it might be argued that the relative inactivity of the Western Allies nourished Nazi ambitions to wipe out the Jews, Britain and the United States never connived in the ethnic reordering of territories as was the case in ex-Yugoslavia in 1994–5 when the UN, NATO and EU intermediaries imposed on Bosnia-Herzegovina partition along ethnic lines. The Nazis were left in no doubt that their incomparably more radical version of ethnic cleansing was abhorred by the Allies.[55]

Western intervention in Bosnia was impelled to an intangible extent by a sense that the events of 1941–5 must never be allowed to recur. This was the explicit meaning of the dramatic visit by President Mitterrand to Sarajevo in 1993, soon after the commemoration of the Warsaw Ghetto uprising. The same sentiment was articulated by Elie Wiesel at the opening of the US National Holocaust Memorial Museum, when he pleaded with President Clinton to commit the United States to an active policy in ex-Yugoslavia. Yet the knowledge of mass murder and ethnic cleansing, the availability of the means by which to intervene and the existence of historical precedents (however attenuated) evidently failed to provide any guarantee that, this time around, something would be done. It merely ensured the inflation of rhetoric and a more elaborate display of posturing.

The most haunting example of history in Europe being allowed to repeat itself was the 'discovery' of Serb-run detention camps in August 1992 and the mass murder of Bosnian Muslims after the fall of Srebrenica in July 1995. The camp at Omerska was located and filmed by British reporters and television news teams in early August 1992. The stories of beatings and shootings by sadistic guards and the images of gaunt men behind barbed wire recalled Belsen, a point made forcefully in the press over succeeding days. The 'exposure' of Omerska is credited with triggering direct international intervention in Bosnia, but it subsequently emerged that international agencies and Western governments had known about such 'detention centres' for months. In fact, to stave off demands for intervention US officials had lied about what they knew of the camp.[56]

The slaughter of up to 8,000 people at Srebrenica occurred when troops from a UN intervention force had been on the ground in Bosnia for four years. The town was a UN-declared 'safe haven' and supposedly protected by a Dutch battalion of the UN intervention force. Relief columns run by the UN High Commission for Refugees, the International Red Cross and a host of aid agencies criss-crossed the country, including Srebrenica. Hundreds of officials from these bodies and a host of international organisations were scattered across Bosnia. Members of the world's media were there in force. And yet the town was overrun by Serb troops who imposed a terrible fate on the defenders. In brazen defiance of the Dutch soldiers, male Bosnian Muslims were rounded up, marched off and shot in secluded fields. Mass graves have since been identified.[57]

A similar story of failure but on an incomparably greater scale took place in Rwanda in spring 1994, according to a report by the Danish Foreign Ministry on behalf of the UN. As in Bosnia there were UN personnel in the country and a plethora of aid agencies. There were warnings that Hutu militias were arming and plotting the massacre of the Tutsi minority. When the killings started their nature and motivation were ill-understood and misreported. International intervention was fatally delayed for ten weeks, partly because of fears of replicating previous intervention missions that had backfired before the world's media. In that time half a million Tutsis were murdered.[58]

Notwithstanding these examples of failure, there was eventually a massive, sustained humanitarian effort in both Bosnia and Rwanda. Many lives were saved by food convoys, medical aid and dramatic acts of rescue, however belated. No such intervention occurred in Hungary in 1944–5. To that extent the situation in 1994–5 was quite different from 1944–5 and manifestly improved. It can only be hoped that if and when genocide recurs the world community and international agencies will act with greater speed and efficacy. Unfortunately, the examples of Bosnia and Rwanda do not bode well. Whatever the world has learned from the fate of the Hungarian Jews has been modestly incremental. The murderers forget nothing; the bystanders remember little; the victims are always the victims.

Notes

1. Diary-Notebook [DN], 22 March 1944, Koestler Archive, Edinburgh University Library [KA], MS2305.
2. See Arthur Koestler, *The Invisible Writing* (London, 1954). For details of Koestler's wartime rescue work, see David Cesarani, *The Homeless Mind: Arthur Koestler, the Jews and the Quest for Identity*, London, 1998 (forthcoming).
3. Tony Kushner, *The Holocaust and the Liberal Imagination*, Oxford, 1994, pp. 139–45, 163–87.

4. On Karski and his mission see E. Thomas Wood and Stanislaw M. Jankowski, *Karski. How One Man Tried to Stop the Holocaust*, New York, 1994.
5. *Horizon*, December 1943. For the controversy, see Michael Sheldon, *Friends of Promise*, London, 1989, pp. 83–4.
6. Republished in *The Yogi and the Commissar*, London, 1945, pp. 94–9.
7. Anglo-Palestine Committee minutes in KA, MS2403/1 and Koestler's correspondence in KA, MS2372/4.
8. DN, 21 June 1944, KA, MS2305.
9. DN, 10 June 1944, KA, MS2305. Notes of conversation, Shertok–Brand, 11 June 1944, Aleppo, KA, MS2403/1. For details of the offer and the Allied response, see chapters 4, 5 and 11. See also Bernard Wasserstein, *Britain and the Jews of Europe 1939–1945*, Oxford, 1979, pp. 249–62; David Wyman, *The Abandonment of the Jews*, New York, 1985, pp 235–54; Yehuda Bauer, *Jews for Sale? Nazi-Jewish Negotiations, 1933–1945*, New Haven, 1994, chs 8–12.
10. DN, 10 June 1944, KA, MS2305 Brockway to Koestler, 1 July 1944 and Laski to Koestler, 13 July 1944, KA, MS2373/2.
11. DN, 11 July 1944, KA, MS2305; 'The case for bombing the Extermination camps in Upper Silesia by the American Air Force', 11 July 1944, KA, MS2403/1. See also, Doris May to Koestler, 13 July 1944, KA, MS2402/4. For the debate over the bombing of Auschwitz see the contributions to Verne W Newton (ed.), *FDR and the Holocaust*, New York, 1996, Pt. 3 and note 9 above.
12. DN, 8 July 1944, KA, MS2305; Koestler to Shertok, 19 July 1944, MS2372/4.
13. DN, 8, 10, 12, 13 July, KA, MS2305.
14. DN, 13, 15, 17 July 1944, KA, MS2305; Foot to Koestler, 11 July 1944, KA, MS2402/4.
15. DN, 25 August 1944, KA, MS2305.
16. See *Arrow in the Blue*, London, 1952, the first volume of Koestler's autobiography.
17. The most exhaustive and authoritative account is by Randolph Braham, *The Politics of Genocide: The Holocaust in Hungary*, 2 vols, New York, 1981; revised edition 1994.
18. See note 9 and Braham, *The Politics of Genocide*, vol. 2, ch. 29
19. Randolph Braham, 'Hungary', in David Wyman (ed.) *The World Reacts to the Holocaust*, Baltimore, 1996, pp. 208–18.
20. Bernard Wasserstein, *The Vanishing Diaspora. The Jews in Europe since 1945*, London, 1996, p. 130.

21. See Michael Marrus, 'The Use and Misuse of the Holocaust', in Peter Hayes (ed.) *Lessons and Legacies. The Meaning of the Holocaust in a Changing World*, Evanston, Ill., 1991, pp. 106–19 and Steven Aschheim, *Culture and Catastrophe: German and Jewish confrontations with National Socialism and other crises*, Basingstoke, 1996.
22. For a lucid exposition of the case and its impact, see Yehiam Weitz, 'Changing Conceptions of the Holocaust: The Kasztner Case', in Jonathan Frankel (ed.), *Studies in Contemporary Jewry*, vol. 10, *Reshaping the Past*, New York, 1994, pp. 211–30.
23. Weitz, 'Changing Conceptions of the Holocaust', p. 216.
24. Ibid., pp. 321–7 and Yehiam Weitz, 'Shaping the Meaning of the Holocaust in Israeli Society of the 1950s', in Yisrael Gutman (ed.), *Major Changes within the Jewish People in the Wake of the Holocaust*, Jerusalem, 1996, pp. 497–518.
25. Walter Laqueur, *The Terrible Secret*, London, 1980; Martin Gilbert, *Auschwitz and the Allies*, London, 1981, and see note 9 above.
26. On Weisel, see Edward T. Linethal, *Preserving Memory: The Struggle to Create America's Holocaust Museum*, New York, 1995. For an insight into the continuing controversy, see David Horowitz, 'Why the Allies Didn't Bomb Auschwitz', *Jerusalem Report*, 12 January 1995 and the contributions by James H. Kitchens III and Richard H. Levy in Newton (ed.), *FDR and the Holocaust*, pp. 183–272.
27. See Bauer, *Jews for Sale?*.
28. Richard Bolchover, *British Jewry and the Holocaust*, Cambridge, 1993; compare Yoav Gelber, 'Moralist and "Realistic" Approaches in the Study of the Allies' Attitude to the Holocaust', in Asher Cohen et al. (eds), *Comprehending the Holocaust*, Frankfurt-am-Main, 1988, pp. 107–23.
29. Braham, *The Politics of Genocide*, vol. 1, pp. 1–78. Raphael Patai, *The Jews of Hungary. History, Culture, Psychology*, Detroit, 1996, pp. 21–115, 141–239; William McCagg, *Jewish Nobles and Geniuses in Modern Hungary*, New York, 1972, pp. 61–3.
30. Patai, *The Jews of Hungary*, pp. 429–41; McCagg, *Jewish Nobles and Geniuses*, p. 30. John Lukacs, *Budapest 1900*, London, 1988, pp. 95–6.
31. Braham, *The Politics of Genocide*, pp. 80–105; Patai, *The Jews of Hungary*, pp. 312–27, 358–86; McCagg, *Jewish Nobles and Geniuses*, pp. 92–3.
32. Patai, *The Jews of Hungary*, pp. 446–57; McCagg, *Jewish Nobles and Geniuses*, pp. 86–7, 169–70, 180–5. Mary Gluck, *Georg Lukacs and his Generation 1900–1918*, Cambridge, MA, 1985, pp. 52–60.

33. Lukacs, *Budapest 1900*, pp. 183–7.
34. Patai, *The Jews of Hungary*, pp. 347–57; Lukacs, *Budapest 1900*, pp. 188–94.
35. Braham, *The Politics of Genocide*, pp. 18–19. Patai, *The Jews of Hungary*, pp. 461–88; Tibor Hajdu and Zsuzsa Nagy, 'Revolution, Counterrevolution, Consolidation', in Peter Sugar, Peter Hanak, Tibor Frank (eds), *A History of Hungary*, London, 1990, pp. 295–318.
36. Asher Cohen, 'The Holocaust of Hungarian Jews in the Light of the Research of Randolph Braham', *Yad Vashem Studies*, vol. 25 (1996), pp. 361–82.
37. Ibid., p. 378.
38. Patai, *The Jews of Hungary*, pp. 500–7, 511–19.
39. Braham, *The Politics of Genocide*, chs 2, 4–6; Patai, *The Jews of Hungary*, pp. 435–47.
40. Braham, *The Politics of Genocide*, pp. 210–35.
41. Cohen, 'The Holocaust of Hungarian Jews in the Light of the Research of Randolph Braham', pp. 380–1.
42. Gerald Jacobs, *Sacred Games*, London, 1995, pp. 25, 28, 34–40.
43. Braham, *The Politics of Genocide*, ch. 10.
44. John S. Conway, 'The Holocaust in Hungary: Recent Controversies and Reconsiderations', in Randolph Braham (ed.), *The Tragedy of Hungarian Jewry*, New York, 1986, pp. 1–48.
45. Cohen, 'The Holocaust of Hungarian Jews in the Light of the Research of Randolph Braham', pp. 371–80.
46. Ibid., pp. 380–1.
47. Braham, *The Politics of Genocide*, pp. 528–690.
48. Maria Schmidt, 'Destruction of Slovakian Jews as Reflected in Hungarian Police Reports', in Randolph Braham (ed.), *Studies on the Holocaust in Hungary*, New York, 1990, pp. 164–74.
49. Trude Levi, *A Cat Called Adolf*, London, 1995, p. 22.
50. Ibid., p. 23.
51. Asher Cohen, *The Halutz Resistance in Hungary, 1942–1944*, New York, 1986.
52. Ernö Szép, *The Smell of Humans*, London, 1994.
53. For Zionist and other rescue efforts, Braham, *The Politics of Genocide*, ch. 29, and Bauer, *Jews for Sale?*, *passim.*
54. See Ed Vulliamy, *Seasons in Hell: Understanding Bosnia's War* (London, 1995) for a journalist's account of this dithering set against a background of ethnic cleansing and mass murder in 1992–4.
55. A passionate account of ethnic cleansing in a local and international context is given by Norman Cigar, *Genocide in Bosnia. The Policy*

of Ethnic Cleansing, Houston, 1995. See also the essays in Part 3 of Rabia Ali and Lawrence Lifschultz, *Why Bosnia*?, Stoney Creek, Conn., 1993. For obvious reasons there are as yet few reliable or scholarly analyses of the war in Bosnia and its effects.

56. See Ed Vulliamy writing in the Focus section, *Guardian*, 22 June 1996, and Noel Malcolm, *Bosnia. A Short History*, London, 1994, pp. 244–5.
57. J. W. Honig and W. Both, *Srebrenica: Record of a War Crime*, London, 1994; David Rohde, *A Safe Haven. Srebrenica: Europe's Worst Massacre since the Second World War*, London, 1997.
58. *The International Response to Conflict and Genocide: Lessons from the Rwanda Experience*, Danish Ministry of Foreign Affairs, March 1996, cited in *Guardian*, 13 March 1996. See also Linda Melvern, 'The UN and Rwanda', *London Review of Books*, 12 December 1996.

–2–

The Holocaust in Hungary: A Retrospective Analysis

Randolph L. Braham

Historical Antecedents

The Holocaust in Hungary was in many respects distinct from the tragedies that befell the other Jewish communities in Nazi-dominated Europe. This distinction is reflected in the disastrous set of historical circumstances which combined to doom Hungarian Jewry in 1944.

The destruction of Hungarian Jewry that year constitutes one of the most perplexing chapters in the history of the Holocaust. It is a tragedy that ought not to have happened, for by then – on the eve of Allied victory – the leaders of the world, including the national and Jewish leaders of Hungary, were already privy to the secrets of Auschwitz. Moreover, except for a few diehards who still believed in Hitler's last-minute wonder weapons, even the perpetrators realized that the Axis had lost the war.

The last major phase in the Nazis' war against the Jews, the Holocaust in Hungary, is replete with paradoxes. The roots of one of the most startling of these paradoxes can be found in the 'Golden Era' of Hungarian Jewry (1867–1918). It was during this period that a cordial, almost symbiotic relationship developed between the aristocratic-conservative and the Jewish elites of Hungary. It was this very close relationship, however, that distorted the Jewish leaders' perception of domestic and world politics during the pre-Holocaust era. While the Jewish elites shared the aristocratic-conservative leaders' abhorrence of Nazism and Bolshevism, they failed to recognize that the fundamental interests of the Hungarians were not always identical with those of Jewry. Their myopic views proved counterproductive during the interwar period and disastrous after the German occupation of 19 March 1944.

After its emancipation in 1867, the Jewish community of Hungary enjoyed an unparalleled level of multilateral development, taking full advantage of the opportunities offered by the so-called 'liberal' regime that ruled the country during the pre-World War I era. The Hungarian ruling classes – the gentry and the conservative-aristocratic leaders – adopted a tolerant position toward the Jews. They were motivated not only by economic considerations, but also by the desire to perpetuate their dominant political role in a multinational empire in which the Hungarians constituted a minority. Because of Hungary's feudal tradition, the ruling classes encouraged the Jews to engage in business and industry, so that in the course of time a friendly, cooperative and mutually advantageous relationship developed between the conservative-aristocratic leaders and the Jewish industrialists, bankers and financiers – a relationship that was to play a fatal role during the Holocaust. The Jews also took full advantage of their new educational opportunities and within a short time came to play an influential, if not dominant, role in the professions, literature and the arts.

As a consequence of the Hungarian policy of tolerance, the Jews of Hungary considered themselves an integral part of the Hungarian nation. They eagerly embraced the process of Magyarization, opting not only to change their names but also to serve as economic modernizers and cultural Magyarizers in the areas inhabited by other nationalities in the polyglot Hungarian Kingdom. The Hungarian Jews, who had no territorial ambitions and naturally supported the group that offered them the greatest protection – as did the Jews of the Diaspora practically everywhere during their long and arduous history – were soon looked upon as agents for the preservation of the status quo by the oppressed nationalities clamouring for self-determination and independence.

The Jews were naturally cognizant of the protection the regime provided against the threat of anti-Semitism. The prompt and forceful intervention of the government in dealing with anti-Jewish manifestations, however sporadic and local they were at the time, further enhanced the fidelity of the Jews to the Magyar state.

In the course of time the Jews, especially the acculturated and assimilated ones, became ever more assertively pro-Magyar. In many cases this allegiance was not only because of expediency or gratitude for the opportunities and the safety afforded by the aristocratic-gentry regime, but also because of fervent patriotism. As Oscar Jaszi, a noted sociologist and social-democratic statesman, correctly observed, 'there is no doubt that a large mass of these assimilated elements adopted their new ideology quite spontaneously and enthusiastically out of a sincere love of the new fatherland'. Jaszi concluded, however, that the 'intolerant Magyar nationalism and chauvinism of the Jews had done a great deal to poison relations between the Hungarians and the other nationalities of the prewar era'.[1]

Paul Ignotus, a noted publicist, echoed these sentiments, arguing that the Jews had become 'more fervently Magyar than the Magyars themselves'. A similar conclusion was reached by the noted British historian Robert Seton-Watson, whose sympathies clearly lay with the oppressed nationalities. He claimed in 1908 that 'the Catholic Church and the Jews form today the two chief bulwarks of Magyar chauvinism'.

It was to some extent the political and economic symbiosis between the conservative-aristocratic and Jewish leaderships during the so-called Golden Era that determined their views and attitudes toward both the Third Reich and the Soviet Union during the interwar and wartime periods. While the Hungarian leaders looked upon the Third Reich as a vehicle for the possible satisfaction of their revisionist ambitions, they shared with the Jewish leaders a fear of both German and Russian expansionism and above all a mortal fear of Bolshevism. It was these attitudes and perceptions that guided both leadership groups during the fateful year of 1944 with almost equally disastrous results.

The signs that the commonality of interests (*Interessengemeinschaft*) between the two groups was in fact limited, fragile and based primarily on expediency were clearly visible even before the end of World War I: despite the eagerness with which the Hungarian Jews embraced the Magyar cause and the enthusiasm with which they acculturated themselves, they failed, with relatively few exceptions, fully to integrate themselves into Hungarian society. Their ultimate assimilationist expectations were frustrated, for they were accepted socially neither by the aristocratic gentry, who exploited them politically and economically for the perpetuation of their feudal privileges, nor by the disenfranchised and impoverished peasantry, which – like a large proportion of the industrial workers – often viewed them as instruments of an oppressive regime.

Christian–Jewish relations were further strained by the presence in the country of a considerable number of mostly impoverished Yiddish-speaking Jews who resisted assimilation, let alone acculturation. In contrast to the assimilated Magyarized Jews, these were pejoratively referred to as 'Eastern' or 'Galician', and almost by definition unworthy of the government's policy of toleration. During the interwar period these Jews became the target of special abuse, for even the 'civilized' anti-Semites regarded them as constituting not only a distinct 'biological race' but also an 'ideological race' representing a grave threat to Christian Magyars. This perception was shared by Miklos Horthy, the Regent of Hungary, who probably also considered this 'threat' when he consented, during his March 1944 meeting with Hitler, to the 'delivery of a few hundred thousand workers' to Germany.

The Interwar Period

The *Interessengemeinschaft* between the Hungarian ruling classes and the Jews came to an end with the collapse of the Habsburg Empire and the dismemberment of the Hungarian Kingdom in 1918. The shortlived Communist dictatorship that followed soon thereafter had a crucial effect upon the evolution of Hungarian domestic and foreign policy during the interwar period. The brief but harsh period of the proletarian dictatorship headed by Bela Kun left a bitter legacy in the nation at large, and had a particularly devastating effect upon the Jews of Hungary. Although the overwhelming majority of Jewry had opposed the proletarian dictatorship and perhaps suffered proportionately more than the rest of the population – they were persecuted both as members of the middle class and as followers of an organized religion – popular opinion tended to attach blame for the abortive dictatorship to the Jews as a whole. In part, this was due to the high visibility of Communists of Jewish origin in the Kun government and administration; however, it was primarily the consequence of the anti-Semitic propaganda and anti-Jewish activities of the counter-revolutionary clericalist-nationalist forces that came to power later in 1919 – forces dedicated to the re-establishment of the status quo ante.

Driven by the so-called 'Szeged Idea' (a nebulous amalgam of political-propagandistic views whose central themes included the struggle against Bolshevism, the fostering of anti-Semitism, chauvinistic nationalism and revisionism – an idea that antedated both Italian Fascism and German Nazism), the counter-revolutionaries engulfed the country in a wave of terror which dwarfed in ferocity and magnitude the Red Terror that had preceded and allegedly warranted it. While their murder squads killed a large number of leftists, including industrial workers and landless peasants as well as opposition intellectuals, their fury was directed primarily against the Jews; their violence claimed thousands of victims.

Radicalized by the national humiliation, social upheavals and catastrophic consequences of the lost war – Hungary lost two-thirds of its historic territory, one-third of its Magyar people, and three-fifths of its total population – the counter-revolutionaries organized themselves in a variety of ultrapatriotic associations devoted primarily to the successful resolution of the two major issues that came to obsess Hungary during the interwar period: revisionism and the Jewish question. In the course of time these two issues became interlocked and formed the foundation not only of Hungary's domestic policies but also of its relations with the Third Reich.

Following the absorption of historic Hungary's major national minorities into the successor states, the Jews suddenly emerged as the country's most vulnerable minority group. With the transformation of Trianon Hungary into a basically homogeneous state, the Jews lost their importance as statistical recruits to the cause of Magyardom. In the new truncated state they came to be exploited for another purpose: as in Nazi Germany a little later, they were conveniently used as scapegoats for most of the country's misfortunes, including its socio-economic dislocations.

In this climate it was no surprise that Hungary – the country in which the Jews had enjoyed a 'Golden Era' just a few years earlier – emerged as the first country in post-World War I Europe to adopt, in the wake of the White Terror, an anti-Jewish legislation. The so-called Numerus Clausus Act (1920), which was adopted in violation of the Minorities Protection Treaty, restricted admission of Jews into institutions of higher learning to 6 per cent of the total enrollment – the alleged percentage of Jews in the total population. Although this particular legislation was allowed to expire a few years later, it sanctified the fundamental principle that was to guide many of the civilized anti-Semites of the 1930s who were eager to solve the Jewish question in an orderly and legal manner. This principle would be formulated by Gyula Gombos, one of the foremost representatives of the Hungarian radical Right, who stipulated that 'the Jews must not be allowed to succeed in any field beyond the level of their ratio in the population'.[3]

At any rate, at that time the Jewish leadership viewed the anti-Jewish measures of the counter-revolutionaries merely as temporary aberrations caused by the unfortunate outcome of the war, and retained its patriotic stance. The leadership not only embraced the cause of revisionism, but actually protested and rejected all 'foreign' interventions on its behalf – including those by the international Jewish organizations – as violations of Hungarian sovereign rights. And indeed, its optimism was for a while reinforced during the 1920s, when Count István Bethlen, a representative of the conservative-aristocratic group of large landholders and financial magnates that had ruled Hungary before World War I, headed the Hungarian government.

The appointment of Gombos as Prime Minister in October 1932, coinciding with the spectacular electoral victories of the Nazi Party in Germany, brought the Jewish question to the fore once again. It soon became a national obsession that frequently rivaled revisionism in intensity. Borrowing a page from the Nazis' propaganda book, the Hungarian radicals depicted the Jews as naturally unpatriotic, parasitically sapping the energy of the nation, and prone to internationalist – i.e. Bolshevik – tendencies. The propaganda campaign was soon coupled with demands for a definitive solution of the Jewish question. The suggestions offered by the radical Right at the time ranged from legal restrictions on the Jews' professional and economic activities to their orderly 'resettlement' out of the country.

Although expediency and temporary tactical considerations induced Gombos to 'revise' his position on the Jewish question, his policies prepared the ground for the disaster that was later to strike Hungary and its Jews. He tied Hungary's destiny almost irrevocably to that of Nazi Germany. He not only abandoned Bethlen's reliance on the Western democracies and the League of Nations as a means to correct 'the injustices of Trianon', but also brought Hungary's foreign policy into line with that of Nazi Germany and made possible the subsequent penetration and direct involvement of the Reich in practically every aspect of the country's life. This was greatly facilitated by the formidable and potentially collaborationist power base Gombos established during his tenure. He was able not only to replace the civil and military bureaucracies of the state apparatus with his own protégés, but also – and this was perhaps more crucial – to pack the upper army hierarchy, including the General Staff, with younger, highly nationalistic Germanophile officers. The stage for anti-Jewish excesses to come was further set through the radicalization of the press and the flourishing of ultra-rightist political movements and parties.

The spectacular domestic and foreign policy successes of the Third Reich, including the Anschluss with Austria by which Germany extended its borders to those of Hungary, were achieved largely because of the shortsighted appeasement policies of the Western democracies. The Nazi victories induced successive Hungarian governments to embrace the Axis ever more tightly. They became increasingly eager to see Hungary involved in the establishment of the 'New Order' in Europe and reaping the benefits of the Nazi revisionist-revanchist policies as an active member of the Axis alliance. The pro-Reich policy was especially supported by the Germanophile General Staff, the Right wing of the dominant Government Life Party and the industrial-banking establishment, including Jews and converts.

While this policy yielded considerable dividends, enabling Hungary to fulfil parts of its revisionist ambitions at the expense of Czechoslovakia, Romania and Yugoslavia, it was in the long run disastrous for the country. It was, of course, even more catastrophic for the country's Jews. In retrospect, the policies of the aristocratic-gentry-dominated conservative governments appear to have been quite unrealistic, if not quixotic. Having embraced the Third Reich for its opposition to Bolshevism and its chief bulwark, the Soviet Union, and for its support of revisionism, these governments were soon compelled to come to grips with the ever more influential Right radicals at home. While they despised and feared these radicals almost as much as the Jews – the Hungarian Nazis had advocated not only the need to solve the Jewish question, but also the necessity to bring about a social revolution that would put an end to the inherited privileges of the conservative-aristocratic elements – the governmental leaders felt compelled to appease them as well as the Germans. In fact, these leaders looked upon the Right radicals' preoccupation with the Jewish question as a blessing in disguise, for it helped deter attention from the grave social-agrarian problems confronting the nation. They were, consequently, ready to adopt a series of anti-Jewish measures. These became more draconian with each territorial acquisition between 1938 and 1941. In addition to passing three major anti-Jewish laws – the third one incorporated some of the basic provisions of the Nuremberg Laws of Nazi Germany – they adopted a discriminatory system of forced labour service for Jews of military age, a unique institution in Nazi-dominated Europe.

These anti-Jewish measures of the various governments, endorsed by the leaders of the Christian churches, were based on the illusions that guided the ruling elites until the German occupation. They thought that by passing laws that would curtail the Jews' economic power and 'harmful' cultural influence, they could not only appease the ultra-rightists who thrived on the social and economic unrest that plagued the country, but also satisfy the Third Reich and at the same time safeguard the vital interests of the Jews themselves. This rationalization was part of the larger quixotic assumption that Hungary could satisfy its revisionist ambitions by embracing the Third Reich without having to jeopardize its own freedom of action.

The upper strata of Hungarian Jewry, including the official national leadership, shared these illusions, convinced that the Jewish community's long history of loyal service to Magyardom would continue to be recognized and their fundamental interests safeguarded by the ruling elite of the country. They accepted, however reluctantly, many of the anti-Jewish measures as reflecting 'the spirit of the times' and as necessary tactical moves to 'take the sting out of the anti-Semitic drive' of the ultra-rightists at home and abroad. They tended to concur with the rationalizations of the governmental leaders that the anti-Jewish laws were 'the best guarantee against anti-Semitism and intolerance'.[4] In consequence, they were convinced that the safety and well-being of the Jews were firmly linked to the preservation of the basically reactionary conservative-aristocratic regime. And, indeed, as long as this aristocratic elite remained in power, the vital interests of Hungarian Jewry were preserved relatively intact.

The Wartime Period

This remained so even after Hungary entered the war against the Soviet Union in June 1941. The Hungarian regime continued not only to provide haven to the many thousands of Polish, Slovak and other refugees, but also consistently to oppose the ever greater pressure by the Germans to bring about the Final Solution of the Jewish question. While the Jews in Nazi-controlled Europe were being systematically annihilated, Hungary continued to protect its 825,000 Jews (including approximately 100,000 converts identified as Jews under Hungary's racial law of 1941) until it virtually lost its independence in March 1944.

The pre-occupation record of Hungary was, of course, not spotless. About 60,000 Jews lost their lives even before the German invasion: over 42,000 labour servicemen died or were killed in the Ukraine and Serbia, close to 18,000 were killed in the drive against 'alien' Jews and about 1,000 were slaughtered in the Bacska area. Nevertheless, Hungarian Jewry continued to dwell in comparative personal and physical safety. There were no restrictions on their freedom of movement and they were treated relatively fairly in the allocation of food. Although the anti-Jewish laws had a particularly severe economic impact on the lower strata of the Jewish population, including both skilled salaried workers and the unskilled labourers, the economic situation of the Jews as a whole was relatively tolerable, primarily because of the well-developed communal self-help system. Also, those in business and industry, while having their activities severely curtailed, were usually able to circumvent some provisions of the anti-Jewish laws or take advantage of loopholes. The relatively few industrial magnates, mostly converts, actually benefited from Hungary's armament programme and dealings with the Third Reich.[5]

The situation of Hungarian Jewry appeared to improve in 1943 despite the Nazis' relentless war against the Jews in the rest of German-occupied Europe. Following the destruction of the Second Hungarian Army near Voronezh and the subsequent defeat of the Germans around Stalingrad early in 1943, the Hungarians began a desperate search for an honourable way out of the war, a search that was intensified after Italy's extrication from the Axis alliance later that summer. It ultimately led to disaster, primarily because of the irreconcilably conflicting political and socio-economic objectives the conservative-aristocratic leaders were pursuing.

The Hungarian leaders were eager not only to safeguard the independence and territorial integrity of the country, including the retention of the areas acquired between 1938 and 1941, but also to preserve the antiquated socio-economic structure of the gentry-dominated society.

While they were apprehensive about a possible German occupation, they were above all paralysed by the fear of the Soviet Union and Communism. They viewed the latter as the ultimate evil to which even Nazism, if it proved unavoidable, was preferable. Ignoring the geopolitical realities of the area, they consequently unrealistically tried to solve their dilemma by manoeuvring 'in secret' for a possible separate peace with the Western Powers. Unaware of the realities of the Grand Alliance, they fervently hoped that the Western Allies would invade Europe from the Balkans and thereby achieve a double military and political objective: the destruction of the Nazi forces and the prevention of Bolshevik penetration into the heart of Europe.

With spies planted in all segments of the Hungarian government, the Germans were fully informed about the nature and scope of the 'secret' negotiations between the emissaries of Prime Minister Miklos Kallay and the representatives of the Western Allies in Italy and Turkey. Reports to the Nazis by their many agents in Hungary about the 'treacherous and pro-Jewish' activities of the Kallay government were reinforced by two secret memoranda by Edmund Veesenmayer, the German expert on East Central Europe who later became Hitler's plenipotentiary in Hungary.

Veesenmayer warned the Führer not only about the untrustworthiness of the government, but also about the 'danger' represented by the Jews. He contended that the Jews were 'Enemy No. 1' and that 'the 1.1 million Jews amount to as many saboteurs . . . who must be viewed as Bolshevik vanguards'.[6] In addition, there were weighty military considerations: extrication of Hungary from the Axis when the Soviet forces were already crossing the Dniester would have deprived Germany of the Romanian oil fields and exposed the German forces in the central and southern parts of Europe to encirclement and possibly an immediate and crushing defeat. It was primarily to safeguard their military security interests that the Germans decided to occupy Hungary and prevent it from emulating Italy.

The German Occupation Era

The destruction of Hungarian Jewry, the last surviving large bloc of European Jewry, was to a large extent the concomitant of this German military decision. Ironically, it appears in retrospect that had Hungary continued to remain a militarily passive but vocally loyal ally of the Third Reich instead of provocatively engaging in essentially fruitless, perhaps even merely alibi-establishing diplomatic manoeuvres, the Jews of Hungary might have survived the war relatively unscathed. But the fundamental interests of the Hungarians were in conflict with those of the

Jews. While the aristocratic-conservative leaders despised the Nazis, they were grateful for the support of the Third Reich in achieving a great part of their revisionist ambitions and mortally fearful of a Bolshevik takeover. Although most of the Jews shared the Hungarians' abhorrence of both Nazism and Bolshevism, they looked upon the Soviet Union – a member of the Grand Alliance – as the only realistic saviour from the threat represented by the Nazis and their local allies.

The German forces which invaded Hungary on 19 March 1944 were accompanied by a small but highly efficient special commando unit (*Sonderkommando*) headed by Adolf Eichmann, which had prepared a number of contingency plans to take advantage of any opportunities to 'solve' the Jewish question that might be provided by the new Hungarian leaders. Two years earlier, Eichmann had been indirectly approached by some high-ranking Hungarian ultra-rightists to help 'resettle' thousands of 'alien' Jews, but had refused to mobilize his deportation apparatus for this small-scale operation, preferring to wait until the Hungarians consented to a total removal of the country's Jews.[7] The occupation provided that opportunity.

It turned out that the Nazis found in Hungary a group of accomplices who outdid even them in their eagerness to eliminate the Jews from the country. And indeed, it was primarily the joint, concerted and single-minded drive by these two groups that made the effectuation of the Final Solution in Hungary possible: neither group could have succeeded without the other. While the Germans were eager to solve the Jewish question, they could not take action without the consent of the newly established Hungarian puppet government and the cooperation of the Hungarian instruments of power. And the Hungarian ultra-rightists, though anxious to emulate their German counterparts, could not have achieved their ideologically defined objectives in the absence of the German occupation.

As a consequence of the occupation the Hungarian Jewish community, which had survived the first four and a half years of the war relatively intact, was subjected to the most ruthless and concentrated destruction process of the Nazis' war against the Jews. The drive against the Hungarian Jews took place on the very eve of Allied victory, when the grisly details of the Final Solution were already known to the leaders of the world, including those of Hungarian and world Jewry. Informed about the barbarity and speed with which the Hungarian Jews were liquidated, Winston Churchill concluded that it was 'probably the greatest and most horrible crime ever committed in the history of the world'.[8]

The liquidation of Hungarian Jewry reminds one of a prophecy by Theodore Herzl. In a letter dated 10 March 1903, when Hungarian Jewry was still in the midst of its 'Golden Era', the father of Zionism cautioned his friend Erno Mezei, a member of the Hungarian Parliament: 'The hand of fate shall also seize Hungarian Jewry. And the later this occurs, and the stronger this Jewry becomes, the more cruel and hard shall be the blow, which shall be delivered with greater savagery. There is no escape.'

Was there no escape? The evidence clearly indicates that had Horthy and the clique around him really wanted to save Hungarian Jewry they could have done so. According to the testimony of Veesenmayer and Otto Winkelmann, the former Higher SS and Police Leader in Hungary, in the postwar trial of Andor Jaross, Laszlo Baky, and Laszlo Endre – the triumvirate primarily responsible for the destruction of Hungarian Jewry – the Final Solution of the Jewish question was only a wish, not an absolute demand of the Germans. The Eichmann-*Sonderkommando*, numbering less than 200, could not possibly have carried out its sinister plans without the wholehearted cooperation of the Hungarians who placed the instruments of state power at its disposal. As the example of Bulgaria, Finland, and Romania reveals – and Horthy's own actions of July 1944 clearly indicate – the Regent and his associates could have saved most of the Jews. Unfortunately, they were interested primarily in protecting the assimilated ones, especially those with whom they had good and mutually advantageous business and financial relations; they were almost as eager as the Right radicals to rid the country of the 'Eastern-Galician' Jews. It was partially for this reason that Horthy, who considered the imminent Nazi occupation less of an evil than a possible Soviet invasion, had made certain concessions that proved fatal for Hungarian Jewry. Meeting Hitler at Schloss Klessheim the day before the occupation, he had consented to 'the delivery of a few hundred thousand Jewish workers to Germany for employment in war-related projects'.[9] Apparently Horthy was convinced that by giving this consent he would not only satisfy Germany's 'legitimate' needs, but also contribute to the struggle against Bolshevism and at the same time get rid of the Galician Jews, whom he openly detested. The Eichmann-*Sonderkommando* and its Hungarian accomplices took full advantage of this agreement to implement the Final Solution programme throughout the country, based on the argument that 'the Jews will be more productive in Germany if they have all members of their families with them'.

Once they were given the green light, the dejewification experts proceeded with lightning speed. Time was of the essence, for the Third Reich was threatened by imminent defeat. And, indeed, in no other country was the Final Solution programme – the establishment of the central and local Jewish Councils, the isolation, expropriation, ghettoization, concentration, entrainment and deportation of the Jews – carried out with as much barbarity and speed as in Hungary. Although the dejewification squads were relatively small, the interplay of many domestic and international factors aided them in the speedy implementation of their sinister designs.

The German and Hungarian agents in charge of the Final Solution programme had at their disposal the instruments of state power – the police, gendarmerie and civil service – and were able to proceed unhindered by any internal or external opposition. The puppet government provided them with 'legal' and administrative cover, and a considerable number of Hungarians proved eager and willing to collaborate for ideological or materialistic reasons. With public opinion having been successfully moulded by years of vicious anti-Semitic agitation, the population at large was at best passive; the bulk of the 'proletariat', including the miners and industrial workers, continued the political stance of the 1930s, embracing the Arrow Cross rather than the leftist parties.

The Passivity of the Non-Jewish World

Postwar Hungarian historiography notwithstanding, there was no meaningful resistance anywhere in the country, let alone organized opposition for the protection of the Jews. This was especially so in the countryside. It was primarily in Budapest that Christians and a variety of Church organizations were ready to offer shelter to Jews, saving thousands of them from certain death. But by that time late in 1944, the countryside was already *judenrein* ('free of Jews'), the Soviet forces were fast approaching the capital and most Hungarians realized that the Allies were bound to win the war.

The Allies, though fully aware of the realities of the Final Solution, were reluctant to get involved in the Nazis' war against the Jews. When the Western Powers were asked, shortly after the beginning of the deportations from Hungary on 15 May 1944, to bomb Auschwitz and the railway lines leading to the camp they declined, stating among other things that they could not spare aircraft for such 'secondary targets'. (A few months later, by contrast, they assembled a large armada to destroy another target without real strategic value: Dresden, the art-laden city.) The Soviet air force, which was strategically in an even better position to bomb the death camps and the railway lines leading to them, also did nothing about them. The record of the leftist, mostly pro-Soviet, underground and partisan forces in Hungary, Slovakia and Poland is no better in this regard. There is no evidence that they engaged in any but the most isolated individual acts of sabotage or resistance to prevent the deportation of the Jews.

During the first phase of the deportations from Hungary, the attitude of the neutral states – Portugal, Turkey, Spain, Sweden and Switzerland – was fundamentally no more positive. But their position, like that of the Vatican and the International Red Cross, changed when late in June 1944 the Swiss press began to publicize the horrors of the Final Solution in Hungary. Their pressure on Horthy, complementing his concerns over the rapidly deteriorating military situation – by that time the Soviet forces were fast approaching the borders of Hungary and the Western Allies had successfully established their beachheads in Normandy – advanced the desired result. Horthy halted the deportations on 7 July. (In fact, the dejewification squads continued their operations around Budapest up to 9 July.) By that date, all of Hungary with the exception of Budapest had been made *judenrein*. The success of Horthy's belated action is another piece of evidence demonstrating that the German demands for the Final Solution could have been refused or sabotaged even after the occupation. Had Horthy and the Hungarian authorities really been concerned with all their citizens of the Jewish faith, they could have refused to cooperate. Without the Hungarian instruments of state power, the Germans would have been as helpless during the first phase of the occupation as they proved to be after early July 1944. Moreover, had Horthy decided not to continue as head of state after the occupation, depriving the quisling government of legitimacy, perhaps even the police, gendarmerie and the civil service would have been less enthusiastic in serving the Germans and their Hungarian accomplices.[10]

What about the victims, the Jewish masses and their leaders? Though the German invasion of Hungary took place on the eve of Allied victory, when the Hungarian and Jewish leaders were already privy to the secrets of Auschwitz, the ghettoization and deportation process in Hungary was carried out as smoothly as it was almost everywhere else in Nazi-dominated Europe. Helpless and defenceless, abandoned by the Christian society surrounding them, the Jews of Hungary – with the notable exception of some young Zionist pioneers in Budapest – displayed little or no opposition throughout the occupation period. In accordance with well-tested Nazi camouflage methods, the Jews were lulled into acquiescence by assurances that the deportations involved merely their relocation for labour within the country and Germany for the duration of the war. They – and the rest of the world – were further assured that the young and the old were included in the transports only out of 'consideration for the close family-life pattern of the Jews'.

Under the conditions of relative normality that prevailed until the German occupation, the predominantly assimilated leaders of Hungarian Jewry were quite effective in serving the community. Firmly committed to the values and principles of the traditional conservative-aristocratic system and convinced that the interests of Jewry were intimately intertwined with those of the Magyars, they never contemplated the use of independent political techniques for the advancement of Jewish interests *per se*. They took pride in calling themselves 'Magyars of the Jewish faith' (*Zsidovallasu magyarok*). The leadership, consisting primarily of patriotic, rich and generally conservative elements, tried to maintain the established order by faithfully obeying the commands of the government and fully associating itself with the values, beliefs and interests of the broader Hungarian society. Consequently, the national Jewish leaders' response to the anti-Jewish measures during the interwar period was apologetic and isolated from the general struggle of European Jewry. Their loyalty to the Hungarian nation, and their attachment to the gentry-aristocratic establishment, remained unshaken. To the end, they followed an ostrich-like policy, hoping against hope that the ruling elite would protect them from the fate of the Jewish communities of the neighbouring countries. As proved by the consequences of the German occupation, the Jews' display of patriotism failed to protect them from the 'exterminationist' anti-Semitism of the Nazis. As Victor Karady, the well-known sociologist, observed:

> [The Jews' display of assimilated status 'worked' only] in a hypothetical way, as a belief in or a hope for such protection, much like wishful thinking or self-fulfilling prophesies. The argument ran that the more Jews kept up their ostensible attachment to Magyardom the more they would be preserved from the worst. Jewish community leadership professed this self-convincing ideology to the end and even collaborated with the Nazi authorities on the strength of this conviction. They thought that it would at least give them a strong moral standing with the Hungarian authorities, a capital potentially convertible into protection. 'Jewish Hungarians stick to Magyardom even in the face of their undeserved persecution.' . . . The continuation of assimilationist attitudes to the very end also made it easier for the community leadership as well as many other Jews to save face and justify their earlier assimilationist commitments.[11]

Of course, neither the Jewish leaders nor the Jewish masses envisioned the possibility that Germany would invade an ally and that the anti-Nazi Christian leadership would also be among the first victims after an occupation. Practically until the beginning of the deportations, the national

Jewish leadership continued to believe that the Hungarian Jewish community, unlike all other large European Jewish communities, would emerge from the war relatively intact even if economically generally ruined. While tragically mistaken, their belief that they would escape the Holocaust – *megusszuk* (we'll get by), they frequently said in self-assurance – was not irrational. After all, Hungary had in fact been an island of safety in an ocean of destruction for four and a half years of the war.

The Jewish leaders' faith in the Hungarian establishment was not entirely groundless. They personally along with close to 150,000 of the 247,000 Jews of Budapest (including some 62,000 converts identified as Jews in 1941) were spared the fate that befell those in the countryside because Horthy, under great diplomatic and military pressure, halted the deportations early in July 1944. In addition, many tens of thousands of Jewish males of military age from all parts of Hungary were saved by the armed forces.

This represents yet another paradox of the Holocaust in Hungary. The Hungarian labour service system, which was unique in Nazi-dominated Europe, had been the major source of Jewish suffering before the German occupation. Deprived of their dignity and rights, the Jewish labour servicemen were compelled to do hard and often hazardous military-related work under the constant prodding of mostly cruel guards and officers. Particularly tragic was the fate of the tens of thousands of labour servicemen who had been deployed, along with the Second Hungarian Army, on the Soviet front and in the copper mines in Bor, Serbia. Yet, after the occupation, the Jewish labour servicemen – unlike the Jews at large who at first were placed under the jurisdiction of the Germans – enjoyed the continued protection of the Hungarian armed forces. Moreover, many Jewish males were recruited by decent military commanders from the ghettos and concentration centres, saving them from deportation and almost certain death.[12]

Postwar Reactions

As elsewhere in the former Nazi-dominated world, in Hungary too the Holocaust became a highly controversial issue after the war. The subject of much public debate during the first postwar years, largely because of the revelations of the war crimes trials, the Holocaust gradually declined as a major public issue and emerged as a very uncomfortable chapter in postwar Hungarian history. Relatively few Christians – whether politicians, professionals or laypersons – managed to come to grips with it honestly either during or after the Communist era. During the Communist era

(1949–89) the Holocaust, like the Jewish question as a whole, was gradually submerged in the Orwellian memory hole of history, although in a more restrained fashion than in the other Soviet-bloc nations. While the Communists never denied the horrendous crimes committed by the Nazis, they systematically ignored or distorted the Holocaust by routinely subsuming the losses of Jewry as losses incurred by their own nations.

During the post-Communist era, the treatment of the Holocaust has varied all across the newly evolved political spectrum. On the extreme Right are the historical revisionists, the charlatans from the lunatic fringes of Hungarian society who specialize in the distortion and outright denial of the Holocaust. Like their counterparts elsewhere, they are engaged in an obscene campaign to absolve the Nazis and their Hungarian accomplices of all crimes committed against the Jews. They are involved in a sinister drive to destroy the historical record – and memory – and make the world forget the consequences of the Nazis' war against the Jews. Among them are anti-Semites who are committed to the Nazi thesis identifying Bolshevism with Jewry. In their reckoning, the suffering of the Jews during the war is more than balanced by the 'even greater suffering' Jews inflicted on their nation through Communism.

The failure to come to grips with the Holocaust is also manifested in less extreme and more benign forms. Many highly respectable individuals acknowledge the mass murder of the Jews, but place exclusive blame on the Germans. Others attempt to generalize the Holocaust by lumping the losses of Jewry with those incurred by the military. Still others, including top officials of the government, would like to close the book on World War II and ease their conscience by honouring all casualties, blurring the fundamental differences between persons who were murdered on racial grounds without regard to age or sex and those who – without minimizing their tragedy – fell as a consequence of hostilities in an aggressive war on the side of the Axis. There are others in this group who try to mitigate the impact of the Holocaust by comparing, if not identifying, the horrors of Nazism with those of Communism and by rationalizing the Hungarian involvement by citing the impact of the 'injustices' of Trianon. And finally there are those who try to ease their conscience by emphasizing the number of Jews who were saved in Hungary. In their drive to rehabilitate Miklos Horthy – and by implication the entire Horthy era – these cleansers of history attribute the survival of the Jews of Budapest exclusively to the Regent's decision of 7 July 1944 to halt the deportations. Eager to assure Hungary's historical continuity as a 'chivalrous' nation, these nationalists fail to acknowledge the important role that others played. In the post-Communist era it has become politically fashionable and historically prudent not to mention the determining role the Red Army played in the liberation of the surviving Jews of Hungary, including those of Budapest.

These negative manifestations notwithstanding, post-Communist Hungary has made considerable progress toward coming to grips with the tragedy of its Jewish community. It decided to make some reparation to the surviving remnant of Hungarian Jewry and passed a law on the rights of ethnic and national minorities. But while the Hungarian government has been forceful in condemning anti-Semitism and eloquent in paying tribute to the victims of the Holocaust, it has failed so far at least to make a national, collective commitment to confront the Holocaust honestly and truthfully.[13]

Notes

1. See his *The Dissolution of the Hapsburg Monarchy*, Chicago, The University of Chicago Press, 1929, p. 825. See also Randolph L. Braham, *The Politics of Genocide. The Holocaust in Hungary*, New York, The Rosenthal Institute for Holocaust Studies, 1994, pp. 5–12.
2. For some details on the Golden Era, see Braham, *Politics*, pp. 1–39.
3. Jenö Lévai, *Zsidósors Magyarországon* (Jewish Fate in Hungary), Budapest, Magyar Téka, 1948, p. 17.
4. Braham, *Politics*, pp. 129–30.
5. For details on the pre-occupation losses of Hungarian Jewry, see ibid., pp. 205–22.
6. 'Edmund Veesenmayer's Memorandum to the German Foreign Office, dated December 10, 1943', in Randolph L. Braham (ed.), *The Destruction of Hungarian Jewry. A Documentary Account*, New York, The World Federation of Hungarian Jews, 1973, pp. 254–84.
7. Braham, *Politics*, pp. 283–93.
8. For details on the Final Solution programme in Hungary, see ibid., chs 17–22.
9. Ibid., pp. 391, 397–401. See also C. A. Macartney, *October Fifteenth. A History of Modern Hungary*, Edinburgh, Edinburgh University Press, 1957, vol. 2, pp. 234, 239.
10. For details on the reaction of the Allies, the neutral states, the Vatican, and the International Red Cross, see Braham, *Politics*, pp. 1205–94.
11. See his 'Identity Strategies Under Duress before and after the Shoah', in Randolph L. Braham and Attila Pók (eds), *The Holocaust in*

Hungary. Fifty Years Later, New York, The Rosenthal Institute for Holocaust Studies of the City University of New York, and Budapest, The Institute of History of the Hungarian Academy of Sciences, 1997, p. 157.

12. For details on all aspects of the labour service system, see Braham, *Politics*, pp. 294–380.
13. For details, see ibid., ch. 33.

–3–

Economic Implications of the Anti-Jewish Legislation in Hungary

Yehuda Don

The Jewish question in interwar Hungary was of immense importance for Hungarian public opinion, and it gained even greater significance in the course of the 1930s. Towards the end of that decade a rather weird, yet very prominent, group of conservative politicians[1] submitted a statement to the Hungarian head of state, Miklós Horthy, in which they warned that Land Reform together with the Jewish question, the two most critical issues on the political and socio-economic agenda of Hungary, must be considered as 'two undefused time bombs'.[2] This rather dramatic wording about the Jewish question by contemporary politicians gained authoritative approval from István Bibó, undoubtedly the most respected Hungarian scholar of the issue, who wrote: 'the solution of the Jewish question . . . appeared to be the Number 1 social problem in the country'.[3]

The authorities' attitude towards the Jewish population, complex and multidimensional as it may have been, boiled down, after the Peace of Trianon, to a fundamentally economic matter. Jews rose to almost unprecedented economic prominence in pre-World War I Hungary due to the fact that 'the capitalist development of modern Hungary . . . has been almost entirely of their making'.[4] An unwritten yet well-functioning division of labour evolved between the Hungarian landed nobility and the Jewish entrepreneurial elements, which 'lent a substantial enrichment to both'.[5] The ruling nobility and the gentry made themselves responsible for the country's politics, occupied all the extravagantly offered and remunerative administrative posts and manned the officers' corps of the army, while the Jews were in charge of economic growth and industrial modernization. However, this 'paradise for the Jews' functioned 'only so long as the country remained a multi-national empire ruled by old regime gentry liberals'.[6]

Following the Peace of Trianon and the dismemberment of Hungary, large numbers of immigrants, members of the old Hungarian gentry classes which had been the masters of the ceded territories, arrived to 'Small Hungary'. They became redundant under the new regimes, and were in fact obliged to return to the 'motherland' to search for the sort of jobs they preferred in an already overcrowded job market. These new circumstances transformed 'Jewish entrepreneurship' into 'Jewish dominance'. They also became the *raison d'être* for the infamous Act 1920:XXV, better known as the *numerus clausus*, which limited, through legislation, the number of Jewish students to be admitted to Hungarian universities to 6 per cent. The *numerus clausus* was essential, wrote A. Kovács, the renowned anti-Semitic head of the Central Statistical Bureau of Hungary, in 1926 'in order to put some limit to the intelligentsia which grew out of proportion through the influx of refugees from the robbed provinces'.[7] Anti-Jewish feeling further mushroomed during the early 1930s, with the global economic depression, which hit Hungary, still an agricultural country, harsher than many other countries in Europe.[8]

The crisis also led to the collapse of the nobility-controlled government of Gyula Károlyi. Political power shifted to the populist radical Right, anti-Semitic National Unity Party. Its leader, Gyula Gömbös, became the Prime Minister in 1932.[9] This new government marked a historical turning point: 'it was clear that the tide was turning against the Jewish interest. The extreme right was there to stay.'[10]

Ideology was converted into actual policy in 1938, when Kálmán Darányi, the successor of Gömbös, in a major policy speech, delivered in the city of Györ, pronounced that 'the solution of the Jewish question (is) the top priority issue of his government'.[11] The prime minister declared that his policy was 'To put an end to the highly disproportionate share of the Jews in certain branches of the economy.' He added that 'the social disproportionality must be uprooted and the influence of the Jewry on the cultural and other spheres of the nation must be reduced to acceptable proportions'.[12] The essence of the Darányi statement was the abolition of Act 1867:XVII, which had stated explicitly that the country's Jewish inhabitants were entitled to all the civil and political rights enjoyed by its Christian inhabitants. In the course of the following four years a series of four anti-Jewish discriminatory laws were put through Parliament which terminated a three-generation-long period of tranquil and productive cooperation between Jews and gentiles in the economy of Hungary. These laws were popularly known as the 'Jewish Laws'.

The first and mildest of the four already heralded a rather radical retrogression from the old free-market principle. Instead of a free labour market, the principle of proportionality was introduced, whereby, in enterprises with more than ten employees, the law would 'not permit the

Jewish share . . . to exceed twenty per cent of the total'.[13] To obstruct the entry of young Jewish professionals into various liberal occupations, the professional chambers in each locality were made instruments for the enforcement of legal discrimination. By the stipulation of practising licences for compulsory membership in such chambers, and by setting an upper limit to the ratio of Jewish members, the number of Jewish practitioners could easily be kept under control. In occupations where no such chambers had existed, but where the control of the number of Jews was considered necessary, such as journalism and the entertainment business, a network of new chambers was to be founded. In occupations with no 'Jewish Menace', such as the public service and the teaching profession, no chambers were needed.

The whole model envisaged for the implementation of the 'First Jewish Law', which implied a sort of partial reconstruction of a guild system, resembled in a way the 'corporate economy' model of Fascist Italy.

The First Jewish Law

Following the Darányi speech, in early March 1938, events moved fast. On 11 March 1938 the Anschluss of Austria made Germany an immediate neighbour of Hungary. On 8 April the Jewish Bill was presented to Parliament under the title of the 'Act for the More Effective Safeguard of the Balanced Social and Economic Life'. Justifications of the need for such a law were submitted one week later.[14] Following its approval in the Lower Chamber by an overwhelming majority, the Upper Chamber debated the Bill on 24 May, again with no surprise regarding the result. Hopes cherished by liberals and Jews with respect to the standing of the clergy's deputies in the Upper Chamber (forty-two in number) proved futile. The bishops of all three major churches supported the Bill as the 'least unfavourable solution'.[15] The Bill became Act 1938:XV late in May 1938.

The very idea of discriminatory legislation raised strong indignation among the Jewish community leaders. They found it particularly annoying that among the reasons for the law was the passage that reckoned the Jews among that 'segment of the population which does not thoroughly sense the nation's historical legacy, which does not represent for them the same values as it does for the rest of the population'.[16] The Jewish community leaders considered this passage as a government statement that the Jews were unassimilable,[17] and reacted to those accusations bitterly and emphatically: 'We have no other homeland in the globe but Hungary, we have no other shield but the constitution of our homeland.'[18]

Apart from the official Jewish protest, a very prominent group of fifty-nine Christian intellectuals also published a strongly worded statement of indignation against the Jewish Law. However they could only publish it in full in two daily newspapers and it left no noticeable impression, either on Parliament or on public opinion.[19]

As stated in Premier Darányi's Györ speech, the prime objective of Act 1938:XV was to reduce Jewish influence in the Hungarian economy, and in particular in certain liberal professions. It has already been mentioned that since the late nineteenth century, there existed a never explicitly declared yet widely accepted symbiosis, whereby there was some kind of division of labour in which the openings in the public sector became the turf of the young (Christian) gentry class, while the liberal professions were open for the children of the Jewish middle class. The difference between these two types of jobs was remarkable. The civil service offered respect, security and employment tenure. Its promotion mechanism functioned mainly through seniority and connections and it provided safe and dependable access to the proper acquaintances and political patronage. Admittedly, for most public sector employees material reward was not very generous, but the work did not require strenuous effort and was quite risk-free.

On the other hand, the occupations often patronized by the children of the Jewish middle class were pursued in highly competitive conditions, required preparedness for risk-taking and demanded long periods of professional training. They also promised highly remunerative rewards for the diligent and the successful.[20] The share of Jews in different areas of the liberal professions – both in the public and the private sectors – visibly demonstrated these trends. Table 3.1 presents this distribution for Hungary as a whole, as well as for the provinces and for Budapest separately. The data were drawn from the 1930 census, the last before the 'Laws'.

Table 3.1 shows very clearly that all occupations in which the employing institution belonged to the public sector showed visible underrepresentation for Jewish employees, while in occupations with private sector dominance Jews held a substantial share of the market. Clergy and secondary school teachers were rather exceptional, as the clergy was employed by the respective Church authorities and many secondary schools were denominational.

Obviously, the First Jewish Law targeted primarily those liberal occupations where the share of Jews was substantial, chiefly the press and the entertainment industry.[21] The decree which restricted the admission of Jews to the professional chambers to 5 per cent, as long as the overall ratio of

Table 3.1. The Share of Jews in Liberal Occupations in 1930 in Budapest, in the Provinces and in Hungary (Jews as per cent of the total)

Occupation	in Budapest column 1	in the Provinces column 2	in Hungary column 3
Civil Service	1.5	1.5	1.5
Judges & Prosecutors	1.7	1.9	1.8
Priests & Clerics	15.3	7.7	7.8
Teachers (elementary)	9.1	2.4	3.3
Teachers (secondary)	12.6	2.7	6.4
Military	–	–	0.5
Veterinary Surgeons	33.7	22.8	24.0
Pharmacists	25.9	10.4	18.9
Actors	30.3	15.1	24.1
Journalists & Editors	36.1	18.2	31.7
Private Engineers	36.1	19.4	30.5
Physicians	40.2	29.7	34.4
Lawyers	55.7	42.7	49.2

Source: G. Zeke (ed.), *Hét évtized a hazai zsidóság életében* (Seven Decades in the Life of the Motherland Jews), Budapest, 1990, vol. I, p. 193; Magyar Statisztikai Közlemények, New Series, vol. 96, pp. 132–53

all Jewish members (including those who had been already in the profession when the Law was enacted) was above 20 per cent, aimed primarily to hinder the career of the young Jewish graduates. They, or many of them, were held back from starting their practice by having been denied admission to their respective chambers. To further reduce jobs in non-physical work occupations, the Law extended the 20 per cent upper limit restriction to all white-collar occupations in enterprises with ten employees or more. White-collar jobs were defined in a very liberal fashion to include even ordinary salespersons in stores. In order to prevent Jewish employees, dismissed from large businesses, from finding employment in small ones (less than ten white-collar employees), the Law prohibited raising the ratio of such Jewish employees even in small businesses. The target date for full implementation was 30 June 1943.

In the first paragraph of the Law it was quite explicitly stated that its central objective was the alleviation of the unemployment problem of the Christian intelligentsia through the creation, by legal measures, of similar unemployment problems for the Jewish Intelligentsia.

On the assumption of a fully implemented First Jewish Law, what would have been its damage on the Jewish labour force in Hungary? No official statement in this respect was issued by the Jewish leadership. P. Bihari, relying on some contemporary projections, claims that the Law would have made about 15,000 Jewish professionals jobless, and that the overall damage to the Jewish labour force could have amounted to close to

50,000.[22] Despite the lack of an official statement on this matter the Jewish authorities earmarked special resources, from the annual budget for the year 1938, towards the establishment of retraining facilities for the predicted unemployed professionals.[23]

In this study an attempt is made quantitatively to estimate the job losses for Jewish professionals and other white-collar employees as a result of the First Jewish Law. To make our calculations intelligible assumptions were considered necessary.

1 The course of events was assumed to remain free from any exogenous disruptions, apart from Act 1938:XV.
2 All business establishments were assumed to have identical ratios of Jewish white-collar employees. This ratio was obviously the overall average ratio.
3 Each establishment was assumed to qualify for the 'ten or more employees' provision.

Naturally, neither assumption '2' nor assumption '3' are close to reality. However, the upward bias caused by assumption '3' is supposed to be, at least partially, countervailed by the downward bias caused by assumption '2'.

Estimates are presented separately for the city of Budapest, which, early in 1938, held about 46 per cent of the total Jewish population of Hungary, for the provinces and for the country as a whole. The estimates are based, as indicated above, on the 1930 Census. The city of Budapest held a separate Census of its own, in 1935. Therefore, we present two estimates for Budapest, one based on the 1930 Census and one on the special city Census of 1935. A distinction is made between professionals and other white-collar employees, although many of those registered as white-collar employees were in fact professionals by training, and worked as salaried employees (such as salaried engineers) in business establishments.

The estimates are presented in Tables 3.2, 3.3 and 3.4, and relate to the situation which would have evolved towards the target date of the Law, 30 June 1943. Columns 2 and 3 in Tables 3.2 and 3.3 are hypothetical, because a few months after the enactment of the First Law, the authorities, in haste to aggravate Jewish persecution, violated Assumption '1' by introducing the Second Jewish Law, which made the implementation of Act 1938:XV irrelevant.

As shown in Table 3.2, had the First Jewish Law been implemented, some 3,242 Jewish professionals would have lost their jobs. A little more than two-thirds of them (68 per cent) would have come from Budapest,

Table 3.2. Hypothesized Employment Damage of Professionals Caused by the First Jewish Law – 1930 Census Figures

Occupation	Ratio of Jews in per cent column 1	Permitted No. of Jews column 2	Jews to be Dismissed column 3
Professionals in Budapest			
Lawyers	55.7	547	976
Physicians	40.2	743	751
Journalists & Editors	36.1	228	184
Private Engineers	36.1	156	126
Actors	30.3	234	120
Pharmacists	25.9	152	45
Veterinary Surgeons	33.7	18	13
Total in No.	4,293	2,078	2,215
Professionals in the Provinces			
Lawyers	38.5	608	562
Physicians	29.7	915	443
Veterinary Surgeons	22.8	153	22
Total in No.	2,703	1,676	1,027

Source: as in Table 3.1.

the rest (32 per cent) from the Provinces. In Budapest alone, over one half (52 per cent) of all professionals, all in the 'over-Judaized' professions, would have become artificially redundant. In the provinces the problem of 'over-Judaization' occurred among the lawyers, the physicians and to a lesser degree among the veterinary surgeons.

Although for the society in general the massive unemployment of professionals was an especially severe economic issue from the point of view of wasted human capital and a painful tragedy for the highly trained individuals, from the plain humanitarian point of view, the First Jewish Law, if implemented, would have caused much more severe employment

Table 3.3. Hypothesized Employment Damage of White-Collar Employees Caused by the First Jewish Law – 1930 Census Figures

Occupation	Ratio of Jews in per cent column 1	Permitted No. of Jews column 2	Jews to be Dismissed column 3
Industry	25.1	14,700	3,800
Trade	69.8	10,100	25,000
Total in No.	53,600	24,800	28,800

Sources: as in Table 3.1.

damage among the salaried white-collar employees. The extent of this damage would have been very wide due to the excessively broad definition of the concept of white-collar workers, which was undoubtedly made with the intention to broaden the applicability of the Law. Table 3.3 quantifies the estimate of damage to white-collar employment.

About 54 per cent of all Jewish white collar employees would have faced unemployment through the implementation of the Law. Total employment losses would have amounted, approximately, to:

	in No.	in per cent
Professionals	3,200	10
White-Collar Employees	28,800	90
Total	32,000	100

During the 1930s there were about 213,000 economically active Jews in Hungary. Consequently, the implementation of the First Jewish Law would have impaired directly the livelihood of some 15 per cent of the Jewish population.

The estimates of Tables 3.2 and 3.3 are based on the 1930 Census figures both for the country, the provinces and the city of Budapest. However, as mentioned above, the city of Budapest held a special Census in 1935. We applied the methods of estimation, used in Tables 3.2 and 3.3 with the data of 1930, to the data of 1935, for Budapest only, with some slightly different definitions in the 1935 Census. The results suggested greater employment damage than that in Tables 3.2 and 3.3, however consistent with it. The author's impression is that the estimates based on the 1935 City Census data are better approximations than those of Tables 3.2 and 3.3. They are summed up in Table 3.4.

Based on the 1935 City Census figures, the number of people laid off in Budapest alone would have been about 18,800. Sixteen per cent of them would have come from the redundant professionals and 84 per cent would have been ex-white-collar employees. Of the 113,000 economically active Jews in the city of Budapest, one out of six (16.7 per cent) would have lost their livelihood.

The Second Jewish Law

The First Jewish Law was, however, never implemented in full. The authorities, who promulgated it as a tool of constitutional anti-Semitism, created it to avert the rage of the radical right-wing zealots, who were

Table 3.4. Hypothesized Employment Damage in Budapest Caused by the First Jewish Law – 1935 City Census Figures

Occupations	Ratio of Jews in per cent column 1	Permitted No. of Jews column 2	Jews to be Dismissed column 3
Professionals			
Lawyers	51.1	723	1,124
Physicians	38.8	852	802
Pharmacists	27.0	188	66
Others	26.1	3,350	1,030
Total in No.	8,135	5,113	3,022
White-Collar Employees			
Industry	43.9	4,494	5,373
Trade & Finance	48.0	7,406	10,359
Mining	47.6	66	91
Total in No.	27,789	11,966	15,823

discontented with the effectiveness and the speed of the Law. Neither were the criteria of Jewishness applied by the legislators, basically religious criteria, satisfactory to the advocates of the racial approach to the Jewish question in Germany and after the Anschluss also in former Austria. The adoption of the German model was thus anticipated, although it entailed the defiance of the churches, which made gains from anti-Semitism due to the proliferation of conversions to Christianity. Therefore it was relatively easy for the churches to go along with Act 1938:XV.[24] However, the prognostications of Count István Bethlen, referring to Act 1938:XV, that 'those who hasten this law will soon realize that it did not solve their problem, and will manipulate the Government . . . to go much further',[25] reads like a prophecy. Indeed, they went much further, first of all in a radical shift in the criteria of applicability of the law.

Race instead of religion.[26] The basic principle now was that if more than one out of the four grandparents was considered a Jew, it sufficed to stigmatize a person as a Jew.[27] The weird aspect of this law was that it divorced Jewishness from Jewish destiny, by invalidating even sincere aspirations to relinquish the Jewish religion through genuine, spiritually motivated, conversion. Some of the forty-two church dignitaries in the Upper Chamber of the Parliament rightly protested against the re-Judaization of the converts. The protest, however, was very meek, and all Christian ecclesiastical members of the Upper Chamber voted for the law, 'partly out of a sense of Realpolitik, having regard to the country's foreign policy position, partly for the sake of communal peace'.[28]

The Bill was submitted to Parliament near to the end of 1938 by Prime Minister Béla Imrédy. Imrédy entered the Hungarian public arena as an anglophile intellectual who specialized in banking. He drifted rapidly during the 1930s to right-wing populism and ended as a whole-hearted collaborator with the monstrous, suicidal Szalasi regime. Imrédy was dismissed by Regent Horthy before the new Bill passed Parliament and his successor Count Pál Teleki carried it on with as much fervour as his predecessor.[29] Early in 1939 the Bill became Act 1939:IV, better known as the Second Jewish Law.

In what way was this law different from its precursor? First, it was brutally undisguised. The Law explicitly stated that it aimed at 'the limitation of the Jews' encroachment in the public life and in the economy'.[30]

Second, the Law extended discrimination deep into all aspects of political and civil life. No Jew, apart from the two officially appointed rabbis in the Upper Chamber, was eligible for election to Parliament or to any elected post in the Comitats or the municipal councils. No more Jews could obtain Hungarian citizenship. No Jew could be appointed to any public office, either at the various levels of state or local administration, or to the legal system. Paragraph 5 of the Law stipulated that all Jewish officials in the public sector, down to the most humble positions of porters and manual workers, had to be dismissed or forced into early retirement. Finally, Jewish citizens of Hungary were deprived of voting rights, unless they could prove the continuous residence of their ancestors in Hungary from 1867 onwards.

Third, and the severest of all, were the economic dimensions of the Law. In these spheres distinction should be made between: (a) exclusion, (b) restriction through quotas and (c) semi-official harassment.

(a) Jewish tradesmen were doomed to exclusion, or banishment from all businesses which required 'professional licenses the appropriation of which depended upon the discretion of the authorities'.[31] Thus, trade in tobacco and liquor (state monopolies) had to be '*Judenfrei*' in two years. The licences of all Jewish pharmacists had to be revoked in five years. Jews were to be excluded from trade in heating fuel, the operation of taxi cabs, peddling and newspaper selling. Jews were to be banned also from trade in wine and wine products (vinegar etc).
(b) The quota restrictions of 20 per cent of the First Law were curtailed to 12 per cent in white-collar jobs and to 6 per cent in the liberal professions. Quota restrictions were also imposed on independent businesses in the various fields of trade, with an upper limit of 6 per cent.

(c) Probably the most annoying discriminatory measures were a wide variety of officially approved or tacitly condoned acts of harassment, which were absolutely arbitrary and unpredictable. In most cases they depended on the mood and disposition of local officials and dignitaries. Among these measures one should also include acts of excess in the administration of the Law, often bordering on atrocities. In certain instances over-zealousness bordered on the ridiculous.[32]

The official institutions of the Jewish communities (conservative, orthodox and status quo) reacted to the new Bill with bitter protest and indignation. They published a joint statement, early in January 1939, in which they argued that the Bill contravened the Hungarian constitution, and violated the basic principles of human justice as well as the Divine Law. After a longish critique of the Bill in which they explained why it would be detrimental to the real interests of Hungary, the statement concluded in a fashion which was painfully consistent with the very ethos of the Jewish existence in Hungary.

> If this bill becomes law, it will result in the compulsion of hundreds of thousands of us and of our children to be banished from our homes. We may change our homes but we shall never change our homeland. Just as no human law can deprive us of our rights to pray to our God, so nothing can deprive us of our Hungarian motherland. Just as none of history's torments . . . deterred us [from our prayers] so shall we never be deterred from our devotion to our Hungarian motherland.[33]

This pathetic statement was made public at a time when the Hungarian Parliament, through its discriminatory legislation, openly pronounced that the Hungarian state did not rely on the patriotism of the Jews and rejected demonstration of their loyalty to the Hungarian motherland.

The sponsors of the Second Jewish Law hoped that it would bring about a radical 'changing of the guard' in the Hungarian economy.[34] In 1938 this was totally unrealistic, disregarding ethical considerations, unless the government was ready to incur immense economic cost. In Hungary there were 80,507 Jewish shopkeepers, of whom 65,113 would have to be replaced by members of the new guard in four years. There were 73,887 independent Jewish artisans, of whom 47,948 were to be replaced by gentile successors.[35] In Budapest alone, which held much of Hungary's manufacturing industry, of the 1,480 non-publicly owned manufacturing establishments (28 were owned by the state or by the city) 869 (58.7 per cent) were owned and/or managed (in the case of public companies) by Jews.[36]

There were close on 2,900 Jewish physicians in Hungary, out of a total of about 8,300 medical doctors. The annual output of the medical schools was some 350 graduates. Close to a fifth of all pharmacists were Jewish and over two-thirds of them were supposed to be replaced by pharmacists of the new guard. Close to one half of all private lawyers were Jews, and close to 90 per cent of them had to be replaced by gentile private lawyers in all parts of the legal profession. The list of the professional fields in which the new guard had to produce appropriate replacements in very large numbers to replace the Jewish practitioners who were to be ousted was long and unattainable. Apparently, neither Regent Horthy's evaluation of the quality of the new guard was ecstatic,[37] nor were the Germans particularly confident that such a change of the guard in the economic life would be easy. The official daily of the National Socialist Party, the *Völkischer Beobachter*, wrote on 24 December 1942 about the 'difficulties in finding "Aryan" successors for the economic life of Hungary . . . In spite of all efforts of responsible circles, the youth still does not want even to hear of commercial or industrial pursuits'.[38]

Obviously, there were important circles in Hungarian public life which were aware of the economic cost that was to be incurred in the event of full implementation of the Second Jewish Law. Among the best-known exponents of this view was Regent Horthy himself. He tried to mitigate the economically harmful effects of drastic and immediate implementation by slowing it down or even holding it back. Other circles took more dogmatic positions, and, induced by their ideological stance, ignored both economic and social costs. During the parliamentary debate on the Bill, the head of the fascist youth organization, the 'Turul Movement', F. Vegvary, stated that 'the most severe *numerus clausus* will have to be implemented among the university and the medical school teachers. . . We shall also have to eliminate from the grammar schools and high schools all the Jewish textbooks'.[39] Such statements obviously reflected the lack of awareness of the availability of proper non-Jewish university teachers and the need to rewrite school texts, or demonstrated willingness to pay the price of such deficiencies. Another example of excessive zeal in speeding up de-Judaization is taken from the state school system of Budapest. This process, according to the instructions of the Law, was to be completed by the end of 1942. However, over-zealous politicians issued regulations to accomplish it by 1 February 1940. A member of the City Council, L. Bánóczy, appealed to the Mayor to cancel the instructions for advanced implementation as they are 'unpedagogical, since the brutal removal of teachers in the middle of the year also damages the education of the Christian children'.[40]

In a way, one may see the interwar years as an epoch of struggle around the Jewish Question, between the pragmatists and the ideologists. It is not within the range of our discussion to investigate whether the pragmatist politicians were less anti-Semitic than the ideologists, (if such phenomena are measurable at all) but it seems certain that the former were reluctant to pay as high a price for their racial principles as the anti-Semitic zealots.

Economic Damage to the Victims

Let us now examine the Second Jewish Law from the economic point of view of the victims. What sacrifices would have been paid by the Jews, in terms of employment and job availability, if the Law had had the chance to run its course to full implementation? Although we know that no such time was given it before the arrival of the Final Solution model, the data nevertheless merit examination.

An early estimate by Dr József Pásztor of M.I.P.I. (Office for the Assistance of the Hungarian Israelites) provided the detailed research of his office on the overall figures of job losses and deprivation of livelihood for the family members of those laid off.[41]

	Lost Jobs	No. of dependants	Total
To 31.12.1940	50,772	82,869	133,641
From 1.1.1941 to 31.12.1941	8,678	12,262	20,940
Estimates to 31.12.1942	32,018	5,279	70,292
Total to 31.12.1942	91,468	130,410	221,896(*sic*)

The 'Total' number constituted slightly over 40 per cent of the Jewish population of 'Trianon Hungary' (within the borders determined after World War I). In 1942, when the Pásztor figures were published, Hungary annexed additional territories, with very substantial Jewish populations, and the ratio of the 'Total' figures to this population was 30 per cent.[42]

Another estimate, probably that of Dr S. Eppler, the Secretary General of the Jewish Religious Community until 1942, mentioned a lower figure of 140,396 Jewish persons who had lost their livelihood by late 1942. The details of this estimate are interesting. The number of persons affected through the loss of jobs for white-collar employees (including dependants) was estimated at 73,487. Parallel numbers were: for salesmen and other commercial representatives: 30,268; for professionals: 2,741; for owners of state monopoly licences (tobacco etc.) 13,500; for owners of trade licences 'earmarked for statutory elimination from social life' 24,400. The total number of potential economic victims would have constituted 31.5 per cent of the total Jewish population of Trianon Hungary.[43] These were, obviously, only estimates of direct damage, not including the indirect effects of secondary livelihood losses through the reduced purchasing power of those directly effected. It would have been very difficult to estimate secondary 'multiplier' effects.

A short time after the final approval of the Second Jewish Law, in May 1939, two of the central figures in the Hungarian Jewry, the President Samu Stern and the Secretary General Dr Sándor Eppler, both of the Neolog community, went to London to appeal for the help of the British Jewry.[44] In their report they estimated the employment damage caused by the First Jewish Law at 15,000 jobs. The immediate effect, to the end of 1939, of the Second Law would be another 10,000, and within the implementation time limit of four years 'a quarter of a million Hungarian Jews would be left without any means of livelihood'.[45]

Our estimates are based on the official statistical returns on Jewish and general occupational patterns in Hungary during the 1930s. They assume that the percentage constraints imposed were fully enforced. Under such circumstances a new occupational pattern could be envisaged for the Jews, which would have reflected the full effect of the implemented Law. Naturally, such an occupational pattern is speculative as long as implementation was not full. However, even as an exercise it is useful to display the dimensions of the economic convulsion which was in the making. As indicated, the Law was never fully implemented, first, because economic rationality overpowered ideological zeal, then, in 1944, because it was substituted by the Final Solution model, which led, in less than one year, not only to the extermination of some 600,000 Hungarian Jews but also to the overall collapse of Hungary.

The statistical basis of our calculations is the Census of the city of Budapest for 1935. Although the coverage is narrower than that of a country-wide census, the Budapest figures were found preferable because the last country-wide census, before the enactment of the Jewish Laws, was held in 1930, so it could not reflect the deep structural impact of the Great Depression of the early 1930s. On the other hand, using the data of the next country-wide census, well after the enactment of the Second Jewish Law, would have obviously biased the estimates, since those data were already infected by the phenomenon which is the subject of this investigation. Furthermore, Hungary of the early 1940s was not, geopolitically at least, the Hungary for which the Jewish Laws were conceived and passed. Consequently, we based our calculations on the 1935 Budapest Census figures, and the results reflect, strictly speaking, only the conditions in that city.

Table 3.5. Occupational Composition of the Economically Active General and Jewish Population in Budapest, 1935 Census Figures (Absolute Numbers and Per Cents)

Occupation	In Numbers		In Per Cents	
	Total	Jews	Total	Jews
Industry	242,048	40,345	45.7	35.9
Commerce & Banking	101,357	45,599	19.1	40.6
Liberal Professions	28,613	9,184	5.4	8.2
Public Sector	65,712	2,983	12.4	2.6
Miscellaneous	91,828	14,241	17.3	12.7
Total	529,558	112,532	100	100

Our point of departure is the occupational composition of the economically active general and Jewish population of Budapest. Table 3.5 presents the absolute numbers as well as the percentage-wise distributions, aggregating all occupations into five major categories. Industry also includes mining (quite insignificant in Budapest); Commerce also includes Finance and Banking; the Liberal Professions also include Journalism and the Arts; the Public Sector also includes the Ecclesiastic Services, Public Transport and Communication; Miscellaneous also include Agriculture and Private Transportation. The figures are displayed in Table 3.5.

The difference between the two distributions is apparent. Let us bring them into even sharper focus by examining the share of the Jews in each occupational grouping. Expressed as percentages, the shares are:

Industry	Commerce	Liberal Professions	Public Sector	Miscellaneous
16.7%	45.0%	32.1%	4.5%	15.7%

The overall share of the Jews in the economically active population of Budapest was 21.2 per cent.

Some conclusions can be drawn from Table 3.5.

(a) In commerce the share of the Jews was high, though by no means dominant. Since the Jews were mostly in the retail trade of basic consumer goods, they were extremely visible. However, quantitatively, they were far from being a majority of all those engaged in commerce.
(b) More than one-third of all economically active Jews were in industry. Many of them did not join the ranks of the typical industrial proletariat, as there was a clearly observable preference for smaller establishments over the stereotyped smoke-stack factories of the 1930.[46]
(c) In Budapest, as in many great urban centres in Europe, Jews displayed a strong inclination to the liberal professions, journalism and the arts. In Budapest and in Vienna this tendency was especially strong.[47]

Nevertheless, in Budapest they were far from being dominant, as they constituted less than one-third of all those active in this branch of the city economy.

(d) As expected, only a very low percentage of all Jews found their way to the public sector, and only a very small percentage of those engaged in the public sector were Jews. This lack of desire on the part of both the authorities and the Jews for an employer–employee relationship was characteristic of most European economies during the interwar years.

The Second Jewish Law imposed a set of quantitative constraints upon Jewish occupational options.

(a) All Jewish employees in the public sector, including the Army, the state school system, the public transport and communication network, had to be dismissed or sent into early retirement. The public sector was to become a '*Judenrein*' zone.

(b) Ownership of agricultural land, or the farming of agricultural estates by Jews, had to be eliminated. Although Act 1939:IV did not stipulate explicitly the expropriation of Jewish landed property, this was amended by a less famous Law, Act 1942:XV, known as the Fourth Jewish Law, which demanded the immediate expropriation of all agricultural estates owned or leased by Jews.[48]

(c) A severe constriction was imposed on Jewish entrepreneurship. The ratio of independent operators or self-employed persons in business establishments had to be reduced to 6 per cent of all the self-employed in each industry. When the ratio was higher, Jewish establishments had to be eliminated, or their ownership passed into gentile hands. This instruction became the cradle of the contrivance known familiarly and widely as the 'Strohman' or 'Aladár' system.

(d) The Second Law severely aggravated the quantitative constraints imposed upon Jews in the liberal professions. The permitted rate of participation was curtailed from 20 per cent to 6 per cent. The immediate implication of the Law was a drastic reduction in the human capital reserves of the country. At the same time a severe unemployment problem was to emerge for those specialists whose chances of finding suitable alternative jobs were close to nil.

(e) Quantitative constraints were also aggravated in the employment of white-collar employees in commerce and industry. The permitted ratio was reduced from 20 per cent to 12 per cent, and worsened the already critical employment conditions of this group of semi-skilled workers.

Summing up the quantitative constraints, the following emerges:

All Jews in the public sector are to be dismissed. Per cent allowed = 0
All Jewish farm owners and operators are to be removed. Per cent allowed = 0
Jewish self-employed in industry, trade and transport: Per cent allowed = 6
Jews in the liberal professions: Per cent allowed = 6
Jewish white-collar employees in the private sector: Per cent allowed =12
Jewish blue-collar employees in the private sector: No restriction

Let us reconstruct in Table 3.6 the occupational composition chart, distinguishing, in each occupational group, between self-employed, white-collar employees and blue-collar workers. In Table 3.6 we separate Agriculture and Private Transport from 'Miscellaneous', because the last includes some groups which can hardly be looked upon as economically active (rentiers etc.), and cannot be divided by status at work.

Let us calculate the employment implications of the participation quotas on the Jewish labour force. For these calculations we resort to the three assumptions used above (see p. 52). Table 3.7 presents the number of legally permitted persons in each occupation in each employment status. It also presents the number of those persons who would have been laid off as a result of the full implementation of the Law.

Table 3.6. Occupational Composition of the Economically Active General and Jewish Population in Budapest in 1935 by Status at Work

Occupation		Total			Jewish	
	S.E.	W.Cr.	B.Cr.	S.E.	W.Cr.	B.Cr.
Industry	33,671	22,801	185,576	10,004	10,024	20,337
Commerce	28,279	37,030	36,048	16,289	17,765	11,545
Agriculture	2,220	484	3,340	335	111	61
Private Transport	1,642	492	5,241	506	141	272

Abbreviations: S.E. = Self-Employed; W.Cr. = White Collar; B.Cr. = Blue Collar.

Table 3.6 omits the public sector, as it was subject to the total dismissal of all Jews, the liberal professions, as they were subject to an overall 6 per cent constraint and the 'Miscellaneous' group, for which we assumed no constraint regulation. The average ratio of the Jews in the different occupations by status at work was:

Status	Industry	Commerce	Agriculture	Private Transport
S.E.	29.7	57.6	15.1	30.8
W.Cr.	44.0	48.0	22.9	28.7
B.Cr.	11.0	32.0	1.8	5.2

Table 3.7. Employment Damage Caused by the Second Jewish Law If Implemented in the City of Budapest – 1935 Census Figures

Occupation	Status at Work	Total No. of Workers	Permitted No. of Jews	Jews to be Dismissed
Industry	S.E.	33,671	2,020	7,984
Industry	W.Cr.	22,801	2,736	7,288
Industry	B.Cr.	185,576	20,337	0
Commerce	S.E.	28,279	1,697	14,592
Commerce	W.Cr.	37,030	5,501	21,073
Commerce	B.Cr.	36,048	2,736(#)	0
Liberal Prof.	W.Cr.	28,613	1,717	7,467
Public Sector	W.Cr.	65,712	101(@)	2,882
Agriculture	S.E.	2,220	0	335
Agriculture	W.Cr.	484	58	53
Agriculture	B.Cr.	3,340	61	0
Transport	S.E.	1,642	99	407
Transport	W.Cr.	492	59	82
Transport	B.Cr.	5,241	272	0
Miscellaneous	(*)	78,409	12,995	0
Total		529,558		62,163

(#) 76.3% of the Jewish blue-collar workers in commerce were registered as sales personnel, and thus considered as employees with a 12% upper constraint. They were added to the white-collar employees. The blue-collar category remained with the rest of the group, 2,736 workers.
(*) The composition of the 'Miscellaneous' group indicates that, possibly, they were subject to no legally required occupational restrictions.
(@) Jewish ecclesiastical workers.

Table 3.7 suggests that about 55 per cent of the economically active Jewish population were exposed to the dangers of losing their work and livelihood. The exclusion of the 'Miscellaneous' group from the economically active population pushes the ratio of the laid-off group to over 62 per cent. A further, detailed breakdown of the internal structure of unemployment thus calculated leads to interesting results. The specific unemployment ratios based on the extrapolated unemployment numbers by groups of professions would have been as follows:

for the self employed	85.9%
for the white-collar employees	79.2%
for all employees in industry	37.8%
for the self-employed in industry	79.8%
for the white-collar employees in industry	72.7%
for all S.E. and W.Cr. in industry	76.3%
for all employees in commerce	78.2%
for the self-employed in commerce	89.6%

for the white-collar employees in commerce	79.3%
for all S.E. and W.Cr. in commerce	83.2%
for the liberal professionals	81.3%

These figures show clearly that the Second Jewish Law would have brought the employment structure of the Jews to a complete collapse. In the provinces the employment damage would have been no lighter. Admittedly the proportion of Jews in the public sector and in the liberal professions was substantially lower than in Budapest. On the other hand, commerce employed relatively more people in the provinces, and the establishments were, on average, smaller than in Budapest. Consequently, the ratio of the self-employed, with the maximum quota constraint of 6 per cent, was relatively high in the provinces.[49]

Also, due to the distance from the centre, control was difficult, and the random factor of arbitrary enforcement by local strongmen was great. One may assume that the harassment effect in the provinces was much stronger than in the capital. On the whole, employment losses in the provinces were also within the range of 60 per cent to two-thirds. However, the problem of substitutability in the provinces must have been more difficult than in Budapest, due to the slimmer reserves of non-Jewish human capital able to replace the ousted Jewish merchants and intellectuals.

The employment flexibility of most Jewish employees who lost, or were to lose, their jobs, particularly in view of the job options realistically left open for them, was extremely low. Most projects sponsored by various bodies within the Jewish Community institutions, to re-train the ousted and the unemployed for blue-collar skills, had little chance of meaningfully alleviating the unemployment crisis. Organizations such as O.R.T. (which came to Hungary only in 1939!),[50] or the M.I.K.É.F.E. and other smaller agricultural training farms,[51] were only of marginal significance in the efforts to solve structurally insoluble unemployment problems. Propositions, therefore, to reform the occupational structure of the Hungarian Jews, to make them into more 'productive' citizens, were nonsensical, unless the authorities were prepared to use physical coercion to carry out their 'reforming' objectives.

Such productivizing efforts through the labour market would have been nonsensical because:

1 The skills of most of the Jewish labour force were totally unfit for the types of work left for them by the legislators responsible for the Jewish Laws.

2 The entrance of the Jews into the unskilled workers' market would have further depressed the very low wages in that market, which behaved like other labour markets in undeveloped economies, displaying huge differences between the wages of the skilled and the unskilled labour force.

Coercive productivization was also practised by the authorities, by calling up large numbers of Jewish males, in the economically most productive years of their working life, to perform navvying jobs, first within the country, and after the involvement of Hungary in the war with the Soviet Union, on the Eastern Front. These were the notorious labour brigades, which, at various times, held in coercive labour service up to 50,000 Jewish men.[52]

Implementation Policies

The Jewish Laws were, as indicated, never systematically implemented. Up to the German occupation of Hungary in March 1944, implementation was haphazard and inconsistent. After that date, the situation was chaotic and lawless.

During the first five years, the determination to implement the Law in full changed with the change in political orientation. Two rather clear-cut subperiods can be distinguished.

1 From May 1939 to March 1942, under the premierships of Pál Teleki and Lászlo Bárdossy.
2 From March 1942 to March 1944 under the premiership of Miklós Kállay.

During the almost three years of the first subperiod the only sector which thoroughly fulfilled the instructions of the Law was the public sector. When the authorities learned that some 'legal nuisance' interfered with their eagerness to eject the Jews from public offices to which they had been duly elected, special legislation was initiated. This was Act 1941: XIX, which went through Parliament on 31 December 1941. Following its enactment twenty-four Jews were suspended from the City Council of Budapest.[53] The judiciary, the civil service and the public communication system sponsored the immediate dismissal of their Jewish officials and workers.[54] Excessive zeal or greed led to the revocation of the licences of all 500 Jewish taxi drivers, of all the Jewish tobacconists and of all Jewish newspaper vendors. The reason given was that all these businesses were state monopolies, and belonged to the public sector. Blunders, when detected, were reprimanded. In October 1941 the Lord Mayor of Budapest censured one of his deputies for some serious 'transgressions' of the Law. The Municipal Electricity Company still employed eighty-one officials of Jewish origin and in the Municipal Gasworks there were still sixty-seven Jewish employees. Worst of all, in the Municipal Waterworks, the administrator in charge of the implementation of the Jewish Law was married to a converted Jewess.[55] If in Budapest such examples of accidental or intentional sloppiness were, apparently, not infrequent, in the provinces they may have been the rule. Local bigwigs virtually had the power of life and death.

In the private sector implementation was uneven. On the one hand, the economic depression, which had lasted for almost a decade, was over. Rearmament projects and the war-induced demand of neighbouring countries, particularly Germany, exerted increasing pressure on the Hungarian economy to produce more. During these years (1938–40) real industrial production increased by 27 per cent. Unemployment, one of the major political reasons for the Jewish Laws, dissipated in the course of 1939. The immediate economic problem became that of inflation. Under such conditions the economic background to the 'Changing of the Guard' ideology disappeared. The macro-economic price of the anti-Jewish policy, in terms of lost economic welfare, rose sharply. Besides, the need to change the guard diminished when everybody had bread. Consequently, the authorities did not press very hard the expropriation of the means of production from Jewish businessmen. So, by the end of 1942 a substantial part of all privately owned industrial plants were still in Jewish hands. This can be seen clearly from Table 3.8.

Although the share of Jewish-controlled plants declined from close to one half to close to one quarter, the Jews remained, even in 1942, the second largest religious group (after the Roman Catholics) among the factory owners. However, even this figure was an underestimate, due to the widespread phenomenon of the 'Strohman' system, which, though not actively encouraged by the authorities, was silently condoned. The

Table 3.8. Jewish Control (Ownership and Leasing) of Industrial Plants Budapest, 1937–42

Year	1937	1938	1939	1940	1941	1942
I. Total No. of plants	3,902	3,990	4,334	4,391	5,066	5,822
II. Jewish-controlled plants	1,834	1,846	1,905	1,820	1,743	1,392
III.=II./I. (in per cent)	47.0	46.3	44.0	41.4	34.4	23.9

Source: *Budapest Statistical Yearbooks*; vol. 1939, p. 99 and vol. 1942, p. 102

'Strohman' system had two advantages for the economic (non-Jewish) elite. First, it safeguarded the professional management of the manufacturing or service companies, without openly violating the provisions of the Jewish Laws. Second, it became a source of rich remuneration to many influential members of the Christian business oligarchy and aristocracy. Thus, Jewish-controlled firms were registered as being run by racially 'pure' Christian directors, so that no objection could be raised against the placement of state orders with such firms. This was especially the case when the government was keen to have its orders promptly fulfilled amid inflationary circumstances, when the government's share in the national income increased from one-third in 1938–9 to close to 72 per cent in 1944.[56] In such circumstances it is obvious that in spite of Act 1942:XV, which ordered the immediate confiscation of all Jewish farmland of 100 acres and above, about 1.5 million acres of farming land were in 1942 still in Jewish hands. So complained Matyas Matolcsy.[57] The dominant reason for such tolerance towards Jewish control of farm land was, probably, that handing out large and very productive estates to small farmers would have jeopardized productivity and reduced the total crop.[58] Yet there might have been another factor which hindered the stringent enforcement of Act 1942:XV. It was probably alarm lest the distribution of Jewish-controlled land could have been interpreted as a beacon for general land reform, an issue dreaded by Regent Horthy and his advisers.[59] This is why most Jewish land which was distributed was given to privileged groups, such as members of the 'Vitéz' order (a distinction given for exceptional heroic deeds for the motherland) or to crippled veterans of World War I.[60]

These were, apparently, the main reasons for the slack enforcement of the Jewish Laws. If, under the Bárdossy government, such slackness may have been the manifestation of bureaucratic inefficiency, it became an implicit signal, one more manifestation of 'goodwill' towards the Western Powers, in the 'see-saw policy' of Premier Miklós Kállay.

The Jewish Laws seemed to make little visible impact on the fortunes of the very large Jewish industrial enterprises. The examination of some of the largest of these during World War II reveals only a few major differences between the activities of the Jewish and the non-Jewish industrial firms.

Take two of the 'flagship' Jewish industrial initiatives, the Weiss Manfred Works and the Goldberger Textile Factory. Both were symbols – positive or negative – of Jewish entrepreneurship in the industrial revolution of Hungary.

The Weiss Manfred Works was the greatest and most important metal and machinery firm in the country. It also manufactured arms, ammunition and military vehicles. In the late 1920s it started to manufacture aeroplanes. Obviously it was indispensable to the economy, and later to the war effort of the Hungarian government. Consequently, the enterprise took its full share in the prosperous war economy, increasing its annual investment almost sixfold, from 6.2 million pengö ($1.2 million) in 1938 to 34.4 million pengö ($6.9 million) in 1942,[61] and its labour force more than threefold, from 18,000 in 1938 to 57,000 in 1944.[62] In the authoritative study on the Weiss Manfred Works nothing was mentioned to suggest discrimination for having been a famous Jewish firm. It shared with all other firms in heavy industry the lavish government orders for the supply of military hardware and ammunition. These prosperous times came to an abrupt end with the German occupation, when the Germans, in a unique coercive deal, 'bought' the firm directly from the family, circumventing the Hungarian authorities, and renamed it the 'Herman Goering Works'.

The economic importance of the Goldberger factory lay mainly in its massive exports, even during the early 1940s, and its reputation as the leading textile establishment in the country. The firm was not totally exempted from the burden of the Jewish Laws, which 'deprived it gradually of its finest craftsmen',[63] sent into retirement some senior executives, also from the Goldberger family, and led the Director General, Leo Goldberger, to give up his personal salary. However, he 'succeeded in persuading' some top politicians, senior public officials and at least one Hohenlohe prince 'to join the Board of Directors'.[64] After these measures the firm prospered. Its net profit soared from an annual average of 340,000 pengo in 1940–2, to 950,000 pengö in 1943. The overall balance-sheet value of the firm, after the deduction of current liabilities, increased from an annual average of 26.3 million pengö ($5.3 million) in 1940–2 to 30 million pengö ($6 million) in 1943.[65] The major troubles of the firm in the early 1940s came not from the Jewish Laws but from the labour unrest which flared up following the wage freeze imposed by the government on the textile industry. The German occupation ended the industrial endeavours of Leo Goldberger, who was deported by the Gestapo to Mauthausen where he died in May 1945.

The business history of other, smaller though still significant, Jewish-controlled industrial enterprises was roughly the same, whether it was the Hungarian Cloth Factory (Magyar Posztógyár), or the Csepel Worsted Yarn Factory (Csepeli Fésüsfonalgyar), both initiatives of the Weiss Manfred conglomerate in the textile industry,[66] or the Mauthner Odon Grain Producers & Traders Ltd (Mauthner Ödön Magtermelö és Mag-kereskedelmi RT.), a coordinated initiative of the Weiss family and another great Jewish Hungarian entrepreneurial family, the Mauthners.[67] Another example is the Csepel Paper Factory (Csepeli Papirgyár), a partnership between the pioneers of the Hungarian paper industry, the Neményi brothers, and the great entrepreneurs of the Hungarian electrical industries, Lipót and Dávid Aschner.[68]

All these firms were Jewish and all of them, after minor or major adjustments, continued to produce, expand and benefit from the war-induced prosperity. The circumstances were similar in the financial sector. Until March 1944 the Jewish financial magnates and their great financial institutions were not seriously affected by the choking regulations of the Jewish Laws. Nor were many senior self-employed practitioners in the liberal professions, such as attorneys, physicians and engineers, seriously affected. They remained in their respective professional chambers and carried on with their practices.

There can be little doubt that such massive and visible violation of the Jewish Laws was not the result of clumsiness or negligence. It must have been inspired, or even instructed, by the supreme decision-making bodies of the state, probably by the Regent himself and his advisers. The basic issue was, as already mentioned above, whether and to what extent was the Christian intelligentsia capable and available, in the short run, to provide, in sufficient numbers, a proficient entrepreneurial and professional labour force to carry out the much-desired 'Changing of the Guard'. When Parliament debated Act 1942:XV, the economic expert of the extreme Right, Mátyás Matolcsy, put the issue most explicitly: 'All those misgivings raised here are unfounded. The Hungarian people and the Hungarian race possesses the strength and the talent to take the place of the Jews.'[69] Regent Horthy, who was also, apparently, keen to implement such a changing of the guard, did not rely on the expectations of politicians like Matolcsy, and turned a blind eye to those Jewish economic activities which he considered essential.

However, this tolerance was discriminatory and selective. The Jewish Laws were of frightful significance to the rank and file of the Jewish white-collar employees and to the great majority of the Jewish intelligentsia. The anticipated employment damage to them and to the operators of the small businesses can be seen from the emergency steps taken by the officers of the Jewish organizations in re-training programmes and in the establishment of relief agencies to aid the needy. The major financial vehicle for such emergency relief was O.M.Z.S.A. (the nation-wide Hungarian Jewish relief campaign), which took upon itself 'to raise the necessary funds to cover the cost of the extraordinary rescue mission of the specific relief organizations'.[70] The principal relief agent for the 'extraordinary rescue missions to be handled centrally' was M.I.P.I. (welfare office of the

Hungarian Jews).[71] Distress forced the community to revitalize old organizations to ease the afflictions of new evils. This was the case with the old art society, O.M.I.K.E., which became a major performing arts centre and provided employment and performing opportunities to some 400 ousted Jewish artists.[72]

The overall economic effects of the Jewish Laws on the Jewish public were highly regressive. They dramatically widened the income and wealth gap within the community, between the well-to-do classes and the lower middle classes. While the income of the upper echelon was hardly impaired and probably improved as a result of wartime prosperity and inflation, the peddler, the artisan, the white-collar employee and the average liberal professional became impoverished, first, by losing their jobs and, second, by losing through inflation the value of their savings. The wealth factor further widened economic inequality. Until the German occupation Jewish wealth, except farmland, was not directly affected. Neither was income from property affected. This applied, naturally, only to those who owned property and did not have to sell it to survive. The wealth factor thus reinforced the regressive tendencies caused by the selective implementation of the Jewish Laws.

Most of these trends came to an abrupt end in March 1944. Indiscriminate deportations which followed the German occupation and the chaotic lawless conditions which prevailed after the Szalasi *putsch* ended everything for the Jews in Hungary. Whatever evolved after the spring of 1945 was a new epoch.

Notes

1. The group was politically weird, as it included, among others, the most prominent member of the landed nobility, Count Istvan Bethlen, and the leader of the smallholders' party, who after 1945 became the President of postwar Hungary, Zoltan Tildy.
2. The expression was used by the above-mentioned group (note 1 above) and was published in M. Szinai and L. Szucs (eds), *Horthy Miklos Titkos Iratai* (The Secret Documents of Miklos Horthy), Budapest, 1963, pp. 206–7.
3. I. Bibó, *Zsidókérdés Magyarországon 1944 Után* (The Jewish Question in Hungary after 1944), Budapest, 1994, p. 12.

4. C.A. Macartney, *The Habsburg Empire, 1780–1918*, New York, 1969, p. 710.
5. W.O. McCagg Jr., *The History of Habsburg Jews 1670–1919*, Bloomington, IN, 1992, p. 133.
6. E. Mendelsohn, *Jews of East Central Europe between the Wars*, Bloomington, IN, 1983, p. 94.
7. The contemporary anti-Semitic literature hailed the *Numerus Clausus* which helps in 'inducing healthy processes among the youth who aspire towards liberal professions'. A. Kovács, *Értelmiségünk Nemzeti Jellegének Biztositása* (Safeguarding the National Character of our Intelligentsia), Budapest, 1926, p. 7.
8. Wheat prices in Budapest fell to a deeper trough in 1933, and recovered more slowly in the mid-1930s than, for instance, in Liverpool, the centre of the European wheat trade. See: K. Rége, '100 év a magyar buza áralakulásának es termelési költségének történetéből' (100 years in the history of the prices and cost of the Hungarian wheat), in *Magyar Nemzetgazdasági Enciklopédia*, Budapest, no date, pp. 380–430.
9. For the radical change of political direction with the arrival of the Gömbös government, see N. Katzburg, *Hungarian Jewry 1920–1943*, Jerusalem, 1992, pp. 59–63 (Hebrew).
10. Mendelsohn, *Jews of East Central Europe*, p. 116.
11. The wording is taken from the quotation in the *Annual Report of the Budapest Jewish Community for the Year 1937*, Budapest, 1938, p. 11.
12. Ibid.
13. L. Ottlik, 'The Hungarian Jewish Law', *The Hungarian Quarterly* no. 4 (1938–9), p. 399.
14. The main reasons raised by the government were: the imbalance caused by Jewish inroads into various professions; the necessity to satisfy Germany with some anti-Jewish legislation; Jews had not truly assimilated and did not deserve equal rights to the Hungarians. See Mendelsohn, *Jews of East Central Europe*, p. 116.
15. Quoted in a review article on the Jewish Laws in the weekly magazine *H.V.G.*, 14 May, 1994, p. 88.
16. *Annual Report of the Community*, p. 12.
17. The idea of unassimilability came out very sharply in the parliamentary debate on the Law. Matyas Matolcsy, a well-known right-wing politician, put it as follows: 'In Hungary there dwell 440,000 Jews. Let us be very clear. It is not a matter of religion but a matter of race.' Scientists quoted by the Speaker were supposed to prove

that 'their assimilation is impossible because, . . . by mixing [the Jews] the contamination of the other race [the Hungarian] will come about'. See: Kirekesztök, *Antiszemita Irások 1881–1992* (Anti-Semitic Writings 1881–1992), Budapest, 1992, p. 81.

18. *Annual Report of the Community*, p. 13.
19. In the opening passage it was stated that 'We Hungarian writers, artists and scientists of various political views and creeds . . . all of us descendants of Christian families . . . raise our voices . . .. This proposal aims primarily at the Jewish poor . . . . Let us think of our responsibility that, if despite our protestation a Law will emerge, it will cause every Hungarian to be ashamed of himself.' Among the signatories were intellectual giants like the composers B. Bartók and Z. Kodály, the writers Zs. Moricz and L. Zilahy, the painter I. Csok and others. See: J. Szekeres (ed.), *Documents from the History of Budapest*, vol. I (henceforth: *Documents*), Budapest, 1972, pp. 447–9.
20. On the issue of Jews in the liberal professions see: Y. Don, *On the Occupational Structure of Jews in Europe*, Discussion Paper 9303, Dept. of Economics, Bar Ilan University, 1993.
21. Of the 10 paragraphs of the Law, 5 dealt with journalism and the performing arts. See the text of the Law in L. Gonda, *A Zsidosag Magyarországon 1526–1945* (The Jews in Hungary 1526–1945), Budapest, 1992, pp. 276–9.
22. P. Bihari, 'A Magyarországi Zsidóság Helyzete a Zsidótörvényektöl a Deportálásig', in P. Horvath (ed.), *Hét Évtized a Hazai Zsidóság Életeben* (Seven Decades in the Life of the Jews at Home), Budapest, 1990, vol. II, p. 19.
23. *Annual Report of the Community*, p. 16.
24. Lászlo Ravasz, the head of the Calvinist congregation of bishops and member of the Parliament's upper chamber, supported, in his speech the First Law, but expressed his hope that it would be the last one. In any case he also voted for the Second Law.
25. From Bethlen's speech in the parliamentary committee in its debate on the First Jewish Law. Quoted in *H.V.G.*, p. 88.
26. Special genealogical charts were distributed to Christians of doubtful origin to be filled in under oath. See the reproduction of the chart in *H.V.G.*, p. 89.
27. The guiding booklet (104 pages long) published to clarify the intricacies of the Law opened with a detailed genealogical preamble on the exact racial definition of Jewishness. See: S.I. Székely (ed.), *A II Zsidótörvény és a Végrehajtási Utasitás* (The Second Jewish Law and its Implementation Ordinances), Budapest, 1939, p. 5.

28. S. Roth, 'Churches and the Jews in Hungary', unpublished manuscript, Budapest, 1991, p. 7.
29. Count Pál Teleki, a prominent scholar and the descendant of a great noble family, was a passionate anti-Semite. He was among the principal sponsors of the *numerus clausus*, which became law under his premiership. As the prime minister who inherited the Second Jewish Bill from his predecessor, he obviously supported it, but remarked that 'his own version of such a Bill would have been more severe'. See K. Froymovich, G. Komoroczy etc., 'A Pesti Gettó 1944' (The Ghetto of Pest 1944), part I, *Szombat*, May 1994, p. 29.
30. This was the officially declared objective of the Law. See: ibid.
31. Paragraph 12 of the Law. See: Székely, *A II Zsidótörvény*, p. 43.
32. A ridiculous case of excessive eagerness to overdo the instructions of the Law was that of Károly Rózsa. Early in 1940, the Lord Mayor of Budapest, Jenö Karafiáth, wrote specially to the Minister of Religion and Culture, Bálint Hóman, and requested the dismissal of the Jewish headmaster Károly Rózsa from a vocational school in the city, three years before the deadline for doing so. The only reason given was the political pressure of the Right wing. See: *Documents*, p. 475.
33. Quoted in *Szombat*, op.cit., p. 43.
34. The expression 'Changing of the Guard' (*Örségváltás*) was very popular in the anti-Semitic press of those days, describing the desire to replace the Jews by the 'New Christian Guard' in the major positions of the economy.
35. The figures are taken from an unpublished paper of Dr A. Ságvári, with the author's kind permission.
36. See the *Statistical Yearbook of Budapest for 1939*, p. 320.
37. Horthy, in a famous letter to Count Teleki, called those unqualified elements who aspired to replace the Jews 'incompetent, vulgar and boorish'. See: Szinai and Szücs, *Horthy Miklós*, pp. 261–2.
38. The quotation from: American Jewish Committee, *The Jewish Communities of Nazi-Occupied Europe*, New York, 1982, The Jews of Hungary, p. 10.
39. Kirekesztök, *Antiszemita Irások*, p. 102.
40. *Documents*, p. 478.
41. *O.M.Z.S.A. Évkönyv 5703 (1942–43)* (O.M.Z.S.A. Yearbook 5703 (1942–3)), Budapest, 1942, p. 205.
42. For the development of the Jewish population in Hungary see: Y. Don and G. Magos, 'The Demographic Development of Hungarian Jewry', *Jewish Social Studies*, vol. XLV, Nos 3–4 (1983), pp. 189–216.

43. The figures are quoted in: American Jewish Committee, *Jewish Communities*, p. 11.
44. For details on the Stern–Eppler mission see: N. Katzburg, *Hungary and the Jews 1920–1943*, Ramat-Gan, 1981, pp. 143–6.
45. Ibid., pp. 145–6.
46. For some characteristics of Jewish industrial preferences see: Y. Don, 'Patterns of Jewish Economic Behavior in Central Europe in the Twentieth Century', in M.K. Silber (ed.), *Jews in the Hungarian Economy 1760–1945*, Jerusalem, 1992, pp. 247–73.
47. An excellent analysis of the social mixing of the Jews in the professional life of Vienna, Budapest and Prague is in McCagg, *The History of Habsburg Jews 1670–1919.*
48. For the text of the Fourth Jewish Law, see: Gonda, *A Zsidóság Magyarországon*, appendix.
49. The occupational composition of the economically active Jews in the provinces, as compared to Budapest, in per cents, was the following:

Occupation	Provinces	Budapest
Industry	35.3	35.9
Commerce	46.8	40.5
Lib. Prof. and Publ. Serv.	5.4	10.8
Transport	3.4	1.0
Miscellaneous	9.1	11.5

Source: The 1930 Census.

50. *O.M.Z.S.A. Évkönyv 5703*, pp. 236–8. The declared objective of O.R.T. for Hungary, reflecting the unique circumstances in which it arrived there, was 'to attract the Jewish youth to careers in manufacturing, and to extend industrially oriented assistance to those who lost their jobs and livelihoods' (ibid., p. 236).
51. Ibid., p. 237.
52. Of the very rich literature on the labour brigades, the most detailed and comprehensive works are still the two-volume book edited by E. Karsai, *Fegyvertelenül Álltak az Aknamezökön* (Armless They Stood in the Minefields), Budapest, 1962, and the long chapter in R. Braham's monumental work *Politics of Genocide – the Holocaust in Hungary*, New York, 1981, 2 vols. See vol. I, pp. 285–361.
53. *Documents*, pp. 449–50.
54. The *American Jewish Yearbook* reported almost annually during these years on the major Jewish events in Hungary. Details on the dismissals in the public sector were reported in volume 1940–1, p. 361 and in volume 1942–3, p. 260.

55. *Documents*, pp. 497–8.
56. T.I. Berend & Gy. Ránki, *A Magyar Gazdaság Száz Éve* (One Hundred Years of the Hungarian Economy), Budapest, 1972, p. 211.
57. M. Matolcsy, *A Zsidóság Házvagyona* (The Real Estate Capital of the Jews), Budapest, 1942, p. 8.
58. Berend and Ránki, *A Magyar Gazdaság*, pp. 218–19.
59. Regent Horthy and the landed nobility behind his regime dreaded the very idea of land reform so much that he dismissed his Prime Minister, Béla Imrédy, for his submission to Parliament of a Land Reform motion.
60. For details, see: Ságvári, unpublished paper (see n. 35 above).
61. T.I. Berend and Gy. Ránki, 'A Csepeli Vasmü Rövid Torténete' (The Short History of the Csepel Ironwork), in *Csepel Története* (The History of Csepel), Budapest, 1965, pp. 33–128, see p. 89.
62. Ibid., pp. 91–2.
63. K. Jenei, F. Gáspár and P. Sipos, *A Pamutnyomoipari Vállalat Goldberger Textilnyomógyárának Története 1784–töl* (The History of the Goldberger Textile Factory from 1784), Budapest, 1970, p. 37.
64. Ibid.
65. Ibid., p. 42.
66. M. Ince and K. Jenei, 'A Csepelen Megtelepült Ipari és Kereskedelmi Vállalatok Története' (The History of the Csepel-Located Industrial and Commercial Enterprises), in *Csepel Torténete*, pp. 129–74.
67. Ibid., pp. 131–42.
68. Ibid., pp. 142–5.
69. Kirekesztök, *Antiszemita Irások*, p. 119.
70. *O.M.Z.S.A. Evkonyv 5703*, p. 221.
71. Ibid.
72. On the history of O.M.I.K.E. see: R. Füzesi, *Szinház az Árnyékban* (A Theater in the Shadow), Budapest, 1990.

—4—

Nazi Jewish Policy in 1944[1]

Richard Breitman

Were Hitler, Himmler, Ernst Kaltenbrunner, Heinrich Müller and Adolf Eichmann all seeking to complete the Final Solution by sending the mass of Hungarian Jewry to Auschwitz? Or was Himmler, with or without Hitler, seeking a separate peace with the West in 1944, and did he try to use Hungarian Jewry (and other surviving Jews) as a pawn in Nazi diplomacy?

Of all the remaining major issues of the Holocaust, these questions are among the most difficult to resolve convincingly. Some intentions and even instructions were never put on paper, and other records apparently did not survive. Postwar testimonies by Himmler's SS subordinates or rival Nazi officials are unreliable, self-serving and/or contradictory. Nor can one assume that whatever statements they made or steps they took accurately reflected the orders or intentions of superior authorities. We have plenty of subsequent examples of rogue intelligence officials or other government officials who falsely claimed authorization from above.

I have attempted to deal with these difficulties here partly by relying on the reports and perceptions of non-Nazis well-informed at the time, partly by uncovering new documentation about Himmler's views and Himmler's conferences with Hitler, and partly by setting all this information into the general context of Nazi policy during 1944. If I pay relatively little attention here to the Joel Brand affair, it is partly because others will doubtlessly present detailed analysis of it, and partly because Joel Brand was not privy to Hitler's or Himmler's intentions. Inevitably, some decisions about the reliability of other evidence and about the context reflect my subjective judgement. Nonetheless, I hope that the array of evidence here, if not necessarily each and every piece of evidence, establishes enough of a foundation for my conclusions.

The Final Solution in Hungary proceeded more or less according to plan during April, May and June 1944. Adolf Eichmann's special unit in Hungary and the Hungarian authorities and gendarmerie arranged the concentration and then deportation of hundreds of thousands of Jews to

Auschwitz-Birkenau. Then, under increasing pressure from Allied and neutral nations to refrain from the deportation of Hungarian Jews (and anticipating eventual German military defeat), Hungary called a halt. On 6 July Hungarian Regent Admiral Horthy 'temporarily' suspended the deportation of Jews, except for two trainloads that Eichmann sneaked out later that month against Horthy's orders. Horthy also tried to oust the Hungarian state secretaries who had worked closely with the German authorities on Jewish matters, but retreated on this issue in the face of protests from the German Plenipotentiary in Hungary, Edmund Veesenmayer.[2]

In response, Hitler then agreed to a suggestion that Foreign Minister Joachim von Ribbentrop had floated earlier – releasing Jews as a gift to Roosevelt and Churchill. What Hitler approved, however, was a far cry from the vast 'blood for trucks' offer made to Joel Brand and then presented by Brand to the Allies. Hitler was willing to release some Jews to Sweden, Switzerland and the United States, provided that Hungary would allow the resumption of deportations.[3] The promise to release Jews abroad had to come from the highest authority, and it certainly did not represent any serious dilution of the Final Solution in Hungary. Rather, this offer represented a way to remove a sudden and serious obstacle to the implementation of the Final Solution.

On 15 July Himmler held a private conference with the Führer. According to his custom, Himmler had prepared a written agenda for the meeting, with brief handwritten items simply designed to remind himself which subjects were to be raised. He outlined what course of action he proposed with regard to the 'Hungarian Jewish question', and he recorded Hitler's approval with a check mark.[4]

The next day Foreign Minister Ribbentrop, apparently operating in conjunction with Himmler for once, sent off to Veesenmayer an ultimatum from the Führer to be delivered to Horthy:

> The Führer expects that the measures against the Budapest Jews will now be carried out without any further delay by the Hungarian government, with those exceptions allowed to the Hungarian government by the German government . . .. No delay of any kind in the execution of the overall measures against Jews must take place because of these exceptions; otherwise the Führer would be compelled to withdraw his consent to these exceptions.[5]

As it happened, Horthy refused to bend to this and other German pressure, in part because Russian troops were beginning to make rapid progress towards Hungary.

The nearly successful assassination attempt on Hitler, which came only four days later, hardly shook his determination to eliminate Hungarian Jewry. In a 21 July conversation with Hungarian Field Marshal Miklos at the Wolf's Lair, Hitler criticized Horthy's intercession on behalf of Jews and then singled them out as the force behind the Allied bombing attacks on Hamburg and other cities. The Jews were responsible for the many thousands of German civilian casualties. If they believed they could destroy Europe, they would find themselves the first to be destroyed, the Führer promised.[6]

Himmler set out even more specific views in a 31 July letter to *Gauleiter* Martin Mutschmann, who had complained about the slow pace of deportations of Jews from France. Himmler blamed the German military for an unwillingness to cooperate with the deportations from France, but he expressed satisfaction with progress in Hungary, where, he wrote, they had already shipped off 450,000 Jews: 'We are now approaching the deportation of the second half [of Hungarian Jewry]. You can rest assured, that precisely in this decisive moment of the war, just as before, I possess the necessary toughness [to complete this task].'[7] Hitler's and Himmler's words and deeds indicate that to the end of July they were willing to bargain Jewish lives on a modest scale only in return for concrete benefits. If Hitler and Himmler actually had been interested in a massive trade of Hungarian Jewry for war *matériel* at this point, they would not have pushed the deportations to Auschwitz-Birkenau over all the obstacles, in the process doing away with a good portion of their bargaining power.

Himmler did not yet have to challenge or plot against Hitler to bring about small exchanges of Jews for goods; he got Hitler's permission.[8] To this point there is no reliable evidence that he sought an end to the Final Solution. The evidence is, rather, to the contrary: Himmler sought to complete the job according to the wishes of the Führer. The Allies' reaction to, and treatment of, Joel Brand in Istanbul and Cairo did not help save Jews, but Brand's detention was not a disaster that doomed hundreds of thousands. The disaster was that Nazi Germany remained on roughly the same course.

The now famous negotiations of Brand with Eichmann and the follow-up negotiations of Rudolph Kasztner with Eichmann and Himmler's economic agent Kurt Becher originated in April 1944 when the Jewish Rescue Committee of Budapest *initiated* the idea of exchanging all Hungarian Jews for trucks and other commodities.[9] As a result of deliberations within the Jewish Rescue Committee, Brand also asked Eichmann to send a transport of 600 to 1,200 Hungarian Jews out simultaneously with Brand's arrival in Istanbul; that first release would demonstrate the

Gestapo's seriousness to the Allies. Eichmann claimed that he accepted the idea in principle, but supposedly ruled out transport to Palestine because of Arab objections. The train would have to go to Portugal, where the Americans would have to take charge and send these Jews to the United States. Whatever Eichmann said in response, he had neither the power nor the desire to spare large numbers of Jews.[10]

Eichmann did inform Becher, who was responsible for acquiring war *matériel.* Becher then consulted Himmler, who wanted Becher to find out whether the offer was real and to report back to him. So Becher returned to Budapest and told Eichmann that Brand could go to Istanbul. Either at that May meeting or a subsequent one, Himmler also told Becher to extract what goods he could and then to disappear. Becher said that Himmler's superficiality had led him to consider seriously the possibility of obtaining trucks from the Allies, in spite of tremendous logistical and political difficulties.[11] He reportedly told Becher that he could act like a South American state and demand a thousand dollars for each permit to emigrate, but what was important to him was not money, but war *matériel.*[12] The limited scope for negotiations on the Nazi side (as well as Himmler's inclination towards bad faith) indicate that in mid-1944 he did not seriously entertain sparing hundreds of thousands of Hungarian Jews.

Those historians unwilling to put any weight in Becher's postwar testimony about Himmler must also confront what Himmler-intimate Felix Kersten told an OSS agent in Stockholm, not according to Kersten's dubious postwar memoirs, but according to OSS records at the time. Kersten's meeting with 'Willard Taylor' (Wilho Tikander, who headed the OSS office in Stockholm?), occurred almost simultaneously with Eichmann's meeting with Joel Brand in Budapest – and one week before the shipments of Hungarian Jews to Auschwitz-Birkenau actually began in May 1944.

Kersten claimed he had been delegated to spread German propaganda in Sweden and then to proceed to Finland, where he would request the government to turn over to Germany all Jews residing in Finland. (Kersten separately told the Finnish military attaché in Stockholm that Himmler had instructed him to demand of Finnish President Ryti at last radical measures against the Jews of Finland, their removal to Germany.[13]) Kersten then let drop the (premature) information that 160,000 Hungarian Jews had already been liquidated. Finally, he explained that Hitler had ordered the murder of all Jews, and that his subordinates (Himmler, et al.) were still carrying out this unrescinded order.[14]

Well-informed Jewish representatives in Budapest reached a similar conclusion about Nazi intentions. After carefully scrutinizing the pace of the deportations as well as the comments of Eichmann, Klages and Becher, the Jewish Rescue Committee of Budapest itself recognized the harshest of realities: the deportations would go on and most Jews would die. A letter written on 18 June by Kasztner, probably to Nathan Schwalb, Zionist emissary in Geneva, specified:

> what previously was current is today no longer the subject of negotiations; there can be no more talk of a cessation of the deportations in general. What can be negotiated is the rescue of a small part of those adults incapable of labor and children . . . [as well as decent treatment for those Jews sent to do labor].[15]

Kasztner's and Biss's subsequent contacts with Becher and Klages in the second half of June confirmed that Himmler might consent to the release of one or more trainloads of Jews abroad in exchange for between $1,000 to $2,000 per head. Kasztner and others on the Jewish Rescue Committee then helped arrange the release of specially selected Hungarian Jews who were supposed to go by train to Portugal. From internal sources the Jewish Rescue Committee could supply only a partial payment for the first transport; the rest had to come from 'world Jewry' after the train arrived safely.[16]

Becher was authorized to negotiate bargains for some Jews to leave Nazi-dominated territory; at the same time, he tried to use his negotiating contacts with the Jewish Rescue Committee in Budapest to reach representatives of world Jewry and to help Himmler float peace feelers to the Allies. Whatever Himmler would have liked to have done regarding contacts with the West, the acquisition of needed commodities would cover him with Hitler and therefore remained an essential part of any bargain. The British and American governments, however, quickly barred any participation of their citizens, and Joseph Schwartz, representative of the American Jewish Joint Distribution Committee (JDC) in Lisbon reluctantly rejected a proposed meeting.[17]

Jewish leaders in Budapest nonetheless persuaded Becher and SD Official Otto Klages that there were still channels for negotiation, and Becher apparently convinced Himmler to make a gesture by releasing 500 Jews to a neutral country.[18] Roswell McClelland, representative of the (American) War Refugee Board in Switzerland, suggested Saly Mayer, Swiss representative of the JDC and not an Allied citizen, as a negotiator in order to gain some time without making any financial (or American) commitments. Mayer then sought and received permission for the first 500 Jews to enter Switzerland.[19]

The arrival of the first train of Jews at the Swiss border on 21 August was to coincide with the beginning of negotiations of a delegation of four from Budapest: Kasztner, Becher, one of Becher's aides, and Wilhelm Billitz, a director of the Manfred Weiss Works, with Saly Mayer. Nothing else was well coordinated. The first meeting was held on the bridge at St Margarethen, on the Austrian–Swiss border, because Mayer could not even win Swiss permission for the delegation to enter the country. It was not a good demonstration of the vast power of international Jewry. The Jewish side, meanwhile, was disillusioned to see that only 318 Jews arrived on the train, well below the 500 Becher had claimed Himmler had approved. Allegedly, Eichmann had unilaterally claimed insufficient transport for 500, and had specifically barred any of Kasztner's and Brand's relatives from the first transport. Nor was Mayer particularly forthcoming. He claimed to be negotiating on behalf of his Swiss refugee organization, not the JDC, and he refused to bow to pressure or accept immoral proposals, such as the extraction of ransom for the preservation of human lives.[20]

The most striking initiative on the German side was the nominal resurrection and expansion of the original Brand 'blood for trucks' proposal. Becher said the Nazis would release not only all Hungarian Jews, but all of the approximately 1 million Jews still in their hands. Becher still asked for 10,000 trucks and agricultural machinery and offered to let Jews leave for the United States on the delivery ships. He chose not to mention the fact that roughly 450,000 Hungarian Jews had already been sent to Auschwitz-Birkenau, which casts some doubt on the seriousness of his offer.

Saly Mayer responded that the US Government would categorically reject the proposed deal; on top of that, he could not be party to any deal that would supply the Germans with war material to use against Allied troops. Becher responded that Kasztner and his group had originated the idea of trucks, which were still of interest to the Nazis. Mayer asked for time to consult his superiors.[21]

During this meeting Mayer was allowed to talk privately to Kasztner, who provided a well-informed assessment of differing opinions on the Nazi side. Kasztner claimed that an extreme group of the 'Gestapo', with Hitler's backing, wanted to liquidate the Jews at all cost; they would not allow emigration, and they would ignore diplomatic intervention or protests. There were some 'Gestapo' people who would abandon extermination if they could. Then there was Himmler's faction, which represented a middle course. It would release Jews if goods of value could be obtained in return, but it had to contend with the opposition of the hardliners. This information, which Mayer passed on to Roswell McClelland of the War Refugee Board who sent it on to Washington, was not correct in all particulars, but captured many of the essential elements of the situation.[22]

Becher tried to put the best face on the meeting by reporting to Himmler that the other side had not believed in the Nazis' good will, but that the unconditional arrival of the first 300-odd Jews had caused the Jewish side to revise its views. Even more optimistically, Becher claimed that the other side's unwillingness to give a clear 'no' represented an acceptance in principle. Still, he had to report that the other side could not arrange for the delivery of trucks even with the best of will, and that Himmler ought to redirect his objectives towards other useful goods that might be obtained in neutral countries. Finally, he reported that any continuation of the deportations would doom further cooperation. The next day Himmler laconically approved continuation of the negotiations along Becher's suggested line.[23]

How seriously did Himmler take this new channel, and what was he prepared to concede in order to exploit it? Kasztner claimed later that Becher actually promised to stop the gassings, but McClelland's report to Washington on 26 August only has Mayer requesting a breathing space of ten days and winning from Becher a promise that he would do all he could to prevent deportations and extermination during that time.[24]

There seem to be separate reasons for Himmler's formal suspension of deportations in the early morning hours of 25 August. Just prior to Himmler's action, the Hungarian Interior Minister, acting upon orders from Horthy, terminated even the pretence of Hungarian cooperation with the RSHA (Reich Security Main Office) deportation team. The Hungarian government informed Eichmann that the Jews of Budapest would be concentrated in large new Hungarian camps outside the city; they would not be deported to Germany. Veesenmayer reported these developments to the Foreign Ministry on 24 August, and Himmler probably was aware of them when he formally suspended deportations, effectively immediately, in the early morning hours of 25 August.[25] Actual deportations had halted more than a month earlier as a result of Hungarian decisions, but with his order of 25 August, Himmler was warning Eichmann's unit not to defy the Hungarian government, as Eichmann had already done on two previous occasions during July.[26]

Under the impact of Nazi military disasters in the East and the defection of Romania, Hungary's tenuous relationship with Germany became all the more obvious in early September when Admiral Horthy told the commanders of the Hungarian gendarmerie that the resolution of the Jewish question had done Hungary much damage. The Jewish question would be an issue in peace negotiations, Horthy said, and he could not tolerate any further deportations. All this information was quickly fed back to Himmler, who could not have been surprised when, about two weeks later, the new Hungarian (Lakatos) government requested a 'free hand' on the Jewish question.[27]

By September Nazi Germany was under intense pressure to loosen the vice of a two-front war. The military situation was deteriorating so rapidly that Himmler could no longer count on inheriting or seizing power should Hitler die. On 12 September Himmler proposed, apparently for the first time to the Führer, the idea of separate peace negotiations. His notes for his private meeting with Hitler indicate 'England or Russia', and his check mark indicates that Hitler approved his proposal. The Soviets were to be approached through the Japanese, Himmler suggested.[28] He did not specify how he proposed to reach the British or the Americans.

Until now the conclusion that Hitler, in September 1944, was willing to accept a separate peace rested largely on the unsupported account in Ribbentrop's memoirs that Hitler approved peace contacts in Stockholm with the *Soviets*.[29] But Himmler's proposal was to negotiate with either side, and he did not propose to use the by now controversial Stockholm channel to Moscow involving German intermediaries Bruno Peter Kleist and Edgar Klaus.[30]

To reach the West, one option was Becher. Becher's team (without Becher) was still meeting with Saly Mayer at the Swiss border during September, discussing now money instead of trucks,[31] but Becher's own position was highly vulnerable. Just when Himmler desperately needed a diplomatic breakthrough, Becher was finding very little give on the other side. He had to convince Himmler to offer more.

In his postwar testimony Becher claimed to have visited Himmler sometime between the middle of September and the middle of October 1944 and persuaded him to stop the deportations in order to negotiate 'further agreements with the Joint [Distribution Committee]'. Himmler supposedly wrote two originals of an order, one for Kaltenbrunner and one for Oswald Pohl (of the SS-*Wirtschaftsverwaltungs-Hauptamt*, which oversaw the concentration and extermination camps), with Becher receiving a carbon copy. The substance of the order was to forbid the further extermination of Jews and to institute adequate care of weak and sick Jews. Becher claimed to have shown the order to Eichmann (who reacted angrily), given it personally to Pohl and left a copy for Kaltenbrunner with his secretary in Berlin.[32]

Evidence from Jewish sources is consistent with Becher's version. On 26 September Mayer cabled Budapest that he was willing to open an account for the Nazis in a Swiss bank. Mayer had not yet cleared this idea with McClelland and the War Refugee Board, but they would eventually agree to set up a blocked bank account as a sign of interest in negotiations, in the hope that this gesture would convince Nazi officials to refrain from further killing of Jews. Mayer knew full well that Washington would never approve actual payments to Nazi officials. Andreas Biss took Mayer's cable to SD official Otto Klages that same day, and Biss wrote later that Klages and Becher not only received the news with relief, even joy, but also promised to send it immediately to Himmler.[33]

Himmler believed that Germany could get through to the West through the Jews. Whatever the Führer's views on a separate peace, however, he was not about to tolerate the use of Jews as intermediaries or release Jews just to gain goodwill with the Allies. In the course of discussing Hungarian matters with Hitler on 27 September, Himmler must have sensed that the Führer would not go along with the release of Jews or with a cessation of the killing.[34]

In early October, and shortly after a meeting with Ernst Kaltenbrunner and Walter Schellenberg of the RSHA,[35] Bruno Peter Kleist made another visit to Stockholm and spoke with Hillel Storch of the World Jewish Congress there. Kleist declared that it was now impossible to buy the release of Jews. There had, however, been a recent meeting in Berlin on the Jewish question, Kleist said vaguely, which had considered various options. The first was kinder treatment of the Jews as well as efforts to prove to the outside world that they had never been abused. The theory here was that surviving Jews who had been treated well would speak up for Nazi officials after the war. A second option was to kill all remaining Jews, which was rejected. The third option still under consideration was the use of Jews as hostages.[36]

Then came another démarche from another source. In September 1944, Walter Schellenberg had enlisted Giselber Wirsing, a prominent nationalist (but non-Nazi) intellectual, to prepare a series of anonymous and unvarnished reports on Germany's foreign policy situation. Wirsing was given access to top secret material compiled by Amt VI of the RSHA. Schellenberg then distributed Wirsing's analyses to a small and select circle including Himmler, Kaltenbrunner, Hermann Fegelein (Himmler's liaison at the Führer's Headquarters) and Ambassador Walter Hewel, but excluding Ribbentrop. These reports were code-named the Egmont Reports, after the sixteenth-century Dutch count (and Goethe's character) who did not hesitate to tell the truth to the Duke of Alba. Wirsing and Schellenberg saw their prime audience as Himmler, and they hoped to be able to move him to break with Hitler.

In October 1944 Wirsing issued the first of thirteen reports designed to create the unavoidable conclusion that Germany needed both an immediate peace with the West, and as a prerequisite, a government capable of negotiating with it, which meant Hitler's resignation or deposition. Himmler was supposedly in accord with the thrust of the reports. Wirsing and Schellenberg also proposed the release of approximately 60,000 Jews among those still alive in German concentration camps to Switzerland, where Swiss Federal Councillor (and former president) Jean-Marie Musy, an old friend of Himmler's, would make arrangements. (Himmler's appointment book indicates that he met with Musy on 25 October and had lunch with Musy and Schellenberg immediately thereafter.[37]) But after the first shipment to Switzerland of some 1,200 Jews in this project (in January 1945), Hitler's veto brought the whole scheme to an abrupt end. Wirsing saw the episode as characteristic of Himmler's inability to live up to commitments to Schellenberg, either because of Hitler's opposition or that of the extreme wing of the SS.[38]

Himmler thus backed away from commitments to both Becher and Schellenberg to halt the Final Solution. His efforts to develop a more moderate position were limited to the protection of small, select groups of Jews, to the shipment of some Jewish labourers to labour camps and East Prussian fortifications, and to the continuing use of Jews as hostages in bargaining efforts. In late October, after German troops had installed a new puppet Arrow Cross government in Hungary, deportations and marches of Jews from Budapest towards Germany – virtual death marches – began. The Final Solution continued into 1945 even though the extermination camps had to be dismantled to keep the incriminating evidence out of the hands of advancing Soviet troops.

Prominent historians of different nationalities have argued that Hitler's two great objectives in World War II were military conquest by the German – 'Aryan' 'race' on a vast scale and the destruction of the Jewish people.[39] Although there is still considerable debate over when Hitler and others first saw the military campaign headed for defeat, even Hitler could not totally blot out reality by the autumn of 1944. If Hitler could not follow the example of Frederick the Great and with the aid of providence gain a last-minute escape from overwhelming defeat, he was determined all the more to destroy his primary racial enemy.

Himmler's more flexible approach has raised or reinforced certain questions about his loyalties. A good number of scholars have maintained that Himmler had turned against Hitler by 1944, if not earlier. Himmler's efforts to arrange for separate peace negotiations have been taken as evidence of his pessimism about the war and his wavering loyalty or actual disloyalty to Hitler. Up to the end of 1944 Himmler was quite capable of exploring diplomatically sensitive possibilities secretly and independently. Yet he continued to pursue both the war and the Final Solution and sooner or later consulted Hitler on both major and minor issues. His initiatives were apparently aimed at moving Hitler towards a more realistic course and/or succeeding him, not at overthrowing him.

There does seem to be a significant alteration in Himmler's diplomacy at the end of August 1944. His concern about military and political collapse in the East induced him to espouse ideologically heterodox proposals directly to Hitler. Hitler was more inclined to accept a separate peace than to abandon or even dilute the Final Solution, but a separate peace by this time was diplomatically and militarily out of reach. The Final Solution continued. Himmler's emerging perception of the need to halt the Final Solution and to improve his image in the eyes of the West then created a gradually widening gap on Jewish policy between himself and Hitler, but that gap did not change the general course of Nazi Jewish policy until 1945.

Notes

1. This chapter is a revised version, with new material, of an article by myself and Shlomo Aronson, 'The End of the Final Solution: Nazi Attempts to Ransom Jews in 1944', *Central European History*, vol. 25, no. 2 (1992), pp. 177–203.
2. Raul Hilberg, *The Destruction of the European Jews*, New York, 1984, vol. 2, pp. 850–3. Randolph L. Braham, *The Politics of Genocide: The Holocaust in Hungary*, New York, 1981, vol. II, pp. 762–74.
3. Ribbentrop to Veesenmayer, 10 July 1944, reprinted in Randolph L. Braham, *The Destruction of Hungarian Jewry: A Documentary Account*, New York, 1963, p. 700.
4. United States National Archives, Record Group (hereafter NA RG) 242, Microfilm Series T-175/Roll 94/Frame 2615074.
5. Memorandum by Altenburg, 21 July 1944, quoted in Hilberg, *Destruction of the European Jews*, vol. II, p. 854.
6. Text in Andreas Hillgruber (ed.), *Staatsmänner und Diplomaten bei Hitler: Vertrauliche Aufzeichnungen über Unterredungen mit Vertretern des Auslandes 1942–1944*, Frankfurt am Main, 1970, pp. 476–77.

7. Himmler to Mutschmann, 31 July 1944, Berlin Document Center, Non-Biographic Order, RFSS 5, SS 704.
8. In addition to the exemption of some Budapest Jews, Hitler had personally approved the release of some Jewish members of the Weiss and Chorin families in return for the SS's gaining control of the Manfred Weiss Works, a Hungarian industrial conglomerate. For general treatment, Braham, *Politics of Genocide*, vol. I, pp. 519–20; Hilberg, *Destruction of the European Jews*, vol. II, p. 829. For Hitler's and Himmler's views, telegram of German Embassy, Budapest, 30 June 1944; Wagner to Rudolf Brandt, 1 July 1944; Himmler to Winkelmann, 8 July 1944, all in NA RG 242, T-175/R 125/2650721-24, 2650739.
9. On the initiative from the Jewish Rescue Committee in Budapest, see interrogation of Becher by Kasztner in the presence of American authorities, 7 July 1947, in *The Holocaust*, ed. John Mendelsohn, New York, 1982, vol. 15, pp. 64–7. Kasztner said quite directly: 'Vielleicht werden Sie sich erinnern, die Initiative ist von uns ausgegangen.' On these negotiations, see in particular, Yehuda Bauer, 'The Mission of Joel Brand', in Michael R. Marrus (ed.), *The Nazi Holocaust: Historical Articles on the Destruction of European Jews*, Westport, CT, 1989, vol. 9, *The End of the Holocaust*, pp. 65–126; Braham, *Politics of Genocide*, vol. II, pp. 932–57.

   Less reliable are Joel Brand, *A Mission on Behalf of the Sentenced to Death*, Tel-Aviv, 1957; Joel and Hansi Brand, *The Devil and the Soul*, Tel-Aviv, 1960, both in Hebrew. For Brand's story in English, if not with careful judgement of its accuracy, see Alex Weissberg, *Desperate Mission: Joel Brand's Story*, New York, 1958.

   Finally, see Kasztner's report, Ernest Landau (ed.), *Der Bericht des jüdischen Rettungskomitees aus Budapest 1942–1945*, Munich, 1961; for Biss's, Andreas Biss, *Der Stopp der Endlösung: Kampf gegen Himmler und Eichmann in Budapest*, Stuttgart-Degerloch, 1966.
10. On Eichmann and Brand, see Braham, *Politics of Genocide*, vol. II, p. 936; Biss, *Stopp der Endlösung*, pp. 53–4.
11. Interrogation of Becher by Kasztner, 7 July 1947, in *The Holocaust*, ed. John Mendelsohn, vol. 15, pp. 64–7, 70–1. On Himmler's schedule, NA RG 242, T-84/R 25/no frames.
12. Interrogation of Becher, 1 Nov. 1947, NA RG 238, M-1019/R 5/534.
13. See Hannu Rautkallio, *Finland and the Holocaust: The Rescue of Finland's Jews*, New York, 1987, p. 256.

14. Johnson (Taylor) to Secretary of State, 5 May 1944, RG 226, Entry 134, Box 304, Folder Stockholm, May–June 1944. This cable describes what an unidentified man told 'Taylor' directly. Kersten's identity is established by the fact that he went to Stockholm at precisely this time and told the Finnish military attaché some of the same information. There was no Willard Taylor working for OSS in Stockholm, according to Legation personnel lists. I am indebted to Meredith Hindley for a copy of this document.

    A very recent article on Kersten fails to mention this trip by Kersten, but argues in favour of a humanitarian interpretation of Kersten's activities towards the end of the war. See Raymond Palmer, 'Felix Kersten and Count Bernadotte: A Question of Rescue', *Journal of Contemporary History*, vol. 29, no. 1 (January 1994), pp. 39–51. It is possible to read Kersten's conversation as an attempt to alert the outside world to forthcoming mass killings or as the utterances of someone who was incapable of keeping a secret.
15. Kasztner to ? [Nathan Schwalb], 18 June 1944, Hagana Archive, Tel-Aviv, Brand/Kasztner files. I am indebted to Shlomo Aronson for a copy of this document.
16. Biss, *Stopp der Endlösung*, pp. 96–9, 105–9. In a 1946 affidavit Kasztner claimed that Hungarian Jewish valuables which Jewish sources estimated at 11 million Swiss francs were delivered to Becher. Kasztner/Boukstein affidavit of 18 Feb. 1946, Hagana Archive, Tel-Aviv, Brand/Kasztner files. Biss, however, claimed that he persuaded Becher's officials to accept an inflated value of various goods in order to promote the train and the negotiations with Jewish representatives outside. In a postwar interrogation Becher gave the much more modest figure of 6 million Pengö for the goods. Interrogation of 1 Nov. 1947, NA RG 238, M-1019/R 5/564. Each source had an interest in establishing his own version, and it now seems impossible to sort out the conflicts.
17. Bauer, 'The Mission of Joel Brand', p. 117; Palestine Censorship, 18 Aug. 1944, with extract of meeting of Middle East Advisory Committee of the JDC with Dr Schwarz, 23 July 1944, NA RG 226, Entry 191, Box 4, Censorship – Belgian Jewry. Many other relevant documents are in *The Holocaust*, ed. John Mendelsohn, vol. 15, pp. 211–45. See also Yehuda Bauer, *American Jewry and the Holocaust: A History of the American Jewish Joint Distribution Committee*, Detroit, 1981, p. 411.
18. Braham, *Politics of Genocide*, vol. II, pp. 957–9. Biss, *Stopp der Endlösung*, pp. 132–48. Biss claims that Becher was ordered to Berlin

to see Himmler on this matter at the end of July and returned to Budapest on 2 August. Himmler's schedule does not survive for this period.

19. Bauer, *American Jewry*, pp. 413–14.
20. Braham, *Politics of Genocide*, p. 960. Biss, *Stopp der Endlösung*, pp. 150–1. Bauer, *American Jewry*, pp. 414–15.
21. Harrison to Department (McClelland to War Refugee Board), 26 Aug. 1944, War Refugee Board Records, Box 56, Jews in Hungary Folder. Braham, *Politics of Genocide*, p. 960.
22. Harrison to Department (McClelland to War Refugee Board), 26 Aug. 1944, War Refugee Board Records, Box 56, Jews in Hungary Folder. The impression that Himmler wished to give was that of the pragmatist who was simply trying to acquire useful goods.
23. Becher's telegram to Himmler, 25 Aug. 1944, and Himmler's response, 26 Aug. 1944, in NA RG 242, T-175/R 59/2574473 and 2574471. Biss, *Stopp der Endlösung*, 153, claims that Kasztner and Billitz persuaded Becher not to send a fully negative report to Himmler.
24. Bauer, *American Jewry*, p. 415. Harrison to State Department (McClelland to War Refugee Board), 26 Aug. 1944, War Refugee Board Records, Box 56, File Jews in Hungary, August 1944, Franklin D. Roosevelt Library.
25. Veesenmayer to Foreign Office, 24 Aug. 1944, and Veesenmayer to Ribbentrop, 25 Aug. 1944, in Braham, *Destruction: Documents*, 480–1. See Braham, *Politics of Genocide*, vol. II, pp. 752–74.
26. Hilberg, *Destruction of the European Jews*, vol. II, pp. 854–5.
27. Schellenberg to RSHA, RFSS Feldkommandostelle, et al., 4 Sept. 1944, NA RG 238, NG-5354, reprinted in Braham, *Destruction: Documents*, 483. Hoffmann (Hungarian Minister in Berlin) to Hennyey (Hungarian Foreign Minister), 22 Sept. 1944, NA RG 238, NG-2604, cited by Hilberg, *Destruction of the European Jews*, vol. II, p. 855.
28. Himmler's agenda notes for meeting with Hitler, 12 Sept. 1944, NA RG 242, T-175/R 94/2615061-62.
29. Joachim von Ribbentrop, *Zwischen London und Moskau. Erinnerungen und letzte Aufzeichungen*, Leoni, 1953, p. 265. This account is accepted by Ingeborg Fleischauer, *Die Chance des Sonderfriedens: Deutsch–sowjetische Geheimgespräche 1941–1945*, Berlin, 1986, p. 259, and tentatively accepted, based on additional sources, by Gerhard L. Weinberg, *The World at Arms: A Global History of World War II*, New York, 1994, p. 720. Two recent American biographers of Ribbentrop entirely ignore the episode: John Weitz, *Hitler's Diplomat: The*

Life and Times of Joachim von Ribbentrop, New York, 1992, and Michael Bloch, *Ribbentrop*, New York, 1992.

30. Himmler had listed 'Schweden' as the next item on his agenda, but crossed it off. Himmler's agenda notes for meeting with Hitler, 12 Sept. 1944, NA RG 242, T-175/R 94/2615061-62. On Hitler's ire at Kleist and Klaus, see Fleischauer, *Die Chance des Sonderfriedens*, pp. 176, 194–5.
31. Braham, *Politics of Genocide*, vol. II, pp. 960–1. Bauer, *American Jewry*, pp. 416–18.
32. Interrogation of Becher, 27 March 1946, reprinted in *The Holocaust*, ed. John Mendelsohn, vol. 14, *Relief and Rescue of Jews from Nazi Oppression, 1943–1945*, pp. 203–6. Becher affidavit of 6 Feb. 1946, NA RG 238, NG-2972, Microfilm T-1139/ R 32/810. On the disbanding of Eichmann's unit, Feine to Veesenmayer, 29 Sept. 1944, NA RG 238, NG-4895, cited by Hilberg, *Destruction of the European Jews*, vol. II, p. 855.
33. Braham, *Politics of Genocide*, vol. II, p. 961; Bauer, *American Jewry*, p. 417; Biss, *Stopp der Endlösung*, pp. 174–5.
34. Himmler met with Hitler on both 26 and 27 September. They did discuss the situation in Hungary, where Germany was about to use force and the kidnapping of Horthy's son to impose a new government headed by Arrow Cross leader Szalasi. The Szalasi government resumed cooperation with the Nazis on the Jewish question. But it is hard to prove that Hitler and Himmler discussed that aspect of the Hungarian problem in late September. See Himmler's agenda notes, NA RG 242, T-175/R 94/2615056-58.
35. The meeting between Kleist and Schellenberg, just before Kleist left for Stockholm on 30 September, is mentioned in Schellenberg to Himmler, 9 Oct. 1944, NA RG 242, T-175/R 579/135. In his postwar interrogation (27 Oct. 1945, NA RG 226, Entry 125, Box 29, Folder 407) Kleist, however, misdates all his September 1944 meetings, listing them as November.
36. See Hershel V. Johnson's cable, 14 Oct. 1944, NA RG 200, Box 29, Folder 364, citing Hillel Storch's contact with Kleist and Kleist's information on what had transpired in Berlin.
37. NA RG 242, T-175/R 112/2637643.
38. Dustbin First Preliminary Interrogation of Giselber Wirsing (18 Jan. 1946), in Saint, Washington to Saint, London, 19 March 1946, NA RG 226, Entry 109, Folder 35, and subsequent interrogation RG 226, Entry 125A, Box 6, Folder 66.
39. Eberhard Jäckel, *Hitler's Weltanschauung: A Blueprint for Power*,

tr. Herbert Arnold, Middletown, CT, 1972, pp. 106–7; Jochen Thies, *Architekt der Weltherrschaft: Die 'Endziele' Hitlers*, Düsseldorf, 1976, p. 61; Gerhard L. Weinberg, *The Foreign Policy of Hitler's Germany*, vol. I, *Diplomatic Revolution in Europe, 1933–36*, Chicago, 1970, pp. 2–22; Sebastian Haffner, *The Meaning of Hitler*, tr. Ewald Osers, New York, 1979, pp. 79–80, 90, 126; Gerald Fleming, *Hitler and the Final Solution*, Berkeley, 1984; Leni Yahil, *The Holocaust: The Fate of European Jewry*, New York, 1990, esp. p. 127. Among the most recent versions: Ian Kershaw, *Hitler*, London, 1991, pp. 18–19; Alan Bullock, *Hitler and Stalin: Parallel Lives*, New York, 1992, pp. 760–1, 764–5.

–5–

The 'Quadruple Trap' and the Holocaust in Hungary

Shlomo Aronson

Introduction

Since 1985, a quantity of historical documentation relating to the Holocaust has been released for research by the American Central Intelligence Agency to the US National Archives. Among others, Record Group 226, Office of Strategic Services (OSS), grew considerably, even though the entire original documentation has not yet been released. Some OSS reports and other documents (especially those originating in its R&A Branch under William Langer) have been accessible for many years.[1] However, the Secret Intelligence files, which originated at the OSS-SI branch headquarters in Washington, or those sent to it by its field units, including raw intelligence reports by agents, headquarters responses to them, censorship intercepts and deciphered German cables, were partially released only recently. Other relevant files, such as the interrogation of Walter Schellenberg, the head of *SD-Ausland*, were also released just a few years ago. When combined with Counter Intelligence Corps (CIC) files at Suitland, MD, with War Refugee Board (WRB) files at the Franklin D. Roosevelt Library in Hyde Park, New York (available for research for many years), with the State Department documentation at the US National Archives in Washington, and with captured German documentation at the same archives (most of which was available for decades), a picture emerges which I chose to describe as the Quadruple Trap of the European Jewry during World War II.

This picture remains incomplete, until we add to the above-mentioned documentation the available British and Jewish primary sources; some of these have been available for many years, but OSS and Allied censorship reports about Jews, Jewish activities and rescue efforts may fill many gaps in the original Jewish documentation itself, because censorship and other British and American wartime controls required caution or caused trouble.

The Quadruple Trap

The Holocaust seems to continue, at least as a subject for a deep controversy about the role of the Zionists and the Jewish leadership in the United States, about rescue options and about moral aspects related to rescue. In particular the Hungarian disaster, which took place late during the war, which was given due publicity in the West after a while, and during which the Allies seem to have won the war, is a subject for deep soul-searching. Survivors and their daughters and sons, among others, blame themselves and mainly the Jewish and Allied leaderships for negligent behaviour during the Holocaust and especially regarding the Hungarian carnage.

This may be seen as the latest phase of a catch situation, into which the European Jewry was manoeuvred in stages; a trap situation, out of which there was no escape until almost at the end, and in which no help could be rendered to its victims in occupied Europe itself, nor from outside of it. Even rescue efforts undertaken by Jewish organizations and individuals through negotiations with the Germans may have become a part of the trap situation itself, although the other option would have been to do nothing or be perceived as collaborating with the Germans after the war. The problem here, among the actual historiographical issues requiring specific research, is that of the political nature of such trap situations, and the political thinking that is necessary to penetrate their murky depths.

A trap situation is a condition in which its victims are caught between several powers whose interrelationships – those which are related to the victims and those which are not – combine to decide the victims' fate. In such conditions everything works against the victims, who are declared to be a principal adversary by an enemy, while they – the victims – become a nuisance to third parties, who are driven to fight the victims' enemy for their own reasons; the enemy may want to be rid of the victims while using them at first as hostage *vis-à-vis* the third parties. In other words, the enemy may deport victims to the third parties' territory in order to get rid of them and create antagonism against them there, in order to serve the enemy's interests; the enemy may then warn the victims and third parties, that victims under his control will be destroyed, should the third parties fight him. In a later phase, the enemy may wait to see which third parties join against him and may still interpret their actual behaviour according to his – wrong – perceptions and order of priorities. This is the hostage-taking phase.

Finally, when the third parties are forced by the enemy's behaviour to fight him, the enemy interprets the third parties' war against him as if it were the victims' doing, having prophesied revenge in advance. The third parties, however, distance themselves from the victims for a variety of reasons; one of these reasons is the war goals and the domestic political consensus which is necessary to achieve those goals. The third parties thus fight their, not the victims', war, and yet their universalistic war aims seem to serve the victims' particularistic interests. In reality, however, the third parties give no special attention to the victims, under severe conditions imposed by the enemy for a long while. Furthermore, during that time and later the third parties refuse to identify with the victims because they believe that this may jeopardize their war effort against the enemy. Worse, sometimes third parties may believe in or develop an explanation of the victims' tragedy which may be influenced by the enemy's own arguments or by the atmosphere created by the enemy's propaganda, blaming a victim at least partially for his condition.[2]

Fearing the impact of his presence in large numbers on their shores, third parties may perceive in the victim a source of trouble that may hamper the national consensus necessary to fight the enemy. At first they perceive other victims of the same enemy (e.g. Poles and many occupied nations in our case), whose sufferings are great but not comparable with those of the principal victims, as victims no less than the actual ones, who will then be destroyed fully and completely by the common enemy. Even when the fate of this particular victim becomes clear, and because of it, third parties are conscious of the political necessity of avoiding the impression that they are fighting for the victim because of his bad reputation or because their peoples believe in it, or that they are ready to make concessions to the enemy because of the victim. This seems to be essential to maintain the fight, which is laid by the enemy at the victim's door, and may combine with prejudices against the victim that are common or perceived to be common among the third parties' nations. Any talk about actively helping the victim may thus endanger the third parties' war effort against the enemy in political and practical terms: diversion of bombing efforts, diversion of shipping necessary for military and other purposes; while the third parties may consider that the enemy would not let the victim go anyway. Yet too much talk – above all *any* talk – about the victims' tragedy may encourage baseless hopes among the victims and dangerous expectations in the enemy's camp that the third parties may go out of their way to help the victim. The third parties may further consider that the price that the enemy would demand for letting the victim go would be too high in domestic, wartime and even postwar terms. The fourth side of the quadruple trap is strategic territories under third parties' control but subject to the consent of fourth parties (such as Arabs and Muslims); their use as safe havens for victims is unacceptable in terms of winning the war against the enemy and may even jeopardize postwar developments.

At the final stage of such a trap situation, the enemy or elements among his leadership may return to the hostage-taking tactics *vis-à-vis* the victim and the third parties alike by using the surviving victims as trump cards against the third parties. The third parties, at least, would perceive such tactics to be possible and would act to avoid falling into that trap. The victim, however, may try to make them respond to such tactics or even initiate such tactics on his own, which in turn would be used by the enemy or elements among the enemy for their own purposes, and which in turn would be avoided by the third parties, and so forth. This was in fact the situation in Hungary late in the war – but it is difficult to understand that stage, the formal subject of this chapter, without understanding the general catch situation outlined above.

Regarding the Hungarian tragedy we can in general argue that even when the victorious third parties were ready to allow large numbers of victims to be evacuated to their own territories, as they finally did with regard to Admiral Horthy's offer in summer 1944,[3] they dealt not with the principal enemy but with one of his former allies, whose freedom of action proved rather limited. Dealing with Hitler was totally out of the question due to the Allies' declared and enshrined war aims, due also to postwar calculations, to the monstrous character of his regime and due to what he had done to the Jews. The 'Führer', who felt victimized by the Jews and hence made them victims, became for these reasons a non-partner in negotiations to save them; thus the negotiations which did take place, finally, between Roswell McClelland, the able representative of the WRB in Switzerland and Himmler's subordinates were indirect and no real power was given to the Allied side to conclude real deals, if they had had any real chance at all. In fact we have proved elsewhere that they had no such chance when large numbers of Jews were at stake.[4] Since Joel Brand's mission – the famous 'million Jews in exchange for ten thousand trucks deal' – and indeed long before, the Allied authorities viewed Hitler's, or possibly his henchmen's, use of Jews as hostages as a means to ransom Jews for military or personal benefits to themselves or to drive a wedge between them and their own masses or between the Western Allies and the Soviets – their unnatural allies. Further, they had to take into account Jewish pressure or Jewish supporters' pressure that might be used by the Nazis to this end, upon the creation of the War Refugee Board and afterwards. This, however, proved not to be the case.[5]

But as far as Hitler was concerned, splitting the Grand Alliance due to war weariness among other things would have been his only hope in the wake of his Hungarian invasion in March 1944, on top of a swift defeat of the forthcoming British–American invasion of the continent. Finally, his uninterrupted pursuance of the 'Final Solution' would be maintained to the very end as a demonstration of victory on at least one – the Jewish – 'front', and as a demonstration of his fanatical devotion to that 'ideal' that might nurture his myth for future generations, as he in fact openly did in his political testament.

We cannot yet say what role was played by the presence of the last large remaining Jewish community in Europe in Hitler's calculations when he decided to invade Hungary, whether he was aware of the establishment of the American War Refugee Board three months beforehand in order to save Jews. Nor can we say what role was played by OSS agents dropped into that country immediately before the invasion, among other measures undertaken by the Allies to divert his attention away from Normandy and disperse his forces.[6] It is possible that these matters, but not the general trap situation, may never be clarified in the sense of obtaining German documentation about them.

The victims were unable and unwilling to accept the logic of this vicious circle; at the time and later, the victims would blame the third parties for not having saved them or at least for not having tried harder. Victims and other observers such as David Wyman would then blame Jewish leaders and Allied leaders for a major misdeed: for not having done more to save the actual victims, or at least warn them or pass the true information among them. Hence the catastrophe became an ongoing process.

In fact the victim had no – and couldn't have had – any real influence over events which determined his fate including upon his own behaviour prior to the Nazi invasion of Hungary and including deeds undertaken by victims' leaders afterwards, which may be judged afterwards to have aggravated that condition. These acts did not help, but they may have been interpreted, then and later, against the victims' leaders by surviving victims, by their contemporaries and by future generations. Some of this may be a conscious political use of the Holocaust for political purposes, which goes beyond the scope of this chapter; some of this may be a genuine, understandable wish to resurrect the dead.

The victims in this case were the European Jews under Hitler's rule, and their brethren in the free world, who escaped the actual fate of the European Jews, but could not help them while being made responsible for the acts of third parties, which contributed to sealing the fate of the European Jews and to their continued murder.

Catch or trap situations are common in everyday life, but astonishingly little, almost no theoretical research has been done on such situations, which do not necessarily lead to fatal results in terms of life and death. When they do, the terminal outcome into which they drive their victims does not lend itself to scholarly speculation and logical development in such terms. Much effort is thus invested in trying to 'open' the trap for possible rescue from it. Otherwise, such a situation may or may not be understood except within a specific historical context; and thus generalizations seem not to offer themselves from the study of a particular case. Yet people or peoples who experience such situations are different from those who didn't; some among them do not even understand them in such terms but suffer from them, as argued above. Research is also needed on the impact of catch situations upon their survivors, or their lack of understanding of them. In this chapter I shall try to deal with a specific trap condition.

In our case, we deal with a 'quadruple trap', whose source was Adolf Hitler and Nazi Germany; to them we can add the various roles of Germany's allies, which require specific treatment.

The other elements in this structure were the Western Allies and the Soviet Union, and the reality of the Middle East in those days, which contributed to the almost complete closure of the trap.

Hitler was of course the principal enemy, and the main cause of the catch situation; his allies – various groups in Hungary, in our case – played their interchangeable roles in response to or in defiance of Allied inputs; the Western Allies did intervene to stop the carnage in this case, but they were hindered by their war aims, war priorities and fighting methods, by their bureaucratic procedures and service frictions in addition to German intentions and goals. Indirect negotiations to save Hungarian Jews did take place, following the initial failure of the Brand–Grosz mission,[7] but both the Germans and the Allies pursued their own – contradictory – policies which could not allow an escape from the trap until Himmler finally broke with Hitler very late in the final stage of the war.[8] Yet Jewish rescue activists, who had initiated deals with SS and SD officials, and medium-level officials' initiatives on the German side created the impression that such deals were possible. This trap within a trap becomes clearer when we realize that rescue workers such as Rezso Kasztner in fact tried to persuade the Allies to deliver things they couldn't, and the Germans who hoped to be delivered things the Allies wouldn't deliver, kept the pressure on Kasztner to deliver things he had no power to promise. On the other hand, making promises that he hoped could be fulfilled, but which later turned out to be empty, as his only way to act – was an alternative to admitting failure or running away; both options were not acceptable to him. Finally, once Saly Mayer entered the negotiations with McClelland behind Mayer but with no power to deliver anything, the promises and urges for German *quid*s ahead of Allied *quo*s combined with Himmler's own needs and with Germany's deteriorating war effort to save Jews; but even then Allied priorities, rules and suspicions on the one hand, and Hitler's determination to pursue the 'Final Solution' to the bitter end on the other, hampered any large scale deal. Hungarian Fascist behaviour played its fatal role in between. At this late stage, and probably long before, Allied calculations were influenced by a major issue for them – Allied POWs. Any action that could have been interpreted by the Germans in terms of wholesale hostage taking or acts of revenge undertaken by the Allies against Germans on an individual basis or on a group basis could have been seen by the Western Allies as endangering their POWs, just a few months before their likely liberation.[9]

The Stages

The stages of the trap may be traced back to the 1920s, to the immigration quotas introduced by the United States Congress in the mid-1920s, or back to Hitler's rise to power in January 1933. We focus on Hitler's ascent to power and maintain that, from then until 1941, his 'Jewish policy' developed towards forced emigration which he coupled with Allied response to his other schemes. Yet the 'Jewish question' was a part of his general concept of a 'New Order' in Europe, rejected by the Western Allies after a long period of contradictory policies known as the period of appeasement in Great Britain, for good reasons that were accepted and supported by every Jew in those countries as a matter of course. Yet until this policy hardened into a war against Germany, many among the ruling circles in Britain – not to mention the American ambassador to St James's Court, Joseph P. Kennedy – believed that 'the Jews' may have had a good reason to have the West fight and destroy Hitler – because their brethren in Germany were persecuted – but not the West itself.[10]

Following the Battle of Britain and Hitler's decision to attack the Soviet Union, in connection with the growing American aid rendered to the British – limited and defensive as it was – the so-called 'Final Solution of the Jewish Question' developed into an industrialized carnage.

The Allies, on the other hand, rejected both Hitler's 'New Order' for Europe and his 'forced emigration' policy aimed at the Jews under his control. The 'Jewish question', a central issue for Hitler, was for the Allies a side issue; later on, when left alone to face the victorious Third Reich, the British – rightly from their point of view and our point of view then and now – having turned down Hitler's peace offers, had to concentrate all their efforts and calculate all their steps under the maxim of fighting him and getting a reluctant America to join them, while seeking and later maintaining an alliance with the Soviet Union.[11] This absolute order of priorities was maintained almost to the end, and assumed a formidable bureaucratic character of its own.[12] Moreover, the Western Allies feared that their decision to fight Hitler first might be perceived by their own non-Jewish citizens as a decision to fight a 'Jew's war'.[13]

Indeed Hitler had always declared that the war – any war – was 'Jewish'. Yet he did not make up his mind before the war became global – thanks very much to his own decisions – and only then did he begin to realize his 'prophecy' of 30 January 1933.[14] He then proclaimed before the Reichstag that should a Second World War break out, this time the war would bring about 'the annihilation of the Jewish race in Europe'. This self-fulfilling prophecy was thus dependent upon a new world war, and hence upon the behaviour of Hitler's adversaries or those to be pursued by him as adversaries alone or with the help of others such as Japan – i.e. Great Britain, the Soviet Union and the United States. Hence the fate of the Jews under Hitler's control was dependent upon Allied or neutral behaviour, upon whom the Jews had no influence as an organized group dedicated to its particularistic interests; yet they were suspected of pursuing such interests since time immemorial.

On the contrary, with the unconditional support of their Jewish citizens, Allied governments fought Hitler for their own sake, and 'for the sake of civilization', Jews included. But they had to recognize the domestic political significance of attempting to absorb large numbers of Jewish immigrants at first or later to rescue Jews during the hostilities. Conscious of the necessary national consensus to fight Hitler, who declared the Jews to be his arch-enemies, and who blamed them, the Allies, of fighting him as Jewish tools, the Western Allies had to approach the issue as a highly sensitive political matter domestically, and *vis-à-vis* Germany itself. Even threats against Germany in retaliation for the crimes against Jews could help Hitler generate a sense of collective guilt that might unite the Germans behind him even more, especially when Jews were the reason for such threats. Using Allied threats related to the Jews killed in order to unite the German people behind Hitler to the last was a devilish, but not an impossible, avenue to be pursued by Hitler and Goebbels. Moreover, Hitler had the power to treat the Jews as he wanted, and even proclaimed the 'Final Solution' to be in force several times in public.[15]

A major political problem here would have been German demands if the Allies had been ready to negotiate on the fate of the Jews, and the use of Jews unilaterally by Germany to hamper the Allied war effort. A proximity between Jews – especially Zionists – and the Germans, in terms of a mutual interest to get Jews out of Europe in such a way as to hamper the Allied war effort, was suspected by British authorities from the beginning of hostilities. It culminated, almost as an expected manoeuvre aimed at driving a wedge between the West and the Soviet Union, in the so-called Brand–Grosz mission of May 1944, and the response was supported by both emissaries when interrogated by Allied officers.[16] Thus the European Jews and their brethren abroad could have been seen as German instruments, if negotiations about their rescue had taken place or even if Jews had been allowed to leave in large numbers with Allied aid. Any active Allied rescue effort could have been regarded, therefore, as a high political matter that could enhance German interests. Indeed, the Allies, President Roosevelt himself included, brought pressure to bear, both publicly and behind the scenes, on the Horthy government and later on the Fascist Szalasi government and helped stop the deportations from Hungary to Auschwitz at least for a while in summer 1944. Allied agents and neutrals such as Raoul Wallenberg were mobilized, and help was rendered now by ICRC officials. The Papacy appealed to the Hungarian government to stop the Hungarian carnage and help save as many victims as the circumstances allowed. Yet this activity avoided any serious negotiations with the Germans themselves, because of Allied fears of German intentions and indeed because of actual German intentions and deeds, which later combined with those of the Hungarian Fascists, who ran amok in the final stages of the Hungarian tragedy.[17]

Summing up, we argue that because the Nazis turned the 'Jewish Question' into a major issue and perceived the Jews under their control as an unacceptable source of racial and political trouble, they finally destroyed them, as no other solution outside Europe – say, settling them on Madagascar – was possible without war and cooperation with the Allies. In other words, in order to save Jews an anti-Semitic common denominator between the Allies and Hitler had to be created, together with Allied acceptance of Hitler's hegemonic plans for Europe. Thus the war to prevent that hegemony which was forced on the Allies sealed the Jews' fate but was not by itself a major concern for the hard-pressed Allies until early 1944, probably not even until the successful breakthrough from the Normandy beachhead. But the war that started in 1939, and its continuation by the British, with American support, and Hitler's own responses to both by invading Soviet Russia and supporting the Japanese in their own attack on the United States, were laid to the door of the Jews as active enemies of the Third Reich. Revenge combined here with ideology, and persisted as a major war aim; and it remained much the same after Germany had lost the war itself. The Hungarian case was a part of this last chapter, and the rescue efforts in this case proved largely futile because of the specific nature of the trap situation in that country, as mirrored in OSS and related documents.

The End of the Deportations

The end of the 'Final Solution' as a systematic, ongoing, universal process allowing the rescue of very few in order to destroy the majority, took place in phases. It is possible that the deteriorating war situation in general, the specific Hungarian conditions, the need for workers in Vienna and elsewhere along Germany's own borders, and rescue efforts undertaken by Jewish organizations including the Rescue Committee in Budapest in conjunction with Himmler's procurement agent Kurt Becher and by the Sternbuch brothers in conjunction with the former Swiss Federal President Jean-Marie Musy, some of which were initiated or supported by Himmler's masseur Felix Kersten in conjunction with the *SD-Ausland* chief Walter Schellenberg, saved the lives of Hungarian and other Jews. Yet this could be seen as the meagre result of Jewish efforts and of Himmler's subordinates' initiatives adopted by Himmler as trial balloons aimed at the Western Allies, covered by Hitler's own prior decision to allow a few Jews to leave in exchange for large sums of foreign currency. Once Hitler suspected that too many were being released, he forbade further releases.[18] Others were sent to work in German fortifications or industrial plants, or interned in camps in Germany itself, in Austria and elsewhere (including Auschwitz), and later were marched on foot from there to Germany. Maintaining alive those who were sent to work or otherwise escaped death at this stage might have been the result of the combined Jewish rescue effort, of Germany's needs and Himmler's and his aides' calculations, and of WRB efforts.

Some Jews were brought to camps in Germany which were finally delivered by Himmler intact to the Allies, when he felt free enough to act on his own, and at last broke with Hitler. We shall return to this in the documentary part of this chapter, by quoting the newly released Schellenberg interrogation at the U.S National Archives and contemporary, i.e. wartime OSS reports, which show how the OSS still saw in each successful rescue operation a German ransom deal aimed at larger achievements.

Yet later on these efforts appear to give the impression that the Jewish and Nazi parties concerned were seeking an alibi, as they did nothing and in fact collaborated in preventing rescue of the many in exchange for rescue of the few.[19]

The point, however, that should be stressed here is that while the rescue workers hoped, and had to hope, that some bargaining with the Germans, at least with some Germans, was possible and the only way out of the otherwise ongoing disaster, the Germans picked up on their ideas, including the truck deal offered by Brand and others or the separate peace negotiations suggested by Bandi Grosz. Thus the initial Jewish proposals, based on their wishful thinking about rescue efforts that seemed to have succeeded thanks to bribes in Slovakia, undertaken by Eichmann's aide Wisliceny, were adopted by Wisliceny and seemingly by Eichmann himself in Hungary.[20] The blame for the deportations, which had started parallel to the Brand–Grosz mission, was laid at the Allied and Zionist door, since they failed to respond to Eichmann's offer, which in fact was a Jewish rescue deal adopted by the Germans for their purposes and uncovered as such by both the Yishuv's leadership and the Western Allies.[21] Yet the argument against the Hungarian Zionist leadership would be that, having trusted a deal with the Germans, they failed to warn the Jews to flee, hide or fight. The German 'deal' thus became a tool in the hands of the Germans with which to kill as many Jews as the alleged deal prevented from fleeing, hiding or fighting. It is not our intention here to discuss these three options, which I have tried to study in a forthcoming book. Only this can be said here: escape in large numbers was extremely difficult psychologically, since Hungarian Jews identified with Hungary, were for four years of war largely protected by the Hungarian government, believed themselves to be inseparable from the Hungarian culture, heritage and economy, the Hungarian elite and the Hungarian war effort itself, but they were hardly able to foresee an ally (Germany) invading yet another ally (Hungary), or they expected an Allied victory soon.[22] Once the Germans occupied Hungary, in practical terms it became very hard to travel, to cross the border to Romania or to Tito partisans in an alien country which offered no forests, marshes or mountains except in Carpathia, where the deportations started immediately, or in Transylvania. The lightning speed with which the deportations from the provinces were carried out to Auschwitz, whose real meaning remained unknown to most of the deportees from the provinces, combined with the specific circumstances of an occupied country, whose state apparatus was nevertheless placed at the occupiers' disposal for the purpose of the deportations. The state forbade travel and the use of one's own bank accounts from the start, and the gentile population was hostile and waited for Jewish possessions and property to be looted and taken over.

Eichmann's intentions in adopting the Brand–Grosz deal were several, I believe, among them the lessons learned from the Warsaw Ghetto uprising which required carrot-and-stick handling of the Zionists – the most politically active element, and yet the least numerous – among the Hungarian Jews. Eichmann knew quite a bit about the Zionist rescue activities in Romania through his representative in Bucharest, Gustav Richter. The Gestapo intercepted or read Zionist letters exchanged between Bucharest, Geneva and Istanbul, in which the Hungarian rescue workers were mentioned as well. The Germans further deciphered American diplomatic messages from Berne, some of which pertained to the Holocaust. The Allies deciphered German cables relating to the same.[23] Under these circumstances, the neutralization of rescue by seeming to adopt rescue schemes was Eichmann's main concern, and indeed he pursued it to the end. The rescue workers, on the other hand, hoped to involve Eichmann and the Allies in rescue as a matter of course and later in spite of themselves. The other option was to try and drive a wedge between the Nazis in Hungary and those at the highest level of the Third Reich. Other than Eichmann, other SS officers such as Himmler's procurement aide Kurt Becher, possibly even Eichmann's subordinates Hermann Krumay and Otto Hunsche, and finally Himmler himself, were ready for some kind of deal concerning the remnants of the Hungarian Jews and others. Yet the very implementation of such deals, even the release of the Kasztner train passengers to Switzerland, and especially the release of some Theresienstadt prisoners – many of Dutch nationality – to Switzerland thanks to a Musy–Schellenberg–Sternbuch agreement, prompted Hitler's order to stop such deals. Rescue thus prompted its prohibition.[24] To complete the trap even at that final stage, one should read OSS reports about German hostage-taking tactics with regard to these releases, as understood in Washington. One sample is quoted below. Of course the Allies would not prevent rescue into Switzerland; by now they actively supported it. But the Germans expected them to pay a price for it, in order to sell the idea to Hitler. He, in turn, would not allow the remnants to escape; unless of course his initial terms were honoured by third parties – acceptance of his regime and goals, coupled with the departure of all Jews from Europe even at that stage.

Since this was by now a daydream more than ever before in each respect, the destruction of the remnants remained the only choice for him, as the one victory he did win, and as a demonstration of Hitler's fanatical devotion to the racial anti-Semitic cause for future generations. There was no escape from this trap as long as Hitler maintained control, perhaps thanks to the collective guilt that he had deliberately created among Germans due also to the 'Final Solution'. Thus the deportations, in terms of death marches and the like, didn't really stop, but served the labour needs of a desperate Germany and the tactics of those among Hitler's cronies who hoped to bargain and thus convince Hitler that they could achieve results – against Allied firm refusal to bargain with Hitler for their good reasons.

The Dwork/Duker Records

American attitudes to rescue of Jews through negotiations with Germany had not basically changed when the War Refugee Board (WRB) was created in January 1944 for the purpose of rescuing Jews. The WRB did its best, however, within the limits imposed on it by both the Germans and Allied governments; its records, scattered in archives of other agencies as well, already told us its story, which David Wyman chose to describe as 'too late and too little'.[25] Yet Wyman ignored the logic of the Quadruple Trap in Hungary, the home of the last large Jewish community in Europe, which was largely destroyed when the WRB was already there, trying to save it. Yet even before the WRB was created, and its records survived to tell us their story, the OSS had established a small section to deal with the Holocaust. Practically a one-man research unit, OSS R&A engaged Dr Charles Irving Dwork, a USC (University of South Carolina, Los Angeles) PhD in Jewish Studies (the well-known reform Rabbi Magnin of San Francisco was his instructor) to create something like a 'Jewish desk', according to William Langer's one-time assistant, the historian Dr Carl Schorske, in response to my query.[26]

The OSS representative in Europe, Allen Dulles, had refused to be directly engaged in rescue efforts, as these interfered with his military mission. The appointment of the able WRB representative in Berne, Roswell McClelland, and the growing cooperation between him and the US Mission in Switzerland generated a larger body of documentation reaching Dwork's desk. His job was to organize and analyse it for the future prosecution of Nazi war criminals. Hence captured German documents also reached him, when OSS and CIC units gathered them in Europe during the later phase of the war, and some primary American intelligence data were given to him when they related to Jews, among secondary sources and dubious reports, press stories and important censorship intercepts. Dwork and other sources were used by the Provost Marshal of the

US Army and the War Crimes Commission in London in their preparations for the war crimes trials in Nuremberg, in which the OSS was involved directly as well. Interestingly enough, his file dealing with the crimes against the Jews remained 'confidential'.[27] Later Justice Robert Jackson took over that effort, and the OSS's role diminished accordingly. Dwork himself collaborated with the office of the Chief of Counsel for Prosecution of Axis Criminality; he tried to build a conspiracy case in regard to the 'Final Solution', but the whole Jewish subject was then incorporated into the complex named 'crimes against humanity' and lost its unique significance. Dwork was then discharged and took some or many of his files, parts or copies of them, home, and kept them for several years. Later, as a successful businessman, he wanted to dispose of the files, but agreed to transfer them to the custody of his former OSS colleague Dr Abraham Duker.[28] Duker, an important Jewish scholar, whose OSS expertise was Polish affairs, kept the files until his death in the early 1990s. The family then transferred them to the US National Archives, which gave them the RG number 200.[29] Largely consisting of copies of WRB, OSS and other agencies reports, RG 200 didn't seem to reveal much in comparison to the giant RG 226 (OSS) itself, and other important NA files. Yet for us RG 200 represents what was reported and known to the OSS 'Jewish expert' in real time and immediately after the war. Moreover, even in comparison to RG 226 itself, RG 200 does reflect the Hungarian trap situation quite clearly. As such I shall use samples from it and related ones from RG 226 and others in this chapter.

The Documentation

A. Anti-Semitism in the West

The first sample that I have chosen from the Dwork/Duker papers would sound rather familiar to Tony Kushner, whose work on anti-Semitism in Great Britain during World War II is known and appreciated by us all. The document is a copy of a Military Attache Report, Gt. Britain, dated 14 September 1944, originated in London.[30] Its contents are repeated here verbatim;

> It has become noticeably apparent that in comparison with the years just prior to the war there has been a marked increase in anti-Semitic feeling in Gt Britain. The basis for this observation is the increased and increasing frequency with which criticism against Jews occurs in conversation; this criticism is not limited to any one class or section of society.

The general tenor of the criticism is based on the following current convictions:

1. That the Jews have avoided playing their full part in the war effort of the country.

2. That they are responsible for the Black Market and have profiteered out of the war.

3. That the Jews are always the first to evacuate London. (This criticism was frequently heard during the flying-bomb raids.)

One aspect worth noting is that prior to the war the great majority of Jews lived in London. The evacuations have distributed them throughout the provinces. Anti-semitic feeling has, therefore, become far more widespread throughout the country.

Comment: [seems to be OSS Washington's, S.A.] The frequent anti-Jewish comments that are now heard in England are directly the result of the war. The general condition of war weariness and aggravation against the restrictions of the war leads naturally to the selection of some scapegoats as a butt for criticism. The Jews have become the scapegoat. Whether the accusations against them are legitimate or not, the conviction that they are exists and has increased with snowball effect. At the present time anti-Semitic feeling goes no deeper than caustic conversational comments.

My comment would differ in several points from the above: that a forthcoming war was perceived in England, and by the American Ambassador in the United Kingdom Joseph Kennedy, as a 'Jew's war' that must be avoided almost at all costs and especially as such, is clear. However, two more points should be stressed here in relation to Hitler's forced emigration policy. The one is related to the alleged growing anti-Semitism resulting from 'distribution of Jews throughout the country'. This may help explain the reluctance to respond to Hitler's forced immigration policy. The other one is related to the argument quoted above, 'whether the accusations against them are legitimate or not'. That is to say, a victim's dubious reputation became a political factor, regardless of the truth, i.e. if he might have been accused of misdeeds which he had not committed. In the case of Jews, their dubious reputation existed in the United Kingdom along similar lines quoted above, especially in regard to black-market profiteering and avoidance of playing 'a full part in the country's war effort' since World War I. Once Hitler had transformed the otherwise – in England – not very major issue of Jews and Jewish influence to a major international and domestic problem, the final decision to fight and destroy him had to be separated in practical and even in various undeclared fashions from the cause of the Jews, in order to maintain the national consensus necessary to fight him.[31] This approach seems to have been valid throughout the war, at least before the successful invasion of France and the Soviet drive westwards in the summer of 1944 seemed to have guaranteed victory and promised to silence the missile bases. Yet the missile threat indeed preoccupied the highest British authorities together with 'Overlord' and its development during the first stages of the Hungarian Holocaust.

B. The Brand–Grosz Mission

The second sample which I have chosen to present here is an OSS R&A report on the Jews in Hungary, dated 19 October 1944.[32] The report covered a large number of issues relating to Hungarian Jewry prior to the German invasion and afterwards quite accurately; regarding the Brand–Grosz mission the report, largely based on an OSS source S, is inaccurate in various details. Yet the final verdict illustrates my arguments as quoted here verbatim:

> This combination of blackmail and political warfare was subject to various interpretations. It was viewed as:
>
> 1. An attempt to split the United Nations by arousing Russian suspicions of the Western Powers' willingness to deal with the common enemy;
> 2. A preliminary, if accepted in principal, to further barter deals to obtain a 'soft' peace or immunity from criminal prosecution for high Nazi officials;
> 3. An instrument of psychological warfare to stir up suspicions and ill feelings among various Jewish and non-Jewish groups, depending upon its acceptance or rejection.

The report concluded, without further comment, that the offer was ultimately rejected by the Allies, but the Germans were informed through the Swiss government that the British and the Americans 'would be willing to cooperate in the transfer of Jews from Axis to Allied and neutral territory but only with due regard for military necessities'. What is missing here is the Jewish initiative in regard to the Brand–Grosz mission, especially Grosz's contribution to it and his initial idea to offer the Western Allies a separate peace, which doomed the mission from the start.[33] In my view this initiative might have been grasped by the SD chief in Budapest, Gerhard (rather than Otto!) Clages (rather than Klages!), and adopted by Kurt Andreas Becher, who obtained a non-committal approval by Himmler. The Reichsführer-SS – the chief executive of the 'Final Solution' – would not release Jews in large numbers anyway, as shown by Richard Breitman and myself elsewhere.[34] Nor would Hitler himself, as shown in great detail by Randolph L. Braham, release Jews in large numbers, but would be willing to release the few in order to secure the murder of the many.[35] Thus the contribution of Jewish activists to the 'Brand–Grosz deal' and to its inevitable failure became the source of ongoing controversy, as if the Allies and Jewish leaders missed an opportunity offered by the Germans – who in fact grasped a Jewish initiative for the purposes of medium-level officials and for the non-committal responses of their superiors, whose attitude toward the 'Final Solution' hadn't changed.[36]

C. Wisliceny in Thessalonica

One of the key figures in the rescue controversy after the war was Eichmann's aide Dieter Wisliceny. Sometimes described as 'Baron von Wisliceny' by rescue workers such as Ze'ev Venia Hadari, as 'a member of Himmler's family' and the like, the SS captain whose medium-level rank probably required such – imagined – title and connections to justify dealing with him, was believed to have ransomed at least a part of the Slovak Jewish community for a while, but could not keep them alive later on due to a major failure of the Jewish leadership abroad to finance the rest of the deal.[37] Yet the Dwork/Duker papers uncover a detailed personal list of Jews from Thessalonica in Greece, who were sent by him to Auschwitz in January 1944, just prior to the invasion of Hungary in March 1944.[38]

Wisliceny counted meticulously all the valuables and the financial assets robbed from the Greek deportees name by name. One could thus infer that money – the 2 million dollars promised to him by the Slovak rescue workers which the Zionists and the American Jewish organizations allegedly failed to deliver – was not the reason for the resumption of the Slovakian Holocaust. Wisliceny's involvement in the Greek disaster was known to the Hungarian rescue workers, but his renewed barter offer in Hungary shortly afterwards – with all its ups and downs as described in the scholarly literature – was still taken seriously, as we learn from Bandi Grosz's interrogation mentioned above. Grosz told the British that he was informed by one of his German *Abwehr* friends about the impending Nazi occupation of Hungary, but hardly believed it. Upon the invasion Grosz was arrested by them, because the *Abwehr* chief in Hungary, one Dr Schmidt, went after his own money 'and the money which had come from Turkey for the Zionists'.[39] Schmidt was quoted by Grosz as if he had learned about the Zionist money from Fritz Laufer, an *Abwehr* and Gestapo operative, who had managed to become an OSS agent and also served the Istanbul Zionists as a courier before the invasion of Hungary.[40] In the meantime, the main Zionist figures who had received the Istanbul money, Rezso Kasztner and Joel Brand, were arrested as well. They were 'clamped on . . . with terroristic methods in order to blackmail them out of their Zionist funds'.

Under this pressure from the *Abwehr* operatives, according to Grosz, Brand asked their chief, Dr Schmidt, 'to be allowed to see Obersturmbannführer 'WILY' [*sic* – Wisliceny] who had formerly been negotiating about improved treatment of the Jews . . . in BRATISLAVA [Slovakia – this is the original interrogation language, capital letters, brackets etc., S.A.] . . . Schmidt (and his accomplice Otto) WINNINGER agreed on condition that BRAND and KASTNER pay them 20,000 dollars. The Zionists paid over the money.' I see no counter-evidence to suggest that Grosz invented this story. On the contrary, it is supported by Hansi Brand's testimony to me of 1986. In my view Kasztner and Brand, strongly supported by Brand's wife Hansi, tried to free themselves from the *Abwehr* net, retrieve their money and suggest to Wisliceny, who was allegedly open to a deal, a 'grand deal' to save all the Hungarian Jewry, as he belonged to the real authority which was to decide the fate of the Jews. Wisliceny seemed ready indeed at least to listen, having brought with him letters of recommendation from Rabbi Weissmandel in Bratislava, who indeed believed that Wisliceny had helped stop the deportations of Slovak Jews thanks to some kind of a deal. Such an illusion was further enhanced by Hermann Krumay, another Eichmann aide, who was ready to allow several hundred Palestine certificate holders to leave Hungary, and then by Eichmann himself, who seemingly endorsed the 'grand deal' offered by Brand to Wisliceny. This is how the 'Brand mission' was born, based on the pretence of the Zionists that the Allies would deliver goods which in fact they had no power to promise. Thus Bandi Grosz came into the picture. I see no reason not to accept his version, when interrogated by the British, that when Grosz had heard of the 'truck deal', he told Brand and Kasztner that the Western Allies would never supply the Axis with war materials; he then told his SD contacts, Gerhard Clages and Fritz Laufer, that if they allowed him to join Brand, he would try to bring about separate peace contacts to be pursued between SD officials and the Western Allies. Hence I maintain, that the 'separate peace' feelers were Grosz's idea endorsed by Clages and Laufer, allowing Grosz to save his own neck to begin with, and not rejected by superior Nazi authorities because of the confusion it would create among the Allies, the possible propaganda value of such a Jewish-conveyed offer, and maybe even because it might yield some effective results. Of course, the logic of the quadruple trap would drive the Allies to fear such 'deals' and offers in advance, and once they were made to reject them. But my contribution to the ongoing agonizing debate about the Brand–Grosz deal is not only to expose it as an impossible deal from an Allied point of view. I argue that the deal was a rescue action initiated by Jews; once the victim tried a rescue option, he was doomed to fail at least in regard to a 'grand deal'. Future generations may still see in this an option that third parties and the Jewish leadership in the free world missed in a negligent or a tragic fashion.

D. Peter Bergson and MI5

A memorandum made available to me from the Stettinius papers,[41] dated 7 January 1944, may shed a light on rescue options just before the Nazi occupation of Hungary. Related to the establishment of the War Refugee Board or to rescue efforts in general, the document carried the header 'Summary of Recommendations for Specific Action':

> I. Release of persons from Axis Europe [underlined in original].
> 1. The President or the Department [of State, in which Stettinius served as the newly appointed Undersecretary, replacing Sumner Wells] should enter into negotiations with Hitler or the German government, through the Pope or through the heads of the governments of Switzerland or Sweden, to reach an understanding which would permit the release of Jews at a certain rate per month consistent with the capacity of available neutral shipping and of Spanish and Turkish railroads. If initial negotiations on humanitarian grounds fail, consideration should be given to further appeals offering a *quid pro quo* to the Germans such as hope of less severe peace terms or the possibility of reduced bombing of certain cities or areas.

Next to this paragraph and underneath it, one word was added – 'no'. We do not know who drafted this document, and who rejected the proposal of hinting at better peace terms with Germany in exchange for Jewish lives, or creating bomb-safe areas in Germany before 'Overlord' or before the liquidation of Germany's war industry and its own aerial bombing potential as a measure to save Jews.

The quoted memorandum further recommended a major change in Allied treatment of those who managed to escape from occupied Europe, by constructing 'healthful and attractive receiving centers', the transportation of the 'appropriate persons' once 'carefully classified as to skills and experience' to countries 'where labor shortages exist'. Finally, the author or authors of the memorandum foresaw 'negotiations . . . with neutrals to obtain shipping to transport refugees to Palestine or to other havens of refuge'. This last sentence prompted yet another handwritten rejection 'in view [of] the Zionists in the Arab World'. We have no evidence to verify the origins of this document, but a reference to suggestions of a similar kind, at least partially, made by Hillel Kook (alias Peter Bergson, a Zionist revisionist, i.e. right-wing operative in the United States) to Assistant Secretary Brekenridge Long was mentioned by Stettinius in a letter to Long of 8 January 1944 – one day later. Stettinius referred to Long's own memo of 27 December 1943, 'relative to the discussion with and communication from Mr. Peter Bergson'. Having studied the file, Stettinius has decided 'not to send a letter to him [Bergson] at this time', but he was 'still considering the possible telegrams to neutrals and the possible warnings to the satellite governments [regarding their Jewish citizens] and will be in touch with you on these matters later'. Stettinius was of a tentative opinion, however, that 'it might be advisable not to send one at this time [due to the peace feelers of the Kalay government, S.A.] to Hungary'.[42] This memo indicates no interest in the above quoted, far-reaching ideas of saving Jews by changing the war aims and/or the bombing policy or adopting a *quid pro quo* approach, which might have served those who hoped to make Hitler change his own policy towards the Jews. Soon after this exchange of memos the War Refugee Board was created, so that Bergson's and others' pressure in this regard did yield fruits; but they had to be 'too late and tool little', due to the logic of the quadruple trap. The Dwork/Duker Papers add to the Bergson story – one of the sources of accusations at that time and later against the mainstream American Jewish leadership which distanced itself from Bergson's aggressive methods – a number of intercepted cables which he and his political friend Yirmiahu Halperin sent from the United States abroad. Both were revisionist Zionists and hence anti-British, whose activities in the United States could have been seen as damaging to the Allied war effort against Fascism, whose main target was the European Jews, and so forth, as the quadruple trap evolved. The Bergson–Halperin cables were thus mailed by the American authorities to British home (and Imperial) Counter-Intelligence MI5, asking for commentary.[43]

E. The Final Stage: Hostages and their Fates

One of the few cases of the release of Jews to Switzerland in the final stages of World War II was the case of the Himmler–Musy–Sternbuch negotiations, which brought about the release of about 1,200 Theresienstadt prisoners into Switzerland on 8 February 1945. The Musy–Himmler talks, in which Schellenberg and an orthodox Jewish group were involved, led to one of Himmler's last-minute efforts to use Jews for his purposes, mainly towards some kind of negotiations for a separate peace with the Western Allies, which he had tried to persuade Hitler to accept late in

1944 but was probably rebuffed or realized that Hitler would not listen. Of course Himmler needed a *quid pro quo* to justify the release, which in turn generated a variety of explanations in Washington.[44] It is quoted here verbatim:

> . . . 4. New procedures for dealing with Jews: During the past week there has accumulated a considerable amount of reliable evidence pointing to a change in Nazi procedures toward the remnants of European Jewry still under Nazi control. The most striking development was the release by the Germans of 1,200 internees from the Jewish reservation at Theresienstadt.[1] In return for a relatively small cash payment this group was given sufficient food and transportation to enable them to get to Switzerland. It is reliably reported that these persons are only the first of many such Jewish groups to be freed under similar conditions.[2] According to M. de Steiger, President of the Swiss Confederation, the negotiations for the liberation of these prisoners were carried on by the former Federal Councillor Musy (in behalf of Orthodox Jewish organizations) and Heinrich Himmler.[3]
>
> Other sources report that commanders of concentration camps and isolated SS groups have become increasingly independent of higher authorities and have adopted a more charitable attitude toward their Jewish prisoners.[4] Thus, the commander of all SS-controlled concentration camps for Jews in the Vienna area, and the SS officer in charge of all Hungarian Jewish deportees in Austria, have announced to neutral official parties their willingness to collaborate in efforts to improve the lot of their Jewish charges. Similar sentiments have recently been expressed by the commanders of the camps of Dachau and Landsberg am Lech (some 12,000 Jews are held in the latter camp).[5] At the same time, there is also considerable evidence that Jewish prisoners have been evacuated prior to retreat to areas where there are labor shortages. In the early fall of 1944, convoys of 3,000–6,000 were withdrawn from Warsaw, Radom, Lodz, and Kielce to the camps at Auschwitz and Birkenau.[6] When this area was threatened by the Russians most of the occupants of these camps were sent (often on foot) to the Sudetenland, the Upper Silesian industrial area, and other manufacturing areas. However, it still appears to be the practice to exterminate elderly people, children, invalids, and others unable to work. The Nazis are also reliably reported to have transferred a great many Jews from Theresienstadt into Germany proper since last October. The number of persons involved in the transfer and the fate of the majority of the inhabitants of the reservation who are unfit for work is not known. However, from postcards, dated at the end of November, which have recently arrived in Switzerland from Theresienstadt contained no indication that the situation in the camps had changed insofar as treatment is concerned . . .
>
> These changes in procedure appear to introduce a more 'lenient' attitude toward the Jews, but there is no indication as to what ultimate purpose these changes are meant to serve. One interpretation is that the Nazis are seeking to

obtain as much ransom as the situation can be made to produce. Another explanation is that, with defeat staring them in the face, the Nazis hope to influence world opinion and thus possibly secure wider political concessions.

1. OSS Source D. 10 February 1945.
2. OSS Source D. 9 February 1945.
3. OSS Source D. 9 February 1945.
4. OSS Source D. 22 January 1945.
5. OSS Source D. 27 January 1945.
6. OSS Source D. 9 February 1945.[45]

Another OSS report dated 24 February 1945[46] tried its own explanations. Generally speaking, OSS had a rather accurate picture of a tragic situation, full of typical contradictions.

The basis for Himmler's sudden interest in facilitating relief for political internees and in aiding Jews to escape to neutral Switzerland is open to considerable speculation. The *Berner Tagwacht* recently reported[1] that in conversations between former Swiss Federal Councillor Jean-Marie Musy and Himmler (which resulted in the release of 1,200 Jews), the question of Jewish rescue projects was merely incidental and that the two were discussing a much bigger issue. A clue to what this matter might be is furnished by a recent unconfirmed report[2] which clearly stated that Musy was to be the intermediary in a scheme whereby the Nazis would use prominent political and military personalities now in their power as hostages to secure the right of exile in Switzerland for top-ranking Nazis. Should the Allies and Swiss refuse these terms, the hostages would share the fate of the Nazis. Musy's efforts to save at least Petain and the King of the Belgians are reported to have the active support of the Vatican which is said to have been approached on this matter by German Ambassador Ernst von Weizsaecker.

Should this report prove true, it would serve to explain the Nazis' simultaneous offer to the Allies of the olive branch and the nailed fist. On the one hand, the Nazis have released a not inconsiderable number of Jews and have taken steps toward ameliorating the living conditions of political internees. (In this connection, Himmler is reported to have inquired of Musy whether the recent better treatment of Jews and other refugees would help to modify public resentment against him)[3] On the other hand, a Nazi official recently used two released prisoners to carry a message to the American Legation in Bern, in which he said that in the event of German collapse the lives of United States nationals held by their Germans would be 'in extreme danger.'[4] The Nazis thus seem to be offering the Allies a Hobson's choice.

8. Nazis seen preparing end of Theresienstadt. Of the 40,000 Jews in Theresienstadt in 1944, only 13,000 now remain according to information furnished

> by persons among the 1,200 recently released internees who have arrived in Switzerland . . .
>
> Conditions in the camp are reported to have deteriorated considerably. The internees are said to be working 15 hours a day and many of the elderly inhabitants are dying of malnutrition notwithstanding the fact that packages are sent to the camp by outside Jewish agencies.
>
> Dissolution of this 'model' camp by the Nazis seems to contradict the previous interpretation of German motives for the creation and continued maintenance of this Jewish Reservation through three years that saw the physical extermination of the vast majority of European Jewry.
>
> Had the Nazis intended to use Theresienstadt as a 'showplace' to 'prove' that they had not maltreated the Jews, they would not liquidate the camp while they stand on the brink of defeat – the only time at which such a policy could bear fruit.
>
> 1. *Berner Tagwacht*, 18 February 1945.
> 2. OSS Source S, 3 February 1945.
> 3. Ibid.
> 4. OSS Source S, S684, 16 February 1945.

On 20 March the American Ambassador in London, John Winant, cabled the director of the Intergovernmental Committee on Refugees, Sir Herbert Emerson, the WRB and the Department of State, regarding the Jewish prisoners released from Theresienstadt in February; Sir Herbert was worried that they might want to go to Palestine, or be pushed to do so by the Zionists; his – and others' – main concern was to return them to their countries of origin. Winant gave those agencies, however, a rather accurate picture about such last-moment rescue efforts which he had received from Sally Mayer, the WRB–JDC negotiator:

> . . . 2. According to Mayer inside story of the arrival of the Theresienstadt group is as follows. Musy, a retired federal councillor, was attacked in the press on account of the high prices he had paid for obtaining the release of a few political and Jewish internees. In order to exonerate himself and at the suggestion of the Vatican and Dr. Steinbuch (Sternbuch)-Montreux of American Orthodox Rabbi Federation, he negotiated release of the Theresienstadt group, stating, without authorization, that Mayer would show gratitude in cash. The sole condition imposed by Himmler was that the group should not include technicians, intellectuals or prominent Jews. Mayer of course refused to make any payment and the arrival of further groups seems unlikely.[47]

But this was not the only reason why the arrival of further groups became 'unlikely'. Hitler was informed about them, exactly as the Western Allies

– who probably were Himmler's target – read about them in the Swiss papers immediately upon their arrival. Hitler then barred any further release of Jews.[48]

Himmler's final efforts to stop the killings and transfer the concentration camps intact to the Allies must have led to his dismissal by the isolated Hitler in his Berlin bunker from all his SS and party offices, on top of the murder of his liaison officer in the Führer's HQ, Hermann Fegelein. Fegelein, married to Eva Braun's sister, was also Kurt Becher's old boss and possibly Becher's initial contact with Himmler.

Notes

1. For a good general description of OSS history and activities published before the release of OSS documentation in 1985 see Bradley F. Smith, *The Shadow Warriors, O.S.S and the Origins of the C.I.A.*, New York, 1983, and see also Ian Sayer and Douglas Botting, *America's Secret Army, The Untold Story of the Counter Intelligence Corps*, London, 1989.
2. For an extended analysis of British and American sources, compared to Nazi allegations about Jewish influence in America, see my forthcoming *Jewish Wars: The Quadruple Trap, its Ramifications and Aftermath*.
3. For the development of Horthy's policies until the Szalasi coup see Randolph L. Braham, *The Politics of Genocide, The Holocaust in Hungary*, vol. II, New York 1981, pp. 743–809, 1113–20, and cf. OSS R&A report of 19 October 1944 #2027, NA RG 226, Entry 191, Box 1, #4, also quoted below.
4. See Richard Breitman and Shlomo Aronson, 'The End of the "Final Solution"?: Nazi Plans to Ransom Jews in 1944', *Central European History*, vol. 25, no. 2 (1993), pp. 177–203.
5. See part D of the Documentation section.
6. I refer here to operation 'Sparrow', which was undertaken from London by OSS-Major Arthur Goldberg, among others – to the great displeasure of the British. For details see my forthcoming *Jewish Wars*, and cf. *Time Magazine*'s illustrated history of World War II, *The Secret War*, New York, 1985, in which an operation 'Zeppelin' is mentioned – aimed at spreading the German forces across the continent, and

especially luring them to the Balkans on the eve of 'Overlord'. No sources were however mentioned, even in reply to my query.

7. Meant here are the Kasztner–Becher–Mayer channel, the Schellenberg–Musy–Sternbuch channel, the Kleist–Storch–Olsen channel, the Kersten–Schellenberg plans related to the former, and finally the Bernadotte–Masur efforts, and cf. Breitman and Aronson, 'The End of the "Final Solution"?', and the literature discussed therein.
8. Ibid.
9. See for example British War Cabinet Documents, CAB 65, vol. 50, meetings 3 April to 18 May, doc. War Cab. 43 (45), meeting of 12 April 1945, PRO, Kew, England.
10. See for more details Tony Kushner's *The Persistence of Prejudice, Antisemitism in British Society during the Second World War*, Manchester and New York, 1989.
11. For a revisionist, but in fact a rather old 'appeasement-like' criticism of Churchill's crusade against Hitler following the fall of France, see John Charmley's *Churchill – End of Glory*, London, 1993.
12. See Documentation.
13. I shall extensively deal with the 'Jews' war' scare in my forthcoming *Quadruple Trap* book, but regarding OSS Washington reactions to the Brand-Grosz mission in this spirit at least one OSS source should be mentioned here: NA, RG 226, Entry 88, Wash-Commo=R+C-381-382.
14. For an annotated, contemporary English translation see Norman H. Baynes, *The Speeches of Adolf Hitler April 1922–August 1939*, vol. I, Oxford and London, 1942, p. 741.
15. See for example Franklin Watts (ed.), *Voices of History 1942–1945*, New York, 1943, p. 121. Hitler's speech as recorded and summerized by the Foreign Broadcast Monitoring Service, FCC; cf. Max Domarus, *Hitler, Reden und Proklamationen 1932–1945*, Wiesbaden, 1973, vol. II, pp. 1828ff.
16. See esp. Grosz's interrogation, Security Intelligence Middle East (SIME), Report no. 3, 22 June 1944, Top Secret, Public Record Office, FO 371 42811 01239.
17. See Braham, *Politics of Genocide*, pp. 820–83.
18. Breitman and Aronson, 'The End of the "Final Solution"?'
19. This is how Judge Benjamin Halevi preferred to explain the Kasztner–Becher effort in the final stage of the war in the so-called 'Kasztner Trial' in Israel in the 1950s. This was the first, and fatal, treatment of the Holocaust in Hungary in Israel, in that Halevi's verdict that 'Kasztner has sold his soul to the devil' took root – perhaps also

because of its bluntness and alleged clarity in spite of and in comparison to the complex and lengthy posthumous exoneration of Kasztner by the Israeli Supreme Court two years later.

20. For Wisliceny's deadly role in Slovakia, which was not changed by any alleged Jewish bribes but interrupted for a while by pure Slovakian reasons, see Braham, *Politics of Genocide*, vol. II, pp. 914–15; see also a related piece of research on the Slovakian Holocaust by Maria Schmidt, 'Destruction of Slovakian Jews as Reflected in Hungarian Police Reports', in Randolph L. Braham (ed.), *Studies on the Holocaust in Hungary*, Boulder and New York, 1990, pp. 164–74. Accordingly, 'the Jewish inhabitants of the northern parts of Hungary not only experienced from close quarters what was happening in their (Slovakian) neighborhood, but most probably also had the opportunity to get first-hand information from the (Slovakian) refugees (about 7,000–8,000) themselves about what they had had to go through' (p. 172).
21. See SIME interrogation quoted in n. 16.
22. See Braham, *Politics of Genocide*, vol. I, p. 85, and cf. Menachem Kish, 'Tales from Peaceful Places', *Davar Hashavua*, 8 April 1994.
23. Regarding the deciphered German cables see documentation below. Regarding German knowledge of rescue efforts undertaken from Istanbul via Bucharest, an archival note is required. The German Legation's archive in Bucharest seems to have been captured wholly intact, following Romania's withdrawal from the Axis camp and its ensuing declaration of war against Germany in the summer of 1944. The Romanian government took over the German Legation building, possibly following an unprovoked German bombing attack against the capital; shortly afterwards an OSS mission was sent to Romania, threatening soon to become a Soviet-dominated nation, under Frank Wiesner, a New York lawyer and reserve Navy Lieutenant-Commander, who beforehand had headed OSS-station Istanbul, and had previously served at the OSS Middle East office in Cairo. Wiesner was able at least to get copies of German Legation records from the Romanians. We do not know whether he received any originals, or whether he was to become the only Western source of such Legation records, as the Romanians were said to have made them accessible after the war to others such as Dr Haim Pozner, a Zionist operative in Switzerland and later one of *Yad-Vashem*'s founders. Upon receiving them, Wiesner realized that he had in his hands 'sensitive' documents from the desk of Adolf Eichmann's man in Bucharest, SS-Captain Gustav Richter, whose official title was that of a

'Judenberater' in the German Legation. Wiesner advised Washington that such 'sensitive' documents revealed internal Jewish feuds in Romania that were reported to Richter by his Jewish and non-Jewish (mainly Swiss) spies and double agents, through Zionist mail pertaining to rescue and to 'illegal money transfers' by Zionists for rescue in occupied Europe which was raised in the United States for the Zionists in Palestine and so forth. See Wiesner's cable to OSS Washington of 27 October 1944, NA, RG 226, Entry 88, box 495, Wash-Commo-R+C-381-382, London-Bern-Ankara-Istanbul; this box also contains documents from Izmir, Sofia, Bucharest and Jerusalem. Some of the Richter documents were incorporated into RG 226 under the synthetic series title DGesBukarest – Deutsche Gesandschaft Bukarest, and registered early in the 1980s in the separate NA guide 81, *Records of the Reichsfuhrer SS*, Part IV, pp. 41–57. The originals were incorporated into OSS files under the designation XL 13163–75, 13177–81, 13709–10. The Dwork/Duker Papers mentioned below also include a large number of German Legation Bucharest material, which seems to be the only regular, daily correspondence between Eichmann and an important subordinate to have survived intact.

24. Regarding the Theresienstadt deal see my 'Theresienstadt im Spiegel Amerikanischer Dokumentation', Prague, November 1994, and Documentation section, above.
25. David S. Wymann, *The Abandonment of the Jews*, New York, 1984.
26. Letter in May 1986.
27. Dwork/Duker Papers, box 17. The folders 'Jewish Partisan Groups in the Balkans' and 'Arabs vs. Jews in Palestine' in box 22 were totally removed by censors. Requests were filed to have them released, under the Freedom of Information Act.
28. Dworks's widow's testimony to the author.
29. The NA archivist Lawrence McDonald who sorted out the files wrote an introduction to RG 200, which accurately describes its origins and limitations.
30. Dwork/Duker Papers, National Archives (NA), RG 200, box 29, #364. On the left upper side the number 93739R is handwritten. Next to the city of origin in brackets, A-1 is added also in handwriting. This is very probably the OSS accuracy rating (the highest).
31. See Kushner, *Persistence of Prejudice*, p. 113: The Nazis were using *The Protocols of the Elders of Zion* in their war propaganda rather extensively, and by 1943 devoted 'between 70% to 80% of their broadcasts to antisemitism. But the influence of *The Protocols* [in

Britain] was more indirect, perhaps most popularly expressed in the "Jews' War" argument, but also in the common belief that Jews controlled public opinion via the press, or culture via dance bands, comedy and the cinema'.

32. NA, RG 226, Entry 191, box 1, #4, R&A No. 2027.
33. See SIME interrogation quoted in n. 16.
34. *CEH* article (see n. 4).
35. Braham, *Politics of Genocide*, vol. II, pp. 1113–20.
36. The initial accusations against the Jewish leadership abroad and especially against the Zionist leadership in Palestine, for having missed the opportunity to ransom Jews was made by the rescue activist in Bratislava, Rabbi Michael Dov-Ber Weissmandel, in his *From the Distress* (Hebrew) Jerusalem, 1960. Similar arguments were made by attorney Shmuel Tamir, a Zionist right-wing activist during the 'Kasztner Trial' in the 1950s, and printed under a false name in Uri Avneri's radical-sensational weekly *Haolam Haze* at the time. Avneri himself adopted those arguments also as a political tool against the Yishuv – now Israeli – state leadership. Somewhat similar accusations were repeated by Ze'ev Venia Hadari, a Labour-Zionist rescue envoy in Istanbul, in his *Against All Odds: Istanbul 1942–1945* (Hebrew), Tel-Aviv, 1992, who after all was there and had his reasons to maintain that he at least tried his best, and by a Tel-Aviv University psychologist who published a totally baseless, hysterical attack on the Yishuv and Jewish leadership in *Ha'aretz* of 8 April and 15 April 1994, probably as a part of a 'post-Zionist' syndrome now current in his circles.
37. See previous note.
38. Dwork/Duker Papers, NA RG 200, Box 28.
39. Ibid., p. 27. Grosz was, among the services he rendered to others, a courier for the Zionist rescue workers in Istanbul.
40. Laufer, alias Schroeder, was believed to have been half-Jewish, but his real employers were the Gestapo-SD. As a result of the Brand–Grosz affair, plus an MI6 interrogation, he was exposed and his American OSS employer, the 'Dogwood' network in Istanbul, was discredited and disbanded; see for the then known details Barry Rubin, *Istanbul Intrigues*, New York, 1989. Yehuda Bauer and myself uncovered some new information on the 'Dogwood' network and about Fritz Laufer himself. See Bauer's *Jews for Sale?*, New Haven, 1994.
41. Edward R. Stettinius Jr. Papers, University of Virginia, courtesy of Richard Breitman.

42. Memo dated 8 January 1944, Stettinius Papers, box 215, folder Assis. Sec. Long Oct. 1943, courtesy of Richard Breitman.
43. Dwork/Duker Papers, box 9. See note 4 above.
44. See for the Musy Affair Breitman and Aronson, 'The End of the "Final Solution"?', esp. 201–2, and WRB report dated 9 February 1945. McClelland via US Legation Berne to WRB Washington. Dwork/Duker Papers, box 29. The document quoted in my text here is an OSS report dated 17 February 1945. The report carries on the top left-hand side a header 'Central Europe'. Its source is RG 226, Entry 191, box 2, folder 18. Secret.
45. In fact most of the artists, doctors, rabbis and others who kept Jewish life at Theresienstadt alive and made it more bearable, among many other inmates, were deported to Auschwitz and killed during the late autumn of 1944.
46. Unsigned, 'Central Europe' top left-hand side. Dwork/Duker Papers, RG 200, box 29, #393. Secret.
47. Winant to Secretary of State, 23 February 1945, telegram no. 1870, confidential. Dwork/Duker Papers, box 29, folder 362.
48. Breitman and Aronson, 'The End of the "Final Solution"?', p. 202.

–6–

Resistance and Rescue in Hungary

Asher Cohen

The *Shoah* is a unique chapter in both European and Jewish history. Based on racialist anti-Semitic ideology, the *Shoah* had been initiated since 1933 by the Nazi persecutions in Germany, but by 1938, and even more evidently during the war, it encompassed the entire continent. Anti-Jewish legislation and the spoliation of the Jews were carried out simultaneously everywhere. Then, following the massacres by the *Einsatzgruppen* in Eastern Europe in the latter half of 1941, the deportations of the Jews were simultaneously undertaken from the ghettos of Poland and from Western Europe. There was an unmistakable similarity in Jewish suffering in both East and West; and it involved not only German persecutors but almost all European governments and nations, which latter were not merely passive spectators. This is why the *Shoah* is a unique and co-ordinated pan-European phenomenon, having a common cause and a clear geographical definition. The operational theatre of the *Shoah* was the European continent. This global perspective is the only one which can give us the necessary comprehensive view of events and a proper historical understanding; and it is into this context that all the events of the *Shoah* must be placed.

On the other hand, it is also evident that an examination of the specific chain of occurrences, differing greatly from one country to the next, is no less essential in this regard. The unique geographic and socio-political situation of each country, the number of its Jewish inhabitants, the character of each community and its specific relation with the non-Jewish environment – all these factors create the scene that defined the fate of the Jews, the extent of their losses and their chances of survival.

Most research on Jewish resistance and rescue has concentrated, with considerable justification, on the local and national levels. The unique circumstances of each case have focused scholars' attentions on the immediate options, possibilities and limits that effectively determined Jewish responses. This appears to have been the only way that basic research could be done. Nevertheless it would seem that the present state of the art permits us to go a step further, and to examine the organizations and events from a more comprehensive point of view, thereby attempting to assign to them a much wider significance, and by the same token also obtaining a better and deeper understanding of the nature of the events.

Studies of Jewish responses have demonstrated the major importance of access to information and, even more, of understanding the information which was received. Obviously every response by way of resistance required an understanding of the actual situation. But it is specific to the character of the *Shoah* that we are faced here with a situation in which reliable information was practically non-existent. The official media were unreliable, and unofficial sources, or so-called hearsay, although eventually shown to be correct, were hard to believe and unverifiable. Even in cases in which information undoubtedly did exist, the specific interpretation given to it by each person or group is often difficult to determine. Thus to understand correctly what the Jews did know, and, even more important, to know what they interpreted as being relevant information, is a precondition for the study of resistance and rescue.

From 1942, when it first became evident that the German aim was the annihilation of *all the Jews of Europe*, the Jewish people were confronted, often unwittingly, with an unexpected new challenge: that of resistance in the face of annihilationist policies.[1] Individual Jews or entire families often tried to hide or to escape from the ghettos in order to evade the deportations.[2] Organized Jewish resistance, however, came mainly from the youth movements.

The first document which reveals an awareness of the Final Solution – one which was apparently more intuitive than rational – was the manifesto issued by *halutz* youth in Vilna in January 1942, only three weeks before the Wannsee Conference.[3] The text is well known, and we mention it only in order to stress that when the young Jews of Vilna called for resistance, their intention was armed resistance and nothing else. It is worth noting that at the same time that the Vilna manifesto was brought out, a group of young people in Toulouse, in the South of France, published a plan of action for an organization which they were already then calling the 'Jewish Army' (*Armée Juive*). The same contains a statement almost identical with that of Vilna: *l'extermination du peuple juif est déjà en cours de réalisation* ('the extermination of the Jewish people is already on the way to realization').[4]

Later, Vilna became the most prominent instance in which a majority of the ghetto population refused to follow the initiative of the youth and persistently opposed any kind of armed resistance.[5] Obviously, this cannot be explained by the lack of well-established information concerning the massacres. Although at first the Jews did not believe the evidence they received of the mass murders in Ponar, very soon the annihilation of 40,000 out of 60,000 people could not be denied. It is entirely evident from this instance that the absence of organized resistance, or even opposition, did not necessarily imply a lack of information. Nor was this reaction unique; rather it was typical. Six months later in Warsaw the Jews did not believe the information from Vilna; and when it was repeatedly confirmed, most Jews persuaded themselves that it could only happen 'there, in the East', and that Vilna's present, in late 1941, should not be interpreted as auguring Warsaw's future.[6] This was well before the mass deportation taking place between July and September 1942 and prior to the establishment of the Jewish Combat Organization. Thus it was not the information received in late 1941 and early 1942, but rather the deportation of more than 400,000 persons observed on the spot that produced the Jewish youth's response in Warsaw.

We know of rescue operations in which 'Aryan' documents were forged and used in organized resistance in almost every country. In Western Europe, the earliest organized underground activity can be seen to emerge only after the first deportations, which began simultaneously in all the countries in July 1942. Similar efforts can be observed in Eastern Europe, sometimes even at an earlier date. The so-called *tiyul* (Hebrew, 'trip' or 'excursion'), or the illegal crossing of the frontier from one country to another, represented a second stage, in the sense that it required sufficient time for organizing and establishing minimal cadres capable of moving about freely by using 'Aryan' papers. An organized *tiyul* was already initiated as early as 1941 by the Polish youth movements and authorized in Warsaw by the *Koordynacja* (the coordinating agency of the youth movements). Other activists left for Slovakia to explore the possibilities of reaching *Eretz Yisrael*. Although this route was discontinued, about thirty-five active members remained in Slovakia. This group concerns us directly because it later reached Hungary.

A second stage began in April 1942, during the initial phase of deportations from Slovakia. It should be recalled that the border between Slovakia and Hungary was relatively new, having been established only in 1938, when parts of southern Slovakia were handed over to Hungary. When the expulsions from Slovakia began, a movement took place of Jews fleeing to the south. The organized *tiyul* undertaken by the Zionist *halutz* movements was an inseparable part of this unorganized flight.[7]

The arrival of the refugees was a long and continuous process. We have no well-established figures on this illegal movement; but by 1944 the number of those involved apparently reached at least 10,000 and probably close to 15,000, among whom several hundred young *halutzim* were included. They were not the sole nor even the initial source of information in Hungary concerning the Final Solution; but their most important contribution was the knowledge they brought of the massacre of the Polish and Slovak Jewry. Between 1942 and 1944 these *halutzim* informed many Jews of the destruction of entire Jewish communities. Certainly not every Hungarian Jew had been informed. However there can be no doubt that it was not only the leadership who received the information; and it would be fair to assume that much of the Jewish population had also been made aware of what was happening. Moreover the very presence of so great a number of illegal refugees for such a prolonged period had for the first time brought up the problem of the production and supply of forged documents in large quantities. Thus some underground experience was required of the members of the *halutz* movements, and the required skills were developed by them to deal with the challenges of Nazi policy some time before the Germans had actually set foot on Hungarian soil.

From all the preceding we can reasonably conclude: first, that there was extensive information available in Hungary about the Final Solution prior to March 1944; and, second, that the information on the mass extermination of vast numbers of Jews appeared to have no practical implications for the future of local Jewry.

It should be clearly understood that however logical these conclusions may seem, they cannot be regarded as having been proved beyond all doubt; just as the contrary, namely that most Jews in 1944 had completely ignored the massacres of the whole of Polish Jewry, could never be established irrefutably. We are in the very uncertain realm of interpretations here. Nevertheless, in the final analysis of the pre-March situation, it seems most logical to assume that the worsening news from Poland was greeted as additional proof of the myth that the Hungarian Regent, Horthy, would continue to safeguard 'his' Jews, as he had apparently done until then. This interpretation (or misinterpretation, rather) of the information received concerning the Final Solution would seem to have recurred repeatedly from 1942 up until 19 March 1944.

Then the German army occupied Hungary. For the Jews, who had deeply assimilated Hungarian national feelings, a re-evaluation had suddenly imposed itself. Unfortunately the re-evaluation of deep-rooted popular beliefs based on a century-old assimilation into Hungarian nationhood would be a painful process requiring time. However, in Hungary after March 1944 there was no time for reconsideration for those who had been unprepared for so long.

If there were any possibility for the rescue of the Hungarian Jews in 1944, it lay in the hands of the Regent. Horthy, however, failed to take advantage of it. He agreed to deliver Jews to Germany, 'for labour'; but he never bothered to set up a mechanism of control regarding who would be given, under what conditions, and where they would be taken to. The new prime minister, Döme Stójay, was explicitly given *carte blanche* in his policy towards the Jews, without needing to consult the Regent or to submit the new measures for his approval. During the entire critical period, until the deportations from the provincial towns were completed at the end of June, Horthy refrained altogether from interfering with the handling of the 'Jewish problem'. By adopting this stance the man who possessed an enormous moral authority, over and beyond the formal powers he was vested with, had in effect forsaken his Jewish citizens.

The rapidity of the deportations from the Hungarian countryside after the occupation is unprecedented in the history of the *Shoah*.[8] Nowhere before was so great a number of Jews deported from so many dispersed locations at such great speed. Except for some isolated cases, no help was given or rescue undertaken that can be mentioned. There was no protest or intervention on behalf of the Jews. Intellectuals and politicians with anti-racialist records remained silent or had been intimidated, even those among them who had protested against the anti-Jewish legislation in 1938. Up to the end of June 1944 no serious protest was submitted by the neutral countries, even though the extent of the deportations was well known.

The Jewish community organizations, which were closely linked with the Hungarian political elite until they had been dropped and disappointed by them, were left disoriented and helpless. Not a single initiative or rescue can be credited to this source. Still, no one can claim that a different kind of leadership would have acted in a more salutary way under the conditions created by Horthy, his government, the entire Hungarian administration and popular opinion.

Nevertheless, there was a sharp difference between the response of the official leadership of the community and that of some of the Zionist leadership. The Hungarian Zionist movement was one of the smallest in interwar Europe and its influence on the community was insignificant. Until March 1944 the Zionist Association had been a legal organization; and if it did play an important role under the occupation, it was surely unexpected. There were four different and nearly independent initiatives to be recorded: that of Otto Komoly, the president of the Zionist Association, who had maintained contact with a number of prominent politicians and in August established the Department A for Children's Protection of the International Red Cross; that of Moshe Krausz, the secretary of the Palestine Office, who was in close contact with the Swiss consul, Karl Lutz, and in response to the 'Horthy Offer' had initiated the extraterritorial status of the so-called Glass House in Vadász Street 29; that of the Relief and Rescue Committee, led by Rudolf Kasztner and Joel Brand; and that of the *halutz* youth movements.

The Rescue Committee was one of the typical creations of the *Shoah*. On one hand its very existence came in response to the problems of the refugees, who were the objects of 'relief and rescue'. On the other hand, it was connected with the *Yishuv* delegation in Istanbul, which had been established at the end of 1942. This delegation financed the rescue activities, and was the principal source of legitimization for the Committee in Hungary. The Committee was one of the main channels for the transmission of accurate and up-to-date information about the destruction of Eastern European Jewry to the world via Istanbul. Information concerning the extermination of Polish Jewry travelled from Budapest to the world, and not vice versa.

Closely related to but independent of the Committee were the members of the Zionist youth movements. There were a few hundred members of these movements in all of Hungary. These were in daily contact with *halutz* comrades from Slovakia and Poland, some of whom had escaped after the Warsaw Ghetto revolt. Indeed so strong and intimate were these ties that the *halutz* movements in 1944 were in reality an amalgam of the local and refugee youth. This twofold contact, with Slovakia and Poland on the one hand, and the free world via Istanbul on the other, created for the Committee and for the *halutz* movements a unique situation in this country. As a result not only were they in possession of information concerning the mass exterminations, but they also understood its significance.

This background enabled the Zionists to grasp relatively quickly that with the German occupation a totally new situation had been created in Hungary. This is why for the very first time in history the Zionists were able to fulfil an important role in the community. In April, Brand and Kasztner initiated negotiations with Eichmann for the rescue of all Hungarian Jewry. The first result was the well-known Brand mission to 'sell a million Jews' in return for 10,000 lorries. The effort failed. Meanwhile, Kasztner, who alone had remained from the Committee in Budapest, continued the negotiations which by the end of June led to the rescue of 1,684 Jews who were taken out of the country in a single train.

At the same time the *halutz* movements, using their accumulated experience, began to turn their previously legal youth movements into underground organizations. During the initial phase their rescue activities were very limited, containing little more than collective self-rescue. Their most important achievement was to consolidate successfully a relatively sophisticated underground organization, and to rescue some of their comrades from the ghettos of the countryside. They also tried to warn the Jews in ghettos against entering the deportation trains, though in this they were quite unsuccessful. In May and June, members of the *Halutz* Resistance arrived in various ghettos with several sets of false identity papers for use by escapees. They certainly did not get to all the ghettos, but frequently the papers remained unused even in those ghettos that they managed to reach. Jews could not believe the youngsters' 'horror stories'.[9]

A more fortunate phase of their activity was the *tiyul*. When existence had become extremely hazardous, and the realization that this was so, had sunk in, the *tiyul* into Romania proved to be a successful means of escape and was extensively developed. Its methods of operation between May and August remained relatively stable. A group of organizers in Budapest prepared the candidates and furnished them with forged papers. Near the Transylvanian border a permanent activist of the Resistance would await them and make contact with the smuggler. The procedure was very risky and many were arrested on trains and in the border towns. All together between 5,000 and 7,000 men and women escaped into Romania. Most of them came from northern Transylvania; only about 2,000 were saved directly by the *Halutz* Resistance. The relatively significant number of individual Transylvanian escapees can obviously be explained by their proximity to the border, and perhaps also by the fact that the danger of the deportations was known by many of them.

In June, during the height of the deportations, three parachutists, including Hanna Szenes, arrived in Hungary. Unfortunately their mission could not contribute to practical rescue activities; but it had important psychological effects on the *Halutz* Resistance as a symbol of the unity of the Jewish people.

Strong international protests took place at the end of June, when no more Jews remained in Hungary apart from those in Budapest and some young men in the labour service battalions. These coincided with the final success of the Allied landing in Normandy. The beginning of July brought two vital changes. The first and most important was that Horthy stopped further deportations. The second was the 'Horthy Offer'. The Regent proposed to allow emigration of a large number of Jews, provided that the neutral states were willing to accept them. The 'Horthy Offer' failed as an initiative for emigration, although some neutral consulates were able to issue a limited number of Protective Passes (*Shutzpässe*) for Jews intending to emigrate. The Swiss legation represented Great Britain in Hungary, and was authorized in this capacity to offer protection to Jews emigrating to Palestine. Then the Glass House was opened and soon became a bizarre scene of licit bureaucratic work, while also functioning as one of the headquarters of the Resistance. Sweden sent Raoul Wallenberg as a special representative for 'humanitarian activities'.[10]

On 15 October, after Horthy's ill-fated attempt at a *volte-face*, the Fascist regime of the Arrow Cross was set up. At the time the Red Army was already in Hungary, only 120 miles from Budapest. Two weeks later, deportations were set in motion once again. However, because of the war conditions and lack of transportation, 80,000 persons, most of them women aged 16 to 60, were marched on foot to the German border. The Resistance and a few dedicated neutral representatives such as Wallenberg had in these dire circumstances managed to save some of the women by using both genuine and false Protective Passes.

The production of forged Protective Passes became an important contribution of the *Halutz* Resistance to the rescue activities. On the basis of 7,800 legal Swiss passes that had been issued, they forged perhaps as many as 100,000 additional documents.

Because of the selective character of these deportations, thousands of children of all ages were left behind with no one to care for them. The *Halutz* Resistance, without preparation and having no plans for such an eventuality, took up the challenge. They were the only ones able to care for these children under the official cover of Department A of the International Red Cross. From October 1944 until the liberation in January 1945, nearly forty children's homes were set up that gave protection to between 5,000 and 6,000 children and to approximately 2,000 adults.

During the same period, the Glass House became a centre of intense activity. The new regime not only honoured the Protective Passes, but also respected the extraterritoriality of the house. In the first weeks of Fascist rule, Jews from all classes looked to this house for their physical protection. The offices quickly became dormitories and in December over 3,000 Jews were living there permanently, and were 'non-existent' as far as the authorities were concerned. At the same time, thousands of others crowded the streets begging for more Protective Passes, which seemed at the time to be the only way of saving their lives. Sometimes they really did.

At that time, the workshop for forged papers of the *Halutz* Resistance was able to produce in quantity any document that was needed. These were not only for the use of their own members, but for many Jews and a great number of non-Jews being persecuted by the Fascists. Most of the identity papers used by the Hungarian Resistance, which began to be active in this period, came from these workshops. The false documents supplied to the non-Jewish Resistance were a prerequisite for their very existence.[11]

After November these newly established underground groups outnumbered the Jewish underground. This enabled them to provide some amount of effective armed protection for important Jewish rescue centres, among them the Glass House, a number of Red Cross bureaux, Children's Homes and several Protected Houses outside the Ghetto. This was a period when official protection had gradually vanished, and the only real authority was the armed Arrow Cross gangs in the streets. Therefore only armed protection could be in any way effective. The instinctive willingness of the rank and file in all the movements brought about the organization of combined armed groups. These carried out a number of effective rescue activities, liberating hundreds and perhaps even thousands of Jews then being force-marched to the banks of the Danube by the Arrow Cross gangs.

In conclusion we can therefore say that until the beginning of July, during the critical period of mass deportations, no important organized rescues were undertaken. The majority of the Hungarian people sympathized more with the persecutors of the Jews than with the victims. Official Jewish leadership fell victim to its own unpolitical background. All the assumptions and anticipations of the assimilationists had proved to be incorrect and failed to save the Jews.

Kasztner's initiative enjoyed a degree of success, although it was fairly limited when set beside the Committee's own expectations and the vast dimensions of the tragedy. After the departure of the famous train, a planned second departure could never be carried out. Krausz was inactive during the deportations, apart from making the one rather significant contribution of being the first to send the well-known Auschwitz protocols to Switzerland.[12] However the report remained unknown to the Jewish population inside Hungary itself. Komoly's effort to establish the Department A for Children's Protection became important only later. The *halutz* movements saved the lives of several hundreds of Jews; and although this was certainly not easily achieved, they had failed to influence the fate of the Jewish masses. Their major success consisted in being able to build a relatively sophisticated underground organization.

The situation after 15 October was quite different from that during the months of mass deportations. For the first time a number of neutral representations in Budapest as well as some of the organized Hungarian Resistance (non-existent prior to November 1944) could be called upon to contribute to rescue operations. But this avenue of course could be efficiently activated only in the presence of a Jewish organization capable of transforming it into a practical large-scale rescue activity. The Arrow Cross regime was characterized by total inefficiency and administrative disorder. The same chaos that made possible the murder of so many Jews in the streets of Budapest was in part turned to advantage and used for the purpose of rescue operations by the members of the *Halutz* Resistance. And though they were not the only rescue organization, they were certainly the best organized and most active. The information that had been accumulated concerning the *Shoah* was used in Hungary in the Zionist initiatives described earlier, and particularly by the *Halutz* Resistance, whose activities derived from this source. Tragically, the rescue operations were belated; they were nevertheless relatively efficient.

The flow of information concerning the realities of the Final Solution followed a pattern rather similar to that observed elsewhere. The information was at first discarded as inaccurate, and later as irrelevant to the local situation. It can be stated as a general rule that even accurate knowledge of the mass killings could not change the behaviour of the Jewish population, not unless atrocities were observed directly.[13] If this misinterpretation is to be judged by historians, it seems to have been even more rational in Hungary than in any other country, and is actually supported by the policies of the Kállay government from 1942 to 1944. Randolph Braham is certainly correct to conclude that prior information concerning the Final Solution was available in Hungary, but that it had no real influence during the period of mass deportations. I should only like to add that Hungarian Jewry was not unique in this respect.

The effectively unique element in the tragedy of Hungarian Jewry was that of chronology. Unlike the situation in Poland, Holland, France and Belgium, there had been no deportations in Hungary prior to 1944, apart from a single case in August 1941. For this very reason Hungarian Jewry could reasonably perpetuate its disastrous illusions that Horthy would protect it. Thus in practical terms, the beginning of the comprehension of the nature of the *Shoah* was belated, and it actually only began some time after the German occupation.

At this moment, which was after March 1944, the timing was once again a unique element here. The exceptional rapidity of the imposition of the Yellow Star, ghettoization and the completion of the deportations (excluding Budapest) had fatal consequences. The same process had taken seven years in Germany and about three years in Poland.

Finally, in contrast to what happened in Holland or in Belgium and France, in Hungary Jews were able to obtain almost no support from the non-Jewish population during the period of deportations. This negative or indifferent attitude changed somewhat in Budapest after October. Thus in making conclusions about the attitudes of the Hungarian population, more careful consideration should perhaps be given to the rapidity of the deportations.

Was resistance and rescue in Hungary basically different from that in other European countries? The answer would seem to be no, when we take into account that local circumstances were of importance everywhere. The unique feature was the chronology of the catastrophe of Hungarian Jewry. When Hungary was occupied and the fate of the Jews was sealed as a consequence, everything could have become known and understood. But this was not the case. Paradoxically, the sequence of the tragedy basically resembled what had already happened elsewhere in Nazi Europe, a year or two earlier.

Notes

1. Two international conferences on these subjects were held at Yad Vashem, and the resulting papers were published: *The Jewish Resistance during the Holocaust*, Jerusalem, 1970; *Rescue Attempts during the Holocaust*, Jerusalem, 1977. For an interesting attempt to define the nature of Jewish resistance, see Roger S. Gottlieb, 'The Concept of Resistance: Jewish Resistance during the Holocaust', *Social Theory and Practice*, vol. 9, no. 1 (1983), pp. 31–49. See also on Jewish resistance, Leni Yahil, *The Holocaust: The Fate of European Jewry, 1932–1945*, New York and Oxford, 1990, pp. 543ff.
2. Among the first instinctive responses to ensure Jewish survival without as yet involving a comprehensive assessment or understanding of the situation beyond the immediate event, we should take into account the *maline* (bunkers) that were built by Jews during the first round-up actions in Vilna, and the 'family camps' in the forests in Eastern Europe. See Yitzhak Arad, 'Mahanot Mishpaha Baya'arot: Derekh Hatzala Mekorit' (Family Camps in the Forests: An Original Approach to Survival), *Yalkut Moreshet*, vol. 35 (1983), p. 12. The article was published in the context of a general discussion of the subject: '40

Shana Lemered Geto Varsha' (Forty Years After the Warsaw Ghetto Revolt), *Yalkut Moreshet*, vol. 35 (1983), pp. 7–77; vol. 36 (1983), pp. 72–7.

3. The manifesto has been published in English: *Documents on the Holocaust*, ed. Y. Arad, Y. Gutman and A. Margaliot, Jerusalem, 1981, pp. 433–4.
4. Quoted from a copy made in 1942: Claude Vigée, *La Lune d'hiver*, Paris, 1970, p. 404.
5. On Vilna, see Yitzhak Arad, *Ghetto in Flames: The Struggle and Destruction of the Jews in Vilna*, Jerusalem, 1980.
6. As regards the understanding of the situation as a whole and the character of German policy, it was not the murders in Vilna but the start of round-ups in the General Government that brought about the change. Israel Gutman, *The Jews of Warsaw, Ghetto, Underground Revolt, 1939–1943*, Bloomington, 1982, pp. 119–80.
7. About the *tiyul* see Asher Cohen, *The Halutz Resistance in Hungary, 1942–1944*, New York, 1986, pp. 16–51.
8. Randolph L. Braham, *The Politics of Genocide: The Holocaust in Hungary*. 2 vols. New York: Columbia University Press, 1981; György Ránki, *1944 március 19* (19 March 1944), Budapest, Kossuth, 1978.
9. Cohen, *The Halutz Resistance*, pp. 52–105.
10. Anger, Per, *With Wallenberg in Budapest* (preface by Elie Wiesel), New York, 1981; Frederick E. Werbel, *Lost Hero; The Mystery of Raoul Wallenberg*, New York, 1982; Alexander Grosman, *Nur das Gewissen; Karl Lutz und seine Budapester Aktion*, Geneva, 1986.
11. Cohen, *The Halutz Resistance*, pp. 155–94.
12. Sándor Szenes, *Befejezetlen mult: Keresztények és zsidók, Sorsok* (Unfinished past: Christians and Jews, Destinies), Budapest, 1986.
13. See for example my 'Comprehension of the Final Solution in France and Hungary: A Comparison', *Comprehending the Holocaust*, ed. A. Cohen, Y. Gelber and Ch. Wardi, Frankfurt and New York, 1988, pp. 243–65.

—7—

Jewish Armed Resistance in Hungary: A Comparative View

Robert Rozett

During the Holocaust, Jewish activists in Hungary did not adopt the idea of armed resistance as the focal point of their response to Nazi murder. This differs greatly from Jewish activists in a number of ghettos in Eastern Europe for whom the notion of fighting with arms came to lie at the heart of their response to the persecution they suffered at the hands of the Nazis and their allies. By comparing the situation of Hungarian Jewry under German occupation with some of these communities, several cardinal reasons for these differences may become clearer.

The idea of organized Jewish armed defence on Hungarian soil was first considered several months before the German occupation began. At a gathering of members of the Zionist youth movement in December 1943, Rezso (Yisrael) Kasztner of the Relief and Rescue Committee advised those present to obtain weapons, outfit themselves with false papers and build hidden bunkers.[1] Shortly thereafter, members of the youth movement Hanoar Hatsioni discussed Kasztner's suggestion at a retreat near the Balaton lake at the resort town of Balatonboglar. They organized lessons in the martial arts and youth movement members who had escaped from Poland to Hungary taught the local youth Morse Code. The fifty or so young people present also decided to establish secret bunkers, as Kasztner had suggested. Eventually they established some in Budapest and the surrounding area, where they stored food and weapons.[2]

The next milestone in the discussion of Jewish armed resistance in Hungary was the arrival of Heike Klinger in the middle of January 1944. She had been active in the Bedzin underground. Lecturing about her experience to Zionist youth in Hungary, she recounted the valiant stand of the Jewish fighters in Warsaw in the spring of 1943. She also told of the final liquidation of the ghetto near Srodula in which the Jews of Bedzin and Sosonowiec had been placed. At the time of the liquidation, in August 1943, the Jewish underground in Srodula had offered armed resistance from bunkers they had established, and then some escaped. Heike Klinger urged her audience to learn the lessons of her experience well and prepare for a German invasion.[3] The primary response of Zionist youth leaders to this information was to warn their comrades in the countryside and bring them to Budapest, with the idea of planning future escape routes from Hungary. Yet the idea of organizing armed defence was also pursued.

Early in February 1944, representatives of the Joint Rescue Committee of the Jewish Agency in Istanbul cabled Kasztner's Relief and Rescue Committee urging the establishment of organized Jewish defence. They suggested that all Zionist leaders meet to determine how best to organize armed resistance. Moreover, they stated that the next messenger sent to Hungary from Turkey would arrive with $15,000, to be used exclusively for the purpose of setting up a defence organization.[4] By early March, it was reported from Budapest to Istanbul that the Zionist youth were enthusiastically engaged in organizing armed defence and that Moshe Schweiger had been chosen to direct a defence committee.[5]

Not long after this note was dispatched, the situation in which the Jews of Hungary found themselves deteriorated precipitously. On 19 March 1944, German forces occupied Hungary and the destruction of the large majority of the Jewish community followed in an intensive rush of isolation, expropriation, concentration and deportation. During the horrible months of the spring and the first weeks of the summer of 1944, organized Jewish armed resistance not only did not emerge as the dominant response of Hungarian Jewish activists to the unfolding catastrophe, but was not offered at all. The defence committee, which had been established in March, met shortly after the occupation. But within a very short time its leader Moshe Schweiger was arrested. Moshe Rosenberg assumed the leadership in his place, yet throughout the spring only limited preparations for armed resistance continued. Some weapons were acquired and some training took place.[6]

At this time, the main outlet for those Zionist youth most interested in fighting the Nazis and their collaborators was flight to Yugoslavia. In the autumn of 1943, well before the Nazi occupation of Hungary, contact between Zionist youth in Hungary and the Yugoslav partisans had been made. After 19 March 1944, many young Zionists still hoped they could join Tito's partisan forces. Crossing the border to Yugoslavia, however, proved extremely difficult and dangerous. Not more than fifty or sixty Jewish fighters managed to reach their goal. By 31 July 1944, it was reported to Istanbul from Budapest that organized attempts from Hungary to reach Yugoslav partisans had ended because of the difficulties encountered, and the feeling that other types of response would yield better results.[7]

For the Zionist youth and the members of the Relief and Rescue Committee it was clear from the outset of the period of German occupation that armed resistance was not their only option. During the next ten months they would engage in a variety of activities that were directed towards facilitating rescue on a large scale. As the letter of 31 July 1944 suggests, those options came to be seen as better courses of action than fighting with weapons. The main activities of the Hungarian Jewish activists included: negotiations with the SS, escape to neighbouring countries, schemes to provide international diplomatic protection for large numbers of Hungarian Jews and the manufacture of false documents towards that end. These activities, based to a large extent on cooperation between local Jewish activists and representatives of the international community, have been well documented by a number of scholars and need not be discussed in detail here.[8]

There are several salient factors which suggest why the Jewish activists in Hungary regarded armed resistance differently from their counterparts in other areas of Nazi-dominated Europe. Perhaps the most outstanding factor is that of 'timing' – timing in two senses of the word. The Jews of Hungary first broached the idea of armed resistance on Hungarian soil before they had direct experience of Nazi occupation and the kind of persecution that culminated in murder. At the time, their knowledge of Nazi atrocities was essentially vicarious. This indicates that immediate experience of Nazi brutality was not necessarily a prerequisite for taking the first steps towards creating an armed underground. Even a brief look at Eastern European Jewish activists, who engaged in armed resistance, suggests that there is no hard and fast rule for designating the exact point at which Jews began seriously to consider taking up arms. However, it does infer – in contradistinction to Hungary – that in most places where Jews focused on fighting with weapons, this course of action was decided upon after they had experienced a great deal of first-hand suffering, ranging from years of ghetto life, through direct experience of mass killing operations and mass deportations to extermination camps.

In Vilna, the decision to organize an armed underground coalesced at the end of 1941 and the first weeks of 1942. This was after the Jews of Vilna had witnessed six months of slaughter, following the German occupation of 24 June 1941. During this time over 33,000 Jews from the city were murdered at Ponary, a ravine on the outskirts of the town. The correlation between the murder and the creation of the underground is clearly evident in the now famous proclamation of Vilna Zionist youth on 1 January 1942:

> All the roads of the Gestapo lead to Ponary. And Ponary is death . . . Let us not go as sheep to the slaughter! It is true that we are weak and defenceless, but resistance is the only reply to the enemy! Brothers! It is better to fall as free fighters than to live by the grace of the murders. Resist! To the last breath.[9]

In the town of Tuczyn in Volhynia, it was not the experience of death in their own community, but the knowledge of murder in nearby Rovno, combined with an order to seal off the Tuczyn ghetto, that led the Jews to plan an armed revolt.[10] In Warsaw, where the largest and longest Jewish uprising took place, the closing-off of the ghetto and news of the murders in other localities was not enough to lead to consolidated planning of armed revolt. It was only after the great wave of deportations that swept the ghetto in the summer of 1942 that earlier and relatively unsuccessful attempts to set up a broad-based armed underground blossomed into an essentially unified fighting organization, supported by the ghetto inhabitants.[11]

Because of their own suffering and the news they had received from surrounding Jewish communities, the Jews in these places had a great deal of knowledge about Nazi intentions. It may be argued whether in a given locality the Jews clearly understood that the Nazis had embarked on a crusade to annihilate all Jews everywhere, or whether they only understood that in their community and the surrounding area Jews were being murdered. But whether they understood that the murder was meant to be all-encompassing or not, by the time they began to focus on organizing armed resistance, they had a great deal of direct experience which had demonstrated to them that their own lives were in immediate danger. But as has been noted, this was not the case of the Jews of Hungary when they first began organizing armed resistance. Perhaps this offers some insight into why immediately after the Germans arrived in Hungary, intensive preparations for armed resistance were not undertaken.

This aspect of 'timing' also helps to explain why the only recorded instances of armed clashes in Hungary between organized Jewish fighters and their persecutors took place several months after the end of the first wave of deportations; and why the clashes generally were not planned attacks, but acts of Jewish self-defence.[12] There were only a handful of attacks by organized Jews against the Nazis and the Hungarian Fascist Arrow Cross. On 29 September 1944, Jews attempted to blow up a German barracks. Jewish labour service men tangled with Arrow Cross units several days after the Arrow Cross came to power, on 15 October 1944.

Jews also took part in a raid with members of the Hungarian underground on Christmas Eve of that year in the Budapest suburb, Kobanya. But more representative were the acts of spontaneous self-defence, such as those of November and December 1944, when Zionist youth fought against Arrow Cross men in order to prevent them from rounding up Jews.[13]

The other sense of the word 'timing' regards the actual period under examination in a particular locality. This aspect of timing had a significant influence on the range of possible responses in a given Jewish community. Most of the planning of ghetto revolts and the armed clashes between the ghetto fighters and their persecutors occurred in 1942 and 1943, while Nazi Germany was still exceedingly strong, the war was far from over and liberation was not in sight. In Hungary, the entire drama was played out in 1944 and the first weeks of 1945. This was the period that saw the Western Allies advance in Italy, land in France and make great headway towards occupying Germany itself. From October 1944 onward, Soviet forces steadily approached Budapest, completely encircling the city on 26 December 1944.[14] Thus rescue in Eastern Europe meant keeping Jews out of harm's way not for months, but for years. Whereas in Hungary, especially during the second wave of deportations in the autumn of 1944, when the approaching front infused the air with the smell of an imminent German defeat, rescue meant preserving Jewish lives for a matter of months. This does not mean that rescue in Hungary was simple to achieve, but in many respects it was easier to carry out large-scale rescue in Hungary than in Eastern Europe. It is clear that, in part, this difference in timing explains why Jewish fighters in Eastern Europe fought out of grievous desperation, whereas in Hungary, even though the situation deteriorated sharply, Jewish activists did not evince the same desperation.[15]

The fact that Hungarian Jews entered the maelstrom of the Holocaust in 1944 affected options of response in other ways as well. Undoubtedly, the intervention of the Western Allies and the international diplomats was a function of the stage of the war in 1944, and the increased availability of information at the time about Nazi atrocities committed against the Jews. Almost immediately after the Germans occupied Hungary, the President of the United States, Franklin D. Roosevelt, and the British Foreign Minister, Anthony Eden, both sent clear messages to the Hungarians warning them not to take part in anti-Jewish measures. The Auschwitz Protocols – the report about murder operations in the extermination camp that was compiled by members of the underground who escaped to Slovakia in April 1944 – and news of the deportations from Hungary which began in mid-May 1944 contributed to heightened diplomatic activity on behalf of Hungarian Jews. This international intervention, combined with the Allied military successes of the first half of the year, contributed to the order issued by the Hungarian Regent, Admiral Miklos Horthy, on 7 July 1944, to end the first wave of deportations.[16] It was also owing to this intervention that much of the joint rescue by the diplomats, Kasztner's committee and the Zionist youth could take place.

Similar large-scale rescue options were not available in Eastern Europe, especially during the height of the murder of the Jews in 1942 and 1943. Jewish leaders in several large ghettos predicated mass rescue on the idea of making Jews useful to the German occupiers, and did not rely on Allied intervention or their imminent liberation by them, which in any case was not yet a possibility. These leaders hoped that if they proved that Jewish labour had significant economic value for the Third Reich, the occupation authorities would improve the conditions under which the Jews were living, and spare them from deportations and death. The most well-known cases in which this policy was adopted by the official Jewish leadership were in Lodz and Vilna.[17] Not all the Jews of the ghettos, however, agreed with this strategy. Some came to oppose the official Jewish leaders openly, and some opponents went on to create undergrounds. Many of the members of the undergrounds eventually committed themselves to what were virtually suicidal acts of armed resistance. In the ghettos, they fought to avenge the murder of their families and friends. They fought for their honour and sense of history. Sometimes they fought to break out of the ghetto and continue the struggle in the forests. Struggle in the forest was certainly closely linked to attempts to survive, even though the odds were overwhelmingly stacked against success. The development and fate of the Jewish family camps, which contained not only partisans, but children and the elderly who could not defend themselves, illustrates this clearly.[18] Nevertheless it may be said of most ghetto revolts that the fighters did not hope to achieve mass rescue first and foremost.[19]

This is not to say that all Jewish fighting in the Holocaust took place against a background of utter hopelessness. In Slovakia, for example, Jewish activists engaged in a broad range of rescue attempts during the same period in which they organized armed resistance. In order to understand the context of armed revolt in Slovakia and compare it with Hungary, it is important first to examine the extent of Slovak rescue activity.

In February 1942 on the eve of the deportations from Slovakia, several members of the official Jewish leadership began trying to prevent transports from leaving Slovak soil. This group, joined by other members of the Jewish community, came to be known as the Working Group. These activists began labouring in two spheres before the deportations began.

Because the Slovak government was headed by a Catholic priest, Father Jozef Tiso, they hoped to make the Holy See aware of the impending deportations, so that the Pope would intervene to have them cancelled before a single transport left Slovakia. Through making contact with Slovak officials and offering them bribes, they also tried to have the planned deportations cancelled.[20] Neither effort succeeded in preventing the first trains laden with Slovak Jews from leaving the town of Poprad for Poland, at the end of March 1942. Additional transports, to the end of July, steadily carried Slovak Jews to their deaths in Poland. Several more transports left in September and October, until the deportations were halted on 20 October 1942. By that time, between 57,000 and 58,000 Slovak Jews had been sent to Auschwitz and the Lublin area.[21]

Although they failed to end the deportations immediately, Slovak Jewish activists did manage to foster the rescue of thousands of members of their community during and after the deportations. Members of the Zionist youth movements, with the support of the Working Group, began smuggling Jews over the Hungarian border in the spring of 1942. At the time, Hungary was a relatively safe haven. Hungarian Zionist youth, the Relief and Rescue Committee and various Hungarian orthodox Jewish groups helped bring the Slovaks into the Hungarian interior, where they also helped provide their basic needs.[22] Through organized rescue and mere flight, several thousand Jews reached Hungary between March 1942 and March 1944.[23]

Another mode of rescue, similar to that employed by the official Jewish leadership in Vilna and Lodz, was based on the idea of keeping valuable Jewish workers in Slovakia. This argument was used with some success by the Working Group, because the Slovak government had claimed that the deportations were for the transfer of Jews to Poland, where they would work.[24] The Working Group convinced the government to allow Jews to enter three work camps on Slovak soil – Novaky, Sered and Vyhne. After the deportations, the ample level of production in the work camps continued to provide the Jewish residents with a measure of security.[25] It was in these camps that much of the preparations for Jewish armed resistance took place.

The last non-violent method employed by Slovak Jewish activists to try to rescue large numbers of Jews was to negotiate with the SS. Much has been written about these negotiations, which at first sought to end the deportations from Slovakia to Poland and later expanded to bargaining for the halting of deportations to Poland from throughout Europe. This later stage of negotiations came to be known as the Europe Plan. As the historians Yehuda Bauer, Gila Fatran and others have shown, the Working Group made great efforts to keep up their part of the agreement reached with the SS, but were unable to do so. By the autumn of 1943, the negotiations in Slovakia had come to a dead end, but they would resurface in a slightly different guise in Hungary following the German occupations.[26]

In the eyes of the Slovak Jewish activists, their preparations for armed resistance were also part of attempts to foster mass rescue. This was because they prepared for armed resistance within the context of the plans for the Slovak national uprising. Fighting, as part of a nation-wide revolt against the Slovak puppet government, meant that victory could conceivably lead to the end of the Nazi-dominated regime and thus to the rescue of the remaining Slovak Jews. When the Slovak national uprising broke out at the end of August 1944, Jewish fighters joined it and played a significant role. With the outbreak of the fighting, the most extreme of measures, all other methods of mass rescue became untenable. When the uprising was crushed at the end of October 1944, the Slovak Jews were left bereft of other means of facilitating organized large-scale rescue.[27]

In Hungary, the gentile underground was rather weak and there were no workable plans for a national uprising. Without this possibility, Hungarian Jewish armed resistance could not be placed in the context of mass rescue. Moreover, most of the Jewish men of fighting age who might have joined the activists to form a broad-based resistance movement had been drafted into the Hungarian forced labour units long ago. This situation contributed significantly to the Jewish activists' emphasis on other activities oriented towards large-scale rescue.[28]

Relatively large-scale rescue was a developing possibility from the start of the Nazi occupation and remained viable until the Soviet conquest of Budapest in early 1945. Although some 560,000 Jews from Hungarian territory were deported to their deaths or murdered on Hungarian soil during the period of the German occupation, tens of thousands were kept alive.[29] Many of the survivors owed their lives to the organized rescue activities of the Jewish activists and their partners. More than any other factor, it was the ongoing possibility of rescue in the unique Hungarian situation of 1944 and early 1945 that led Jewish activists away from focusing on organized armed resistance.

Notes

1. Beit Lohamai Hagetaot Archive (hereafter BLHA), joint testimony of Bnai Akiva members; Institute for Contemporary Jewry, Hebrew University, Oral History Division (hereafter OHD), Budapest child rescue, Yeshayahu Rosenblum testimony.
2. OHD, Budapest child rescue, Shmuel Levenheim testimony.
3. Moreshet Archive (hereafter MA), A665.1, Hehalutz in Hungary.
4. Central Zionist Archives, S26/1440, 8 February 1944, unsigned cable from Istanbul.
5. BLHA Z1063, 2 March 1944, Rezso Kasztner and Joel Brand to Istanbul.
6. MA, A665.1; Asher Cohen, 'Hehalutz Underground in Hungary, March–August 1944', *Yad Vashem Studies*, vol. 14 (1981), p. 251; Eichmann Trial, session 60, 31 May 1961, Moshe Rosenberg testimony.
7. BLHA Z1063/h4, 31 July 1944, Peretz Revesz et al. to Istanbul.
8. For more information on this topic see: Yehuda Bauer, *The Holocaust in Historical Perspective*, Seattle, 1978, pp. 94–156; Arieh Ben-Tov, *Facing the Holocaust in Budapest; The International Red Cross and the Jews of Hungary, 1943–1945*, Dordrecht, 1988; Asher Cohen, *The Hehalutz Underground in Hungary, 1942–1944*, New York, 1986.
9. Yitzhak Arad et al. (eds), *Documents on the Holocaust*, Jerusalem, 1981, p. 433.
10. Shmuel Spector, *The Holocaust of Volhynian Jews, 1941–1944*, Jerusalem, 1990, pp. 214–15.
11. Yisrael Gutman, *The Jews of Warsaw, 1939–1943; Ghetto Underground, Revolt*, Bloomington, 1982, p. 284.
12. For more information on this topic see: Robert Rozett, 'Jewish and Hungarian Armed Resistance in Hungary', *Yad Vashem Studies*, vol. 19 (1988), pp. 269–88.
13. Joint Distribution Committee Archives, Hungary General 1941–1944, Sept. 29, 1944, Raoul Wallenberg; Yad Vashem Archives, 03/3384, Zvi Goldfarb Testimony; Randolf Braham, *The Politics of Genocide*, New York, 1981, pp. 997–8; Rafi Ben-Shalom, *Neevaknu lemaan hahayim*, Givat Haviva, 1977 (Hebrew), pp. 154–9.
14. Peter Gosztony, *Der Kampf um Budapest, 1944–1945*, Munich, 1964, pp. 12–67.
15. Modechai Tenenbaum, leader of the Bialystok ghetto uprising voiced this idea clearly, 'The force that has overcome Europe and destroyed entire states within days could cope with us, a handful of youngsters.

It was an act of desperation . . . We aspired to only one thing: to sell our lives for the highest possible price' (Yitzhak Arad, *Ghetto in Flames; The Struggle and Destruction of the Jews of Vilna in the Holocaust*, Jerusalem, 1980, p. 230).

16. War Refugee Board, 'Report on the Treatment of Jews in Hungary', no date, unsigned; Robert Rozett, 'Auschwitz Protocols', *The Encyclopedia of the Holocaust*, Israel Gutman (ed. in chief), New York, 1990, pp. 121–2; Henry Feingold, *The Politics of Rescue; The Roosevelt Administration and the Holocaust, 1938–1945*, New York, 1970, pp. 252–3; Per Anger, *With Raoul Wallenberg in Budapest*, New York, 1981, p. 43.
17. Arad et al., *Documents on the Holocaust*, pp. 237, 283–6, 438–56.
18. For more information on this topic see: Shmuel Krakowski, *The War of the Doomed; Jewish Armed Resistance in Poland, 1942–1944*, New York, 1984.
19. Arad, *Ghetto in Flames*, p. 412; Arad et al., *Documents on the Holocaust*, pp. 435–8; Gutman, *The Jews of Warsaw*, p. 294.
20. OHD, (8) 48, Symposium on Slovak Jewry during the Holocaust; Gila Fatran, *Haim maavak al hisadrut; hanhagat yehudai slovakia beshoah 1938–1945*, Givat Haviva, 1992 (Hebrew), pp. 162–8; Yeshayahu Jelinek, 'Catholics and Jewish Persecution in Slovakia', in *Jews and Non-Jews in Eastern Europe*, Bela Vago and George L. Mosse (eds) New York, 1974, pp. 221–56; Livia Rothkirchen, *The Destruction of Slovak Jewry*, Jerusalem, 1961, p. 27.
21. Yehosua Buechler, 'The Deportation of Slovakian Jews to the Lublin District of Poland in 1942', *Holocaust and Genocide Studies*, vol. 6, no. 2 (1991), pp. 151–66; Rothkirchen, *The Destruction of Slovak Jewry*, pp. 22–6.
22. YVA, 03/3384, Zvi Goldfarb testimony, Joint Distribution Committee Archive (hereafter JDC), SM 38, 'Report on Jewish children in Hungary', undated; JDC, SM 38, Rezso Kasztner and Shmuel Springmann note, 15 December 1943; Zvi Goldfarb, *Ad Kav Haketz*, Tel Aviv, 1981 (Hebrew), p. 30.
23. OHD, (8) 4, Akiva Nir testimony, (8) 16, Yochanan Blaufeder testimony.
24. OHD, (8) 3, Moshe Daks testimony.
25. CZA, L15/89, 12 December 1943, unsigned note; Fatran, *Haim maavak al hisadrut; hanhagat yehudai slovakia beshoah 1938–1945*, pp. 250–7.
26. For more information on this topic see: Yehuda Bauer, *American Jewry and the Holocaust*, Detroit, 1981, pp. 356–400; idem, *The*

Holocaust in Historical Perspective, pp. 94–156; Avraham Fuchs, *The Unheeded Cry*, New York, 1984, pp. 97–127; Fatran, *Haim maavak al hisadrut; hanhagat yehudai slovakia beshoah 1938–1945*, pp. 162–208.

27. OHD (8) 11, Juraj Revesz testimony; Emile Knieza, 'The Resistance of the Slovak Jews', *They Fought Back*, Yuri Suhl (ed.), New York, 1967, p. 181; Ladislav Lipscher, 'Helkam shel hayehudim bemilhemet hamagen haantifashisti beslovakia be milhemet haolam hashnia', *Yalkut Moreshet*, vol. 14, April 1972 (Hebrew), pp. 117–42.
28. Rozett, 'Jewish and Hungarian Armed Resistance in Hungary'.
29. Israel Gutman and Robert Rozett, 'Estimated Jewish Losses in the Holocaust', *The Encyclopedia of the Holocaust*, Israel Gutman (ed. in chief), New York, 1990, pp. 1800–1.

—8—

Germans, Hungarians and the Destruction of Hungarian Jewry

Attila Pók

This chapter discusses some aspects of German and Hungarian responsibility for the unprecedented tragedy of modern Hungarian history: the deportation and murder of hundreds of thousands of Jewish Hungarians.[1]

Before turning to the actual topic, two preliminary remarks that help clarify the approach and method applied here seem to be necessary.

(1) I share the view (as described for example by the Hungarian writer Imre Kertész[2]) that the Holocaust is perhaps the most memorable event since the crucifixion, and that the flames of the Holocaust came close to destroying what we can describe as modern civilization.

(2) My second preliminary remark brings me to the method I apply in this chapter: Elie Wiesel says[3] that scholarship can have no vocabulary for the horror of Auschwitz. Historical scholarship can shed light on the number of victims and analyse the related political manoeuvres in the foreground and in the background, but it has no key to the essence of that tragedy. The history of anti-Semitism prior to the Holocaust can be studied with the traditional methods of economic, social, political and intellectual history but historians working after the Holocaust can hardly do with that; seemingly ahistorically, they have to look for the antecedents of the later tragedy by utilizing, among others, the findings of social psychology. On the basis of this consideration I apply the social psychological concept of scapegoating in my present investigation.

It was mainly Allport, Heider and Lewin who in their works on group dynamics and prejudices extensively dwelt on this issue.[4] The analysis of the behaviour of smaller and larger groups shows that whenever tensions of any kind accumulate, there also appears the demand for finding a scapegoat (be it an individual or a group) who is presented as the ultimate cause of all troubles. The prevailing attitude towards the scapegoat in the group is violent. Both individual and group scapegoats serve for transferring responsibility: a well-selected scapegoat might ease tensions.

Responsibility, however, can be defined from at least three points of view: it can be legally interpreted (this is not unambiguous either, as the formally perfect civil and penal codes of dictatorships can serve absolute injustice) but also understood in a moral or historical-political sense. Scapegoats are easily born in situations like that – especially when not only legal norms but moral and historical-political values change frequently as well. The less definable responsibility is and the less responsibilities in the legal, moral and historical-political sense of the word overlap, the easier it is for scapegoats to be born. Scapegoats are also important as objects of common hatred when radical political mass movements aiming at dictatorial rule use the hostility towards a group or a person as a mobilizing force for easy manipulation. Scapegoating, of course, is not a legal procedure; therefore the measures and sanctions taken against scapegoats cannot be legally regulated either – which might have tragic consequences.

After these lengthy preliminary remarks the main issue this chapter will address is the relationship between the various forms and stages of Hungarian anti-Semitism and the destruction of the Hungarian Jewry – to what extent is there a continuity, a direct connection between them? Did anti-Semitism necessarily lead to the Holocaust?

Anti-Semitism has always been a kind of a seismograph sensitively showing when the accumulation of social, economic and interethnic tensions reached critical dimensions. In the early 1880s the anti-Semitic ideological motives, which had already existed for a long time, were synthesized into the groundwork of a political movement, then a party, and this fact reflected a qualitative change in major economic and social processes. In the political climate created by the 1873 economic crisis, the impoverished, indebted, declining Hungarian gentry considered the Jews as obstacles to their own 'modernization', as threats to the 'organic' national development. Istóczy, a leading figure of the Hungarian anti-Semitism of the time said in the Hungarian Parliament in March 1881: 'The Jewish problem is not a religious issue, it is a social, national, economic, political and first of all a racial question.'[5] His Anti-Semitic Party (founded in 1883) was present from 1884 to 1892 in Parliament and is in fact the first factor in modern Hungarian party politics which in its programme and activity subordinates the questions related to Hungary's constitutional, legal status in the Habsburg Monarchy to social and economic issues. The party's short-lived success can perhaps be best explained by the fact that its leaders strongly sensed the short- and long-term changes inherent in the decline of big segments of the middle layers of the Hungarian nobility. Instead of a critical self-examination – unlike the great figures of Hungarian liberalism – they transferred responsibility to the Jewish scapegoat. The social psychological phenomenon of organizing movements by offering a well-defined object of common hatred to potential members is at work here. Still, this first major anti-Semitic upsurge in Hungarian history failed quite quickly because the dominant trend of Hungarian liberalism considered assimilating Jews as allies in the actual and potential conflicts between Hungarians and the national minorities of the country in the struggle for maintaining the political and cultural supremacy of Hungarians in multi-ethnic Hungary.

The next, most critical, juncture in the growth of anti-Semitism in Hungary is the aftermath of World War I when – according to the argumentation of contemporary anti-Semites – it turned out that in spite of the 'generous liberal assimilationist policy' Jews had a leading role in the anti-national communist Hungarian Soviet republic and this contributed to the substantial Hungarian territorial losses, to the 'Trianon disaster'. This argumentation points out that there was something basically wrong with the Hungarian liberalism of the nineteenth and early twentieth centuries. I have chosen two case studies from 1920 to illustrate how even most self-critical, intellectually high-level analyses of the Hungarian national tragedy after World War I also led to presenting Jews as scapegoats. The first case study is the most influential book in twentieth-century Hungarian political literature. Under the title 'Three Generations'[6] it aimed at pointing out the 'deeper-lying' causes of Hungary's post-World War I tragedy. The author, the 37-year-old Vienna archivist and historian, Gyula Szekfû (well known by that time for his realistic book on Ferenc Rákóczi's exile years which among extreme nationalists earned him the label of a 'traitor' to the sacred Hungarian traditions) found the causes of Hungary's tragedy mainly in the series of futile attempts at the liberal transformation of Hungary. Three generations were misled by the illusions of Western liberalism which could not take root in Hungary. The backbone of the Hungarian nation, the traditional Hungarian middle class, turned out to be a loser in the emerging liberal market economy – no indigenous Hungarian bourgeoisie could develop and the economic-cultural gap was filled by the alien Jewish upper and middle class. The liberal state did not care about the impoverished layers. This unhealthy development of Hungarian society led to a power vacuum after World War I, to the revolutions which (rather than the military defeat of the monarchy) caused the loss of two-thirds of Hungary's prewar territory. The result of the attempt at the implementation of liberal principles in Hungary was a total failure: Hungarian national interests were pushed into the background, and the non-Hungarian national minorities and especially the Jews were gaining ground. A careful reading of the book shows that Szekfû blames more the Hungarian liberals who gave way to the Jews than the Jews themselves. Nevertheless, the Hungarian public opinion of the 1920s concentrated on the anti-Semitic implications of his argumentation, i.e. blaming the Jews for the Hungarian national catastrophe. This interpretation could have the fatal function of mobilizing anti-Semitic feelings. In his book Szekfû devotes a special chapter to those tendencies in late nineteenth–early twentieth-century Hungarian political and intellectual life which – one way or another – were in opposition to the dominant liberalism. He deals quite a lot with the so-called bourgeois radicals who, from a leftish platform, criticized pre-World War I Hungarian political regimes. They studied modern French, English and American sociology and wanted to apply their newly acquired intellectual arsenal for working out a plan for the modernization of Hungarian society. They concentrated their attacks on the 'feudal-clerical' reactionary forces, the 'noble-plutocratic' class rule which, in their interpretation, is a peculiar kind of scapegoat.

Oszkár Jászi, the leading figure of this group, was forced into exile (to Vienna) after World War I and in the same year as Szekfû he also published a book on the causes of Hungary's post-World War I tragedy. His *Hungarian Calvary, Hungarian Resurrection*[7] also addresses the Jewish problem. As different as his personality and the framework of his analysis might be, at this crucial point he seemingly gets very close to Szekfû's conclusions. According to his argumentation the deepest root of the problem was that real liberalism could not gain ground in Hungary 'as the noble-plutocratic class-rule was unable to do any organisational and creative work'. The Hungarian soul turned out to be sterile and the thinning ranks of the army of culture were increasingly filled by aliens, above all Jews, 'which in turn led to a disgusting mixture of feudalism and usury'.[8] Szekfû thus blames a rootless liberalism imposed on Hungary, whereas Jászi blames the lack of real liberalism for the enfeeblement of Hungarian society. Still, it follows from both argumentations that part of a successful therapy of the fatally sick Hungarian society should be to set borders to, to limit Jewish presence in Hungarian economic, social and cultural life.

A practical implementation of this demand was the *numerus clausus* law of 1920.[9] Szekfû and Jászi, of course, had nothing in common with the radical right-wing students and politicians who argued in favour of the limitation of the number of Jewish students at universities, but it was quite impossible to keep anti-Semitism within moderate bounds.

The *numerus clausus* law was only the tip of the iceberg of this second major upsurge of anti-Semitism in Hungary. In his excellent monograph,[10]

Rolf Fischer lists numerous examples from various fields of public life for the policy of dissimilation on national and local level. He mentions Prime Minister Pál Teleki's 1921 proposal of a separate labour service for Jews who cannot be drafted for regular military service or a decision of a chief judge in a village not very far from Budapest (Derecske) who, in 1922, when refusing to grant permission for a Jewish entrepreneur to start an industry, argued as follows: 'The request will be refused because on the territory of truncated Hungary the primary task of officials is to guarantee the living conditions of Hungarians. If he granted the request of a member of a different race, a chief judge would act against his obligations.'[11] A failed therapy again – the re-emergence of anti-Semitic views – as a peculiar kind of seismograph – shows that the accumulation of social, economic and political tensions had again reached a critical level.

Though by the late 1920s and early 1930s anti-Semitic views and movements were – parallel with the gradual recovery of the country – pushed back, if one searches for the changing role of anti-Semitism in Hungarian society, there is an obvious, striking difference between the pre- and the post-World War I period. Whereas before the war anti-Semitism was against the main trend of Hungarian politics, during the interwar period it became part of governmental policy and legislation. And it is at this point that I should like to introduce the problem of German responsibility for the destruction of Hungarian Jewry.

The 1938–41 period, on the one hand, marks the return of much of the 'mother country'; on the other, it also marks stages of increasing discrimination against Jews – including those living on the regained territories. Even if the first anti-Jewish law of 1938[12] can in no way be attributed to German pressure, it can hardly be denied that both processes were greatly determined by the 'German factor' in Hungarian politics. The German–Hungarian relationship after Hitler's coming to power was shaped by three major factors:[13] Hungary's economic dependence on Germany, the shared interest of the revision of the post-World War I peace treaties, and certain similarities in internal power structure. We know of a great number of sources that testify to the Germans' growing impatience because of the 'too generous' treatment of Jews in Hungary. In spite of the cruelty of the labour service, the third anti-Jewish law,[14] Kamenyec-Podolsk and Novi Sad, Antonescu, Pavelic and Tiso kept complaining to Hitler about Hungarian leniency in this respect. Prime Minister Miklós Kállay and similar-minded politicians believed that it was possible to work out a middle way in this respect as well, which might in turn also help Hungary get out of the war.

The nineteenth of March 1944 brought an end to such illusions. With the Germans occupying Hungary, the conservative elite, undoubtedly, also suffered serious losses. This elite, indeed, had helped to preserve some elements of constitutional order and a relatively normal framework of everyday life, but in spite of all the good intentions, the outcome was an unprecedented disaster for modern Hungary. The members of the so-called Christian national middle classes held leading positions in public administration and the army and some of them were part of the machinery of deportations. They, of course, also suffered losses. Still, this is not an acceptable argument for relativizing the losses of Hungarian Jewry. No doubt, if the Germans had not occupied Hungary in March 1944, the Holocaust would not have extended to this country. However, we immediately have to add to this commonplace statement that a long series of failures of an antiquated authoritarian regime which, on the one hand, had managed to keep the extreme Right out of power for many years, and on the other hand had incorporated 'moderate' anti-Semitism into government policy, greatly contributed to Hungary's being pushed into this situation. It must also be said that the same policy which was responsible for paving the way to the Hungarian Holocaust, also led to an overall national catastrophe, to a catastrophe which endangered the culture and civilization jointly created by Hungarians, Germans and Slavs, by the followers of all religions, by all the people living in Hungary. Furthermore, we can never forget the outstanding figures of intellectual and practical opposition to anti-Semitism in Hungary, nor the eternal merits of righteous gentiles. Many of them belonged to the ranks of the conservative elite and the Christian middle classes whose responsibility I have referred to. The fact that they did not, could not, set the main trend, must not obliterate their merits. There is no collective guilt, but there is no collective innocence either.

Let me try to summarize by calling again on the scapegoat theory of social psychology to help. Jews, as I have just discussed, have often been forced into the positions of scapegoats in modern Hungarian history. Scapegoats have the primary social psychological function of carrying transferred guilt. Here the question logically arises: what kind of guilt in modern Hungarian history was transferred onto them? I think the answer can be one single world: failure. National and economic failures could easily be explained by transferring guilt and responsibility onto Jews.

Jews in Hungary also fulfilled another important social psychological function of scapegoating: they were often presented as objects of common hatred, they functioned as 'mobilizing scapegoats' for different types of rightish political movements and parties.

Looking for scapegoats is an unavoidable social psychological process. Scapegoats, however, in a classical biblical sense were known to be innocent. Contrary to that, anti-Semites considered Jews to be guilty of all kinds of evil. Still, the various forms of anti-Semitism in Hungary did not necessarily lead to the Holocaust. There is not, I think, a wide gulf between anti-Semitic parties, movements, various forms of anti-Jewish legislation and the Holocaust, only temporary planks. As Lesek Kolakowski put it: the seemingly quite harmless, dispersed, in themselves weak elements of anti-Semitism can easily and quickly be united into an explosive mixture.[15] This comparison might help me to reach my final conclusion: to an ever increasing extent, different forms of anti-Semitism can be observed in Hungary since the 1880s: up to World War I against the main trend of political life and after World War I as part of the main trend. It was German pressure, then direct intervention that laid down the planks between anti-Semitism and the Holocaust, that fused elements of anti-Semitism into a most dangerous mixture, bringing about the greatest tragedy of modern Hungarian history.

A Note on the Literature

The political, ideological and intellectual climate of Hungary in the aftermath of World War II was far from being favourable for serious scholarly research into the history of Hungarian anti-Semitism, although the issue of tracing the connections between 'traditional' non-violent anti-Semitism and the unprecedented mass murder of Jews (around 560,000 victims in Hungary) was an essential problem of debates in intellectual and non-intellectual circles alike. By now it is clear that the most important contribution to this debate during the short period of democracy (1945–8) was an essay by a Protestant legal scholar and specialist in public administration, István Bibó (1911–79). Under the title 'Zsidókérdés Magyarországon 1944 után' (The Jewish Problem in Hungary after 1944), first published in the review *Válasz* (Answer) in 1948 (the most accessible later edition is that in his *Válogatott tanulmányok* (Selected Studies, vol. 2, Budapest, Magvetô, 1986, pp. 621–797), he raises the problem of the responsibility of Hungarian society for the Holocaust. He looks very deeply into the components of modern anti-Semitism, listing medieval anti-Jewish prejudices, the bulk of experiences accumulated in Jewish–non-Jewish relations and the deficiencies of modern social development as the main causes of anti-Jewish thoughts and actions. He warns against identifying anti-Semitic declarations with the ideology of mass murder but insists on the necessity of a national self-examination. Bibó did his best in this direction but the monolithic Communist system in Hungary from 1948 did not tolerate the *Vergangenheitsbewältigung* he initiated.

From the late 1950s on, some Hungarian historians produced important source-publications about the Hungarian Holocaust (the most important work is Ilona Benoschowsky and Elek Karsai (eds), *Vádirat a nácizmus ellen* (Indictment against Nazism), 3 vols, Budapest, 1958–67). Such serious scholarly works on this most sensitive issue were quite rare in the countries of the region during these years, and their impact on Hungarian society was limited as well.

It was only during the second half of the 1970s that a Christian writer, György Száraz, could publish a longer essay under the title 'Egy elôitélet nyomában' (In Pursuit of a Prejudice), first published in *Valóság* (Reality) 1975/8, then extended to a book under the same title (published by Magvetô, Budapest, 1976) which had great resonance in most layers of Hungarian society. The essay came out at a time when the pro-Arab official Hungarian position in the Arab–Israeli conflict was the cause of some compunction for a number of Jewish Hungarian Communist officials. The lack of an open and sincere re-examination of Hungarian society's attitude towards the Holocaust, the shocking ignorance of numerous young people born after World War II concerning the facts of this most tragic chapter of Hungarian history and also an emerging strong collective identity among young Jewish intellectuals, many of them pessimistic about the possibility of a Jewish–non-Jewish dialogue – all these factors pushed Száraz's work into the foreground of public interest. Száraz pointed out the late nineteenth/early twentieth century as the time when the religious type of anti-Semitism was transformed into a socially motivated anti-Semitism. According to his argumentation, influential groups of the Christian upper and middle classes felt threatened both by Jewish capitalists in search of more political influence and also by the aspirations of socially marginal critics of the establishment, some of the latter being active in the socialist movement. These fears led to the birth of legends about the 'anti-national Jewish conspiracy' which played a very important role in influential explanations of Hungary's tragic truncation (with two-thirds of the former state territories lost) after World War I. Now, for the first time in Hungarian history the whole of Hungarian Jewry was blamed and in many cases brutally persecuted, which, as Száraz argues, 'forecasted the horrible shadow of 1944'.

A young scholar, Judit Kubinszky, published an analysis of the early phase of Hungarian anti-Semitism in 1976 (Judit Kubinszky, *Politikai antiszemitizmus Magyarországon 1875–1890* (Political Anti-Semitism in Hungary 1875–1890) Kossuth, Budapest, 1976). She describes the first wave of anti-Semitism in Hungary which, seemingly, had completely disappeared by the late 1880s. But 'in fact it left deep traces behind – its arguments were disseminated by various social groups which, by distorting facts, stirred up hatred appealing to instincts and sentiments. It created . . . an anti-Semitic ideology and phraseology.'

A number of works were published about the history of Hungarian Jewry in the 1970s and 1980s, especially about various aspects of their assimilation. (For a survey cf. Péter Váry, 'Befejezetlen múlt-mai magyar zsidó valóság' (Unfinished Past–Present Day Hungarian Jewish Reality) in Róbert Simon (ed.), *Zsidókérdés Kelet- és Közép-Európában* (The Jewish Problem in Eastern and Central Europe), Budapest, 1985, pp. 455–83.) In comparison with this literature, the number of works on the history of Hungarian anti-Semitism is much smaller. The first comprehensive works raising the question of the relationship between pre-1938 anti-Semitism and the Holocaust were published outside Hungary: first of all, the first ten chapters of Randolph L. Braham's monumental work (*The Politics of Genocide. The Holocaust in Hungary*, 2 vols, Columbia University Press, New York, 1981. In Hungarian: *A Magyar Holocaust*, Gondolat-Budapest, Blackburn International Incorporation, Wilmington, 1988) and Nathaniel Katzburg's analysis of official Hungarian policy towards the Jews and of the anti-Jewish laws (*Hungary and the Jews, 1920–1943*, Bar-Ilan University, Ramat-Gan, 1981). In Hungary it was especially Miklós Szabó who, tracing the origins of conservative political thought, published some important studies on these issues during these years (collected in a volume entitled *Politikai kultúra Magyarországon 1896–1986* (Political Culture in Hungary 1896–1986), Atlantis Program, Budapest, 1989). As an example of his balanced evaluations, I quote from an article on Dezsô Szabó, a most influential Hungarian writer and political thinker of the interwar period:

> [Dezsô Szabó's] greatest achievement is that he was able to write about social problems in a racist language without being dissolved in racism, the problems preserving their social character – unlike in Fascist racisms. This helped him work in both right and wrong directions. The wrong direction was that he gave a tool to racist ideologies, the right direction was that social problems presented in racist language could appeal to middle-class layers which could not understand any other language.

The fortieth anniversary of the Holocaust brought about a major breakthrough. Numerous publications came out, meetings and conferences were held, including an Israeli–Hungarian symposium about the Hungarian Holocaust. The most important publication was a book edited by Péter

Hanák, the internationally well-known and respected author, on the history of the Austro-Hungarian monarchy (*Zsidókérdés, asszimiláció, antiszemitizmus* (The Jewish Problem, Assimilation, Anti-Semitism), Gondolat, Budapest, 1984). Among others, this volume included Bibó's and Száraz's above-mentioned works, a Communist scholar's and politician's article from 1946 (Erik Molnár, 'Zsidókérdés Magyarországon' (The Jewish Problem in Hungary)), and Péter Hanák's analysis of the assimilation of Jews in the Austro-Hungarian monarchy. The introduction to the book was written by a senior leader of the Communist Party, Imre Pozsgay. His position reflected the views of a number of historians (Iván T. Berend, Ferenc Glatz, Tibor Hajdu, György Ránki, Péter Sipos, Loránt Tilkovszky, etc.) who clearly differentiate between the conservative, right-wing, authoritarian interwar Hungarian regime and the Hungarian Fascists who came to power only after the German occupation of Hungary. The open Fascist rule after 15 October 1944 and the Holocaust in Hungary are not considered to be the unavoidable consequences of the anti-Semitic policy of Governor Horthy's regime, the thesis about the 'collective guilt' of all non-Jews is clearly rejected, but exactly for this reason the significance of personal decisions in critical situations is emphasized. At the same time Pozsgay's article shows the willingness of an influential group within the party to accept the party's responsibility for national unity without enforced assimilation of any type.

It was around this time that serious research programmes were started on the history of Hungarian Jewry mainly within the framework of the Hungarian Academy of Sciences, co-sponsored by the Hungarian-born American billionaire György Soros, who set up his foundation in Hungary in 1985. Important results of this work were summarized in a two-volume work edited by the Institute of Philosophy of the Hungarian Academy of Sciences (*Hét évtized a hazai zsidóság életében* (Seven Decades in the History of Hungarian Jewry) Budapest, 1990) or a publication of the Hungarian Statistical Office (*A zsidó népesség száma településenként 1840–1941* (The Number of Jews in Hungarian Settlements 1840–1941), Budapest, 1993). The most comprehensive scholarly work about the history of Hungarian anti-Semitism, however, was published by a German scholar, Rolf Fischer (*Entwicklungsstufen des Antisemitismus in Ungarn 1867–1939*, R. Oldenbourg Verlag, Munich, 1988 with a rich bibliography). This very well-documented book also supports the dominant view among Hungarian scholars of the topic: anti-Semitism has long-standing traditions in Hungarian political and intellectual life but the mass murder of Hungarian Jews could not have taken place without the German factor. Fischer goes even further: according to his view, the Second Anti-Jewish

Law (in 1939) 'endete jener Abschnitt der Geschichte des ungarischen Antisemitismus, der weitgehend aus den innerungarischen Verhältnissen erklärt werden konnte' ('terminated the period of the history of Hungarian anti-Semitism that could basically be explained by Hungarian domestic political factors'). The dramatic transformations of 1989–90, bringing about a complete freedom of thought, i.e. a political climate in which practically everything could be printed, opened the way for anti-Semitic views as well. The results of the free elections in 1990 and 1994 clearly proved that the number of the supporters of these often very loudly expressed anti-Semitic views is quite negligible. Still, a number of scholars felt the need to be alert. László Karsai, author of important monographs and source-publications on the Hungarian Holocaust, published an anthology (*Kirekesztôk* (Exclusionists), Aura, Budapest, 1992) which emphasized the continuity in the history of Hungarian anti-Semitism from the 1880s to the 1990s. A year later Karsai published another anthology of works by critics of anti-Semitism (*Befogadók* (Inclusionists), Aura, Budapest, 1993) showing the continuous presence of liberal, open-minded, tolerant views in Hungarian political and cultural life.

More recently, a number of younger scholars, born after World War II, have been carrying on extensive research on various aspects of the history of the Hungarian Holocaust (László Karsai, Judit Molnár, Tamás Stark, etc.). The results of their work are substantial contributions to the nation's coming to terms with the burden of the greatest tragedy in modern Hungarian history.

Notes

1. Very consciously I use the term Jewish Hungarians and not Hungarian Jews in order to emphasize that Jews – just as Catholics, Lutherans or Calvinists – are one of the denominations in Hungary and not a race or other segregated group.
2. Cf. e.g. Imre Kertész, *A holocaust mint kultúra. Három elôadás* (The Holocaust as Culture – Three Lectures), Budapest, Századvég, 1993.
3. Cf. Ellie Wiesel, *Against Silence. The Voice and Vision of Ellie Wiesel*, ed. Irving Abrahamson, New York, Holocaust Library, 1985.
4. Cf. the excellent study of Ferenc Pataki, *Bûnbakképzési folyamatok a társadalomban* (Scapegoating in Society), in id., *Rendszerváltás után:*

Társadalomlélektani terepszemle (After the Change of Political Systems: A Social Psychological Perspective), Budapest, Scientia Humana, 1993, pp. 83–126.

5. Quoted in *Zsidókérdés, asszimiláció, antiszemitizmus. Tanulmányok a zsidókérdésrôl a huszadik századi Magyarországon* (Jewish Question, Assimilation, Anti-Semitism. Studies on the Jewish Question in Twentieth-Century Hungary), Budapest, 1984, p. 18.
6. Gyula Szekfû, *Három nemzedék* (Three Generations), Budapest, Királyi Magyar Egyetemi Nyomda, 1920. Reprinted with an introduction by Ferenc Glatz, Akv-Maceneas, Budapest, 1989.
7. Oszkár Jászi, *Magyar Kálvária, magyar feltámadás* (Hungarian Calvary, Hungarian Resurrection), Vienna, Bécsi Magyar Kiadó, 1920. Reprinted Munich, Auróra, 1969.
8. Ibid. 154.
9. Passed by the Hungarian Parliament on 26 September 1920 as Act 1920:XXV.
10. Rolf Fischer, *Entwicklungsstufen des Antisemitismus in Ungarn 1987–1939*, Südosteuropäische Arbeiten 85, Munich, R. Oldenbourg Verlag, 1988.
11. Ibid. 156, 159.
12. Passed by Parliament on 29 May 1938 as Act 1938:XV.
13. Cf. György Ránki, *A németek szerepe a magyar zsidók elpusztításában* (The Role of Germans in the Destruction of Hungarian Jewry) *Az 1944: év históriája* (The History of the Year 1944) ed. Ferenc Glatz, Budapest, 1984, pp. 64–8.
14. Passed by Parliament on 8 August 1941 as Act 1941:XV.
15. Quoted by Péter Kende, *Röpirat a zsidókérdésrôl* (Reflections on the Jewish Question), Budapest, Magvetõ, 1989, p. 146.

–9–

The Meaning of Auschwitz: Anglo-American Responses to the Hungarian Jewish Tragedy

Tony Kushner

> One would think that in the last fortnight or so most of the members of the [British] Government would have been greatly preoccupied by these flying bombs. I can tell you that we have another preoccupation, to some of us a great preoccupation, and that is the dreadful situation in Hungary today. I cannot exaggerate the brutality of the Germans in Hungary . . .. What the Germans are doing is nothing less than setting up abattoirs in Europe into which are shepherded thousands of Jews. They are dispatched with the sort of brutal efficiency in which the Prussians delight. This is the biggest scandal in the history of human crime.[1]

> While assurances of 'warmest support and sympathy' have not been lacking, we have received little active cooperation to date from the British in connection with refugee rescue and relief . . .. There is, of course, in the British Government no really comparable agency [to the American War Refugee Board] whose function it would be to cooperate with us in concrete measures. While the absence of a comparable agency does not necessarily preclude active cooperation any more than the establishment of such an agency would automatically guarantee it, our experience with the British to date suggests that this absence of even the framework for cooperative action has been a real stumbling block.[2]

These two perspectives, articulated only a few weeks apart in the summer of 1944, reveal much about the tensions generated between Britain and the United States over the fate of Hungarian Jewry. They were, however, equally (if not more) concerned with the liberal reputation of both countries – especially in relationship to one another. The first was made by Brendan Bracken, the British Minister of Information (representing one of his few utterances during the war concerning the plight of European Jewry), and was made at a time of renewed allegations of British government indifference in this area. The second, a critique of British state responses, was made by the American government-sponsored War Refugee Board (WRB) which was formed in January 1944 with the explicit goal of carrying out a policy of rescue and relief and, through the Office of War Information, 'bring[ing] home to the people in Germany and the satellite countries our determination in this matter'.[3] Yet the differences that emerged between the governments of the two countries over the Holocaust in Hungary were in marked contrast to the near-trouble-free Anglo-American consensus that had grown with regard to helping the Jews of Europe since the Nazi rise to power. Moreover, the divergent paths taken by Britain and the United States in 1944 went beyond the worlds of Whitehall and Washington: the responses of American churches, trade unions, Jewish communities, media and public opinion as a whole were far more intensive than was the case across the Atlantic. This chapter highlights these differing responses but ultimately asks what Auschwitz meant to either society as the war in Europe came towards its bloody end.

I

That Britain would lag behind in its state and popular responses to the fate of European Jewry compared to the United States was far from obvious from the standpoint of 1943. Indeed, it was pressure from the Foreign Office and the Cabinet itself that led to the summoning of the Anglo-American Refugee Conference held in Bermuda during April 1943. The lead from the British government itself reflected demands from the population as a whole after the disclosures concerning the extermination of the Jews at the end of 1942. Pressure from Christian and Jewish bodies in Britain, the World Jewish Congress and the Polish government in exile culminated in the Allied Declaration of December 1942 and in turn led to public demands, channelled so ably by Victor Gollancz and Eleanor Rathbone, that something be done to 'rescue the perishing'. Nothing of this sort occurred in the United States at this time.[4] The contrast between British and American popular responses was acknowledged in February 1943 by those fighting for a radical change in American policy towards the Jews of Europe. The Committee for a Jewish Army of Stateless and Palestinian Jews, the so-called 'Bergson Boys', called for

> an all-out campaign to save European Jewry. We will spare no effort and have no rest until the American public will be fully informed of the facts and aroused to its responsibilities. We believe in the overwhelming power of public opinion, as the greatest, if not the only, power, in democracy. Governments in democratic countries like the United States and Great Britain can act only when they feel

> sure that they are backed by a powerful movement of public opinion. We plead with everyone to help and co-operate in this sacred campaign we have launched. Join in the fight – write to your Congressman, contribute to our work, so that this message may be carried to every city and hamlet in the United States *as is being done in Great Britain* [my emphasis].[5]

When such campaigning, with its particularistic message of saving the remnants of European Jewry, led to mass demonstrations in the United States during the summer of 1943, the State Department had no hesitation in blaming it on 'England, where certain emotionalists and impractical dreamers adopted it and shipped it on to Rabbi Wise and Goldman in New York'. It was somewhat ironic, therefore, that by the time public activities in the United States had developed momentum, those in Britain had almost faded away. Although suspicious of the apparent inertia following the Bermuda conference, British campaigners, organized through the National Committee for Rescue from Nazi Terror, believed they had little choice but to accept that all was being done that could be done on behalf of the persecuted Jews.[6]

Much has been made in recent scholarship of the divisions within British Jewry (and especially between Zionists and non-Zionists) with regard to rescue of the Jews in 1943. It would be misleading to deny that time, energy and money were not wasted because of clashes of ideology and personality in the first months of that year. Nevertheless, they mattered little in the sense that the British government from the spring of 1943 was impervious to all demands – public and private, angry and reserved – for changes in policy until the matter had been discussed with the Americans at Bermuda.[7]

It is easy to be cynical about the Bermuda conference and to see it as an excuse for inactivity. But such an interpretation does not explain the full complexity of the event and the policies that were agreed between the two countries with regard to the Jews of Europe. Both British and American governments had no desire to appear unfeeling but they also wanted to keep the issue under control. Richard Law of the Foreign Office summarized the situation neatly in September 1943: 'the persistent propaganda of large-scale "rescue" remains as unreal as ever, short of victory. Nevertheless since the Bermuda conference distinct progress within practical limits has been made.' Yet when it came to the possibility of mass rescue in the case of Romania and Bulgaria, the Foreign Office, sharing the same view as the State Department, feared 'a quite unmanageable flood' of Jews. Instead, help and support in the form of transit visas to Palestine and neutral countries were given to small numbers of usually prominent, hand-picked Jews through the re-established InterGovernmental Committee (initially created at the Evian conference in July 1938).[8] This management of the refugee question in the summer and autumn of 1943 was successful in Britain. Public protests were shelved as British campaigners gave the government the benefit of the doubt. The net result, however, was that the persecution of the Jews lost any public or media prominence. By the end of 1943 the very real concern that had been articulated at the start of the year had dissipated; without a lead from the state or campaigners, the plight of the Jews lost its relevance to the fighting of the war as a whole. It became hard or unrewarding to identify with a people both physically and psychologically a long way removed from the British Home Front. Ignacy Schwartzbart of the London-based Polish government in exile reported in December 1943 – just a year after the Allied Declaration which outlined 'this bestial policy of cold-blooded extermination' – that stories connected to the Jews were now being 'dismissed as propaganda'. Nothing, as we shall see, was to change that pattern in the British case throughout 1944 and until the end of the war.[9]

II

Why was it, however, that in 1944 the lead in terms of rescue and relief for the persecuted Jews was to come from the United States government? This was far from predictable if the American record in 1943 is examined. In the vital early months of 1943 it was delay from the State Department which held up the response of the British government. Until Bermuda, American officials were still suspicious that pro-Jewish activists had somehow convinced the British government that urgent action was both necessary and feasible. Nevertheless, during and after the Bermuda conference and for the rest of 1943 there was relative harmony between the two governments on this issue (even if the State Department, and especially Breckinridge Long, appeared even more inflexible than the Foreign Office with regard to relaxing restrictions on Jewish movement and responding to information on the extermination of the Jews). The American immigration quota system and British policy with regard to Jewish immigration to Palestine were subjects that were generally avoided by mutual agreement.[10] But while public campaigning in Britain declined, it intensified in the United States in the second half of 1943. A range of American Jewish groups were joined by Christian and labour organizations in demanding action on behalf of the remnants of European Jewry. Pressure inside and outside of Congress built up but was steadfastly ignored by the State Department. Ultimately, however, the intransigence of the State Department (and especially its refusal to pass on the increasing evidence of the Nazis' extermination programme) proved to be the undoing of American official inertia. Henry Morgenthau, joined by non-Jewish colleagues within the Treasury Department, forced Roosevelt into action by threatening to expose the non-response of the American government and thereby indirectly implicating the President. As Morgenthau put it: 'You can't hold it; it is going to pop, and you have either got to move very fast, or the Congress of the United States will do it for you.' The net result of this near-blackmail was the creation of the War Refugee Board in January 1944.[11]

At first the British welcomed the Board, believing it to be a window-dressing aimed at wooing the Jewish voters of New York in an electoral year. British complacency was soon removed, however, when it was realized in the words of Sir Herbert Emerson, director of the Intergovernmental Committee, that its staff were 'young, able and keen. They feel they have a job of work to do and they have to do it quickly.' A sharper analysis, which confirmed all British fears, was provided by a British Treasury Department official: John Pehle, the Executive Director of the Board, 'feels that his first loyalty is not to Anglo-American co-operation nor to the British conception of a financial blockade but to the Jews in Europe'. By as early as March 1944 Anthony Eden reported 'serious differences of opinion between HMG and the United States Government over details of refugee policy'. These came to a head in the next four months over the fate of Hungarian Jews.[12]

British government strategy was to back the Intergovernmental Committee which was in favour of using practical, limited relief measures – primarily through credit payments to help Jews via postwar pledges of payment. This system meant that rescue measures could be controlled both in the cost and numbers involved. Moreover, it would involve no negotiations with the enemy or payments that contradicted the financial blockade of the enemy. This system was already in place through the Joint Distribution Committee and its agent in Switzerland, Saly Mayer. Throughout 1944, the British Cabinet Committee on Refugees used the existence of this system and other means to secure visas for a few thousand Jews – details that were endlessly reproduced to prove that not 'only the United States Government takes the refugee problem seriously'.[13] As soon as it became clear that the Americans were considering a more imaginative system with the use of licences to pay for goods for the relief of Jews in occupied countries, there were major objections from the Ministry of Economic Warfare. By March 1944 tensions were openly exposed and the War Refugee Board decided that whilst they would keep the British informed of what they were doing 'and to consider any objections they may have, we do not contemplate clearing our programs with them, as that has not been the procedure in this field in the past'. Indeed, rather optimistically, the Board hoped 'that the British Government would see fit to change its policy so as to conform with the policy this Government has been following in this field'.[14]

In early 1943, it was the American government that feared that its British counterparts had been influenced by unrealistic campaigners. A year later, when mass rescue of Jews in the case of Hungary now looked, from the Allied perspective, a distinct possibility, the tables were turned. The British state believed that the Board was peddling 'extravagant hopes' which could not be met. At the same time, however, there was a widespread fear that the Nazis could create a flood of Jewish refugees so as to embarrass the Allies. In the summer of 1944 the ambiguities in British government policy towards the Jews of Europe threatened to be exposed with the Hungarian Jewish crisis.[15]

In May/June 1944 the British Cabinet Committee on Refugees was presented with the notorious offer of Adolf Eichmann. In the proposals brought by the Hungarian Zionist, Joel Brand, Hungarian Jews would be released and swapped for goods including lorries and foodstuffs. The Committee wanted nothing to do with what it rightly saw as blackmail and there was great relief when it became apparent that the Americans also refused to take the offer seriously. The British government was wary of being embarrassed by the United States and told Washington at the time of the Brand proposals that it 'realised [the] importance of not [being] negative to any genuine proposals involving the rescue of any Jewish or other victims which merit serious consideration of the Allied Government'.[16] The test of this resolve was to come shortly after with the offer of Horthy to let the Jews leave Hungary. Eden and other senior British figures believed that *this* offer was genuine and that some response would be required. More than anything, its consideration was based on the possible consequences of hundreds of thousands of Jews flooding the Middle East and other British-controlled areas. The issue thus brought into sharp focus the differences between the Cabinet Committee and the WRB. The latter wanted immediate action taken, fearing that any delay would show a lack of Allied resolve. In contrast, the British wanted a more cautious approach – in the first place to consult the InterGovernmental Committee. They also warned that 'strong military reasons' should also be taken into consideration with regard to any rescue plan. In short, British universalism – winning the war at all costs – was at loggerheads with the particularism of the War Refugee Board – saving the remnants of Hungarian Jewry. After three weeks of delay the British Cabinet Committee finally consented and accepted the Horthy offer. By this stage, the Hungarians agreed to resume the deportations to Auschwitz.[17]

Was this delay crucial? Some campaigners, such as Eleanor Rathbone, believed it was. This, of course, is 'if history', but it is the significance of the British delay on its own terms that is important here. In essence, there was an absence of urgency about official responses in late July and early August which in turn reflected the lack of prominence the issue was receiving at both state and public level. In contrast, the response of campaigners in the United States was, relatively, far more dynamic. The forces of the churches and organized labour were mobilized and the War Refugee Board was far more up to date about developments. How are we to explain these differences?[18]

III

At its most basic level, the greater power of Jews in the United States compared to those in Britain might appear to be the key to unlocking this question. Jewish pressure was instrumental in the creation of the War Refugee Board and the vast majority of this agency's finance would come from American Jewry. In contrast, British Jews had neither the financial or electoral clout to worry their government.[19] Money and power politics are undoubtedly important but they are not enough to explain the huge divergences between Britain and the United States with regard to responses towards the Jews of Hungary. It was the willingness (even if it had been a reluctant one) of Roosevelt to accept the realities of ethnic politics that marked out the differences between the two countries. On the one hand, the British government would not accept the War Refugee Board because it was perceived as pursuing Jewish, anti-universalistic aims. On the other, the American government had to incorporate the Board into the state apparatus *because* of its particularism.

In terms of timing, the American campaigners were far luckier than their British counterparts. The latter saw their efforts climax with the Bermuda conference which brought little tangible reward. There was nothing to show for those who had identified with the persecuted Jews and demanded action to help them. In contrast, the growing public activities in the United States in the latter part of 1943 appeared to reach a speedy and successful fruition with the creation of a new official organization concerned only with rescue and relief and initiated by the President himself. Continued campaigning in Britain after 1943 brought with it the possibility of frustration, anger and demoralization. In contrast, the experience in late 1943 and early 1944 led in the United States to a far more optimistic outlook.

The paucity of the British response in 1944 is evident in many different spheres. Even the British campaigners on behalf of the Jews had failed to realize the enormity of the catastrophe by the summer of 1944. As late as August the National Committee for Rescue from Nazi Terror wrote that 'perhaps as many as 100,000 [Hungarian Jews] have already been exterminated by the Nazis' – in fact roughly one-fourth of those killed in the death camps by that stage. Yet less than two years before in December 1942, Eleanor Rathbone MP, the power behind the National Committee and a tireless campaigner on behalf of refugees, had prepared a speech to follow the Allied Declaration on behalf of the persecuted Jews of Europe. Rathbone wished to highlight that although much of European Jewry had already been wiped out and that 'the best we can now do will be too little and too late', it was still essential to see 'that even that little is not left undone'. Rathbone was clear where attention should be focused – the Balkan states:

> It should not be assumed that even Hitler's unwilling Allies – Hungary, Roumania, Bulgaria – cannot be influenced. In their treatment of their own Jews, these states have indeed a *Black Record* . . .. But by this time they must know in their hearts that the United Nations are going to win the War. They must be haunted by the fear of retribution . . . by showing a *reluctance to participate* in this last and worst of Nazi crimes – the extermination of a whole people.[20]

From a position of acute perception of the current situation and awareness of future dangers to the Jews of Europe, British activists were exhausted and demoralized by the summer of 1944 and beginning to get out of touch with the situation on the continent. In terms of public and private campaigning, much depended on the National Committee which ran on a tiny annual budget consisting of as little as hundreds of pounds. But so desperate had the situation got by the autumn that its executive was even considering the question of its continued existence.[21] Rathbone and the National Committee saw themselves in a no-win situation. Their power to embarrass the British government was minimal and they thus depended on the goodwill of the state. When it became apparent that one of the factors supposedly stopping the British government pursuing a more generous policy was the fear of domestic anti-Semitism, the National Committee put its scarce resources into a futile anti-defamation campaign.

In fact, anti-Semitism in Britain, as measured by the British government, was at its lowest war level in 1944. The situation in the United States was perhaps the reverse – hostility to Jews as measured by opinion polls peaked in that year but this did not stop a more open and innovative approach to the rescue and relief of European Jewry.[22] In Britain, anti-Semitism and Jewish difference were equated – the one the corollary of the other. Focusing specifically on the plight of the Jews or even granting them special status was anathema to the British state. Thus when the Chief Rabbi asked that Hungarian Jews be given a special status of British protection in the summer of 1944, the response was clear: 'it is not the policy of HMG to regard Jews as belonging to a separate category. It is felt that discrimination of this kind savours too strongly of the Nazi attitude towards Jews.'[23] There was little that campaigners felt they could do to break through these ideological restraints.

Although news of the Jewish plight in Hungary in early July 1944 created minor ripples of popular concern – the government's Home Intelligence unit reported 'Horror at [the Jews] treatment and sympathy with the victims' in July 1944 – there was nothing even approximating to the mass public demonstrations that occurred in the United States or had been witnessed in Britain eighteen months previously. Church leaders such as William Temple, the Archbishop of Canterbury, and trade union leaders such as Mr Marchbank of the Transport Workers' Union were encouraged to speak out on behalf of Hungarian Jewry, yet there was little or nothing in the way of grassroots campaigning as had been the case in late 1942 and early 1943.[24]

Much the same was true of British Jewish responses as a whole. Delegations to the government on behalf of European Jewry in the war had been marked by a sense of indebtedness and an unwillingness to embarrass the state. By 1944 this 'cult of gratitude' reached astonishing levels. On 26 July 1944 a delegation consisting of Jewish and Christian leaders was received by the Foreign Office. The delegation put forward suggestions aimed at saving the remaining Hungarian Jews most of which the Foreign Office rejected out of hand. It fell to the Chief Rabbi, Joseph Hertz, to offer thanks for the privilege of the meeting. Hertz ended by stating that

> because every one of us feels that nothing humanly possible will be left undone by H.M. Government, we assure you of the lasting gratitude of men with human hearts the world over. With these words, I wish formally to extend to you the warmest thanks of this deputation, for giving us so much of your immeasurably precious time, and for the sympathy with which you have listened to our representations.[25]

Hertz reflected the insecurity of British Jewry – frightened by the continuation of domestic anti-Semitism in the war, financially weak and worn down by the pressures of living on the Home Front (with the additional burden of having to worry about having a large percentage of its members in the Forces). Even so, the response of British Jewry at an institutional and popular level to the European Jewish crisis was particularly meagre. As the prominent Zionist Maurice Rosetté put it to the editor of the *Jewish Chronicle* at the start of 1944:

> In the matter . . . of saying that [Jewry] in this country has not done enough, I am unrepentant . . . Even Eleanor Rathbone has privately from time to time expressed amazement at the way in which we are dealing with the situation here.
>
> I am not at all in agreement with you that no appeal for money could have been made. You probably know . . . that there is work going on of which we cannot speak publicly, and whilst no one can pretend that it is saving large numbers of Jews, it is at least saving some, and it is done at the cost of enormous sums of money and prodigious human effort. Where is this money coming from? Either the Yishuv, at tremendous sacrifice, or even from the Joint in America. What have we done in this country to help? . . .
>
> As for public agitation, can we honestly say that we have done anything approaching even that which is being done in America, and I would not exonerate them entirely. The American Government has, however, moved and allowing for the fact that in some respects this is a political move, nevertheless it appears to mean business, and American Jewish opinion has played some part.[26]

In fact the chasm between British and American Jewish responses widened even further throughout 1944. Awakened to its potential power and with a growing sense of responsibility, some $20 million were donated to the American Jewish Joint Distribution Committee in 1944 for rescue and relief in Europe – double that of the preceding year.[27] In Britain, although emergency meetings were held with regard to Hungarian Jewry, there was little in the way of sustained campaigning from the major Jewish organizations. For example, the Anglo-Jewish Association (whose goals were to look after the needs of Jews in foreign countries) only mentioned Hungarian Jews in four of its meetings in 1944 and finally delegated the matter to the National Committee for Rescue from Nazi Terror in July 1944. In short, the British government had little to worry about in terms of pressure from Jewish and non-Jewish groups on behalf of Hungarian Jewry – its only major concern was criticism from across the Atlantic.[28]

IV

It is clear that the Holocaust in Hungary made very limited impact on contemporary Britain. Indeed, throughout 1944 the state-sponsored Royal Institute of International Affairs had published three-monthly chronologies of 'principal events' of the war. The fate of the Jews of Hungary was not mentioned once. The *Jewish Chronicle* in late June 1944 went as far as to say that the slaughter of Hungarian Jewry had 'passe[d] unnoticed'. Why was this the case? The *Chronicle* believed that 'Few cries of indignation are heard in this country, perhaps because the chords of human sympathy have been dulled or atrophied by sheer over-use.' A close reading of the responses of ordinary people in Britain reveals, however, that this was not really the case and that other explanations have to be found for the near-silence on Hungarian Jews.[29]

Indeed, what emerges in the first four months of 1944 is outrage at the stories of Japanese atrocities committed on British prisoners of war which, given official backing, received extensive media and parliamentary attention: 'What a terrible business this is about the treatment of prisoners of war in . . . Japanese camps . . . How one's blood boils at the indignities of the human beings, apart from the physical pain and degradation caused', to quote a typical example. Two factors are particularly noticeable in these British responses. First, there is a sense of despair – nothing can be done to help those suffering Japanese atrocities until the war is over. Second, a parochialism at work. These are 'our boys' and therefore in a different category from others suffering in the war.[30] The refusal of the British government to give the Jewish fate any great public prominence throughout 1944 made it hard to connect with the Jews – identification ran the risk of frustration. In the United States major public speeches were made by Roosevelt and Cordell Hull, Secretary of State at the State Department, on the destruction of Hungarian Jewry. In July 1944 Hull made clear that

> The entire Jewish community in Hungary, which numbered nearly 1,000,000 souls is threatened with extermination.
>
> The horror and indignation felt by the American people at these cold-blooded tortures and massacres has been voiced by the President, by the Congress and by hundreds of private organizations throughout the country . . .
>
> This government will not slacken its efforts to rescue as many of these unfortunate people as can be saved from persecution and death.[31]

There was nothing of this nature in Britain. The fate of Hungarian Jews was mentioned only five times in the House of Commons throughout 1944 and there was nothing approximating a full debate on the subject. The mood of the British government was summarized by the response from the Foreign Secretary to a question by the Jewish MP, Sidney Silverman, in early July 1944; Eden refused to give any detailed information about the numbers killed and confirmed that 'The principal hope of terminating this tragic state of affairs must remain the speedy victory of the Allied nations.'[32] Although the British press gave some prominence to the deportation of Hungarian Jews in the first ten days of July 1944, it is noticeable that the editorial tone was one of despair – postwar retribution was demanded rather than action to save the Jews now.[33] Those campaigning on behalf of the Jews had to make it clear to the British public as well as the state 'that something *can* be done'. In this they never succeeded. The dramatic narrative of the war with D-Day and the speedy if bloody military successes dominated all British considerations. In late June 1944, the National Committee for Rescue from Nazi Terror reminded its supporters that whilst for the common people of Europe liberation had started, the plight of Hitler's victims 'will become worse than ever before'. It pointed particularly to the reign of unmitigated terror in Hungary and that, according to the WRB, some 500,000 Hungarian Jews were 'threatened by deportation to an "unknown destination"'.[34] This process of the marginalization of the Jewish fate intensified through the summer of 1944. In August 1944 a meeting of the Intergovernmental Committee involving representatives of thirty-seven governments remained largely unnoticed by the British press. The National Committee concluded that although it was not surprising that the 'world-shaking' developments on the battlefields had grabbed the headlines, it was still 'a deplorable fact that the British public was not better informed as to the proceedings of a conference which . . . dealt with the problem of many millions'.[35] The official backing of rescue and relief campaigns by the American state, as well as the encouragement of the media by the WRB, meant that awareness of the fate of the Jews of Hungary was far more intensive in 1944 than was the case in Britain. Although it is true, as Deborah Lipstadt suggests, that American press interest waned in late summer, this occurred later than in Britain. Moreover, with the exception of the remarkable *Manchester Guardian* and, to a lesser extent, *News Chronicle*, British newspapers gave far less extensive coverage to Hungarian Jewry in early 1944 than their American counterparts.[36] There was simply less national attention in Britain given to the Jewish plight in Hungary whether it be from the government, press or public. Furthermore, Hungarian Jews in Britain, even when they were as prominent as the writer Arthur Koestler or the cartoonist Vicky Weisz, remained powerless individuals without the backing of communal organizations or a government in exile when it came to the rescue of their national co-religionists.[37] The Hungarian Jewish tragedy could be, and in fact was, very easily lost in bigger issues. Was this the case also with knowledge of the site of the murder of the majority of Hungarian Jewry, Auschwitz-Birkenau?

On 16 May 1945 a question was asked in the House of Commons whether any British subjects 'were confined in Aeschwitz [*sic*] camp in Germany'. The index to the debate adds on another layer of confusion by referring to 'Aeshwald'. Did Auschwitz have *no* meaning in the Anglo-American world by the end of the war?[38]

On 26 November 1944 the WRB published two detailed accounts of the camp by escapees from Auschwitz-Birkenau which corroborated the number of Jews killed there as over 1.5 million. News dispatches were carried in eighty-three American newspapers with a further twenty-four editorials devoted to the accounts. The eye-witness accounts received very limited attention in Britain – even in the Jewish press – continuing a trend throughout the summer of 1944 when other Auschwitz-linked reports received very limited attention (although they were quite easily available through Polish Jewish circles).[39] Yet even with the greater backing of the state and the press, the *scale* of the Hungarian Jewish disaster ultimately bypassed the public in the United States. Neither society seemed to comprehend the size or nature of the Nazi extermination programme. The Holocaust went beyond the scope of liberal imagining or explanation; no crime committed by the Jews could possibly justify Nazi actions. In a revealing editorial, *The Times* pointed out the *particular* unreasonableness of the persecution of the Jews in Hungary:

> In spite of a temporary outbreak of anti-Semitism after the brief Communist regime of 1919 most Hungarians were then averse to reprisals on a large, useful, and patriotic community for the misdeeds of a tiny minority; and it has been observed that in no continental country were Jewish assimilation and inter-marriage between Jews and non-Jews more prevalent. This circumstance adds to the disgust excited by the measures which are being carried out by the Hungarian Government.

Unable to face the irrationality of Nazi anti-Semitism (which threatened to suggest that *all* forms of antipathy towards Jews were unjustified), many people in the liberal democracies took solace in a form of denial. Thus, for example, in December 1944 the American public gave, as its most common response to a Gallup poll, the figure of 100,000 or less for those killed in the Nazi concentration camps and at the same point only 37 per cent of the British population felt that the atrocity stories were true.[40]

V

In conclusion, although this chapter has highlighted the differences between British and American responses in 1944 – relating this to questions of pluralism, national exclusivity, ethnic particularism and liberal universalism – their common ground should not be minimized. Although it is clear that Brendan Bracken was grossly exaggerating British governmental vexation over the plight of Hungarian Jewry in the summer of 1944, it was far from the case that this was a problem of obsessive concern within the American government. It is true that the WRB did see the plight of the Jews in Hungary as being their *raison d'être* throughout the year, but it remains the case that the vast majority of its funding came from American Jewry. Only $500,000 came out of official funds whereas the British government, in spite of all the criticisms levelled at it by the WRB, was willing to fund the Intergovernmental Committee to a tune of £1.5 million. The WRB, as Yehuda Bauer puts it bluntly, 'was an expression of moral and political support by the administration to save Jews with Jewish means'.[41] Nevertheless, such particularism, even if costing the American taxpayer little, would have been hard to imagine or realize in the British case. In the last count, if mass rescue of the Jews of Hungary proved impossible through Nazi intransigence, smaller numbers of Jews could be and were rescued and kept alive by the spending of quite spectacular sums of money. Thus in late June 1944, an appeal was made to the American Jewish Joint Committee that there was a 'possibility that an additional 8,000 persons c[ould] be rescued from the Balkans at an approximate cost of two to two and one-half million dollars'. Much of this funding was channelled through the offices of the WRB with the Intergovernmental Committee playing a far less significant role. Finally, although the WRB was justly proud of its efforts (it claimed to have saved between 100,000 and 200,000 Jews), it was aware that its efforts were 'too little and too late'.[42] Although effective in distributing resources in places where it was most needed, it still occupied an uncertain status within the American state apparatus as a whole. When it came to the question of the bombing of Auschwitz, whatever the problems involved in this complicated question, the respective Air Ministries of the British and American governments were unwilling to risk the lives of Allied forces in what was seen as an essentially non-military operation. In Britain there was no mechanism to channel sustained pressure on this issue and in the United States, even the WRB was powerless to change high-level state policy.[43] In both countries, therefore, the fate of Hungarian Jews was ultimately marginalized in the increasingly exclusive nationalistic atmosphere dominated by D-Day and the successful invasion of Europe. The meaning of Auschwitz and the specific Holocaust in Hungary was lost amidst wider universalistic considerations – just as it was to be generally forgotten in popular memory as the Normandy landing commemorations took place half a century later.[44]

Notes

1. Brendan Bracken at Brigadier Kirsch Memorial Committee luncheon, 6 July 1944, quoted by *The Times*, 7 July 1944 and *Jewish Telegraphic Agency Daily News Bulletin* (hereafter *JTA Daily News Bulletin*), 7 July 1944.
2. War Refugee Board, 'Weekly Reports', 29 May–3 June 1944: 'Relations With Great Britain', in David Wyman (ed.), *America and the Holocaust*, vol. 11, New York and London, Garland, 1989, p. 165.
3. 'Significant Activities of the War Refugee Board January 22–1 March, 1944', in Wyman, *America and the Holocaust*, vol. 11, p. 33.
4. See Tony Kushner, *The Holocaust and the Liberal Imagination: A Social and Cultural History*, Oxford, Blackwell, 1994, ch. 6; Eleanor Rathbone, *Rescue the Perishing*, London, National Committee for Rescue from Nazi Terror, 1943.
5. Full-page advert in *New York Times*, 8 February 1943; more generally see Monty Penkower, 'In Dramatic Dissent: The Bergson Boys', *American Jewish History*, vol. LXX (March 1981), pp. 281–309.
6. Department of State Visa Department, confidential memorandum, 7 May 1943 in Wyman, *America and the Holocaust*, vol. 2, New York and London, Garland, 1990, p. 266; on the decline of British campaigning see Tony Kushner, 'Rules of the Game: Britain, America and the Holocaust in 1944', *Holocaust and Genocide Studies*, vol. 5, no. 4 (1990), pp. 386–9.
7. See Geoffrey Alderman, *Modern British Jewry*, Oxford, Oxford University Press, 1992, pp. 304–5; *Sunday Telegraph*, 18 October 1992. For British Jewish internal divisions, see letter from Solomon Schonfeld in *Jewish Chronicle*, 29 January 1943. Calls for a rescue motion to be discussed in the House of Commons were repetitively refused by the government in spring 1943 – see the records of the Committee for the Rescue of Jewry in Nazi Germany in the Schonfeld papers, 153/1, University of Southampton archive (SUA).

8. Law, memorandum, 'The Refugee Situation', 3 September 1943 in PRO FO 371/36666 W12841; for a perceptive account of the flexibility within specific parameters operated by the Foreign Office see Anthony Bevins, 'British Wartime Policy Towards European Jewry', University of Reading Department of Politics, *Occasional Paper*, no. 5 (March 1991); Tommie Sjoberg, *The Powers and the Persecuted: The Refugee Problem and the Inter-governmental Committee on Refugees*, Lund, Lund University Press, 1991.
9. Schwartzbart in National Council Minutes of the World Jewish Congress, British Section, 13 December 1943, C2/279, Central Zionist Archives.
10. Sjoberg, *The Powers and the Persecuted*, ch. 4; Fred Israel (ed.), *The War Diary of Breckinridge Long: Selections from the Years 1939–1944*, Lincoln, Nebr., University of Nebraska Press, 1966, *passim*.
11. The origins of the War Refugee Board can be followed in Michael Mashberg, 'Documents Concerning the American State Department and the Stateless European Jews, 1942–1944', *Jewish Social Studies*, vol. 39 (1977), pp. 163–79 and in Morgenthau's diary entries reproduced in Seymour Maxwell Finger (ed.), *American Jewry During the Holocaust*, New York, Holmes and Meier, 1984, appendix 6, item 5.
12. Emerson memorandum on the WRB, JR 44 (12), 16 May 1944 in PRO CAB 95/15; Treasury official, 1 May 1944 quoted by Louise London, 'British Immigration Control Procedures and Jewish Refugees, 1933–1949' (unpublished paper, University of Bristol, History Research Seminar, February 1990); Eden, 7 February 1944, JR (44) 1 and 10 March 1944, JR (44) 4, PRO CAB 95/15.
13. 9th meeting of the Cabinet Committee on Refugees, 14 March 1944, PRO CAB 95/15 on the credit system; Eden, 29 June 1944, JR (44) 16, PRO CAB 95/15.
14. WRB 'Weekly Report', 6–11 March, 13–18 March, 1–6 May 1944, in Wyman, *America and the Holocaust*, vol. 11, pp. 38, 45 and 112.
15. Sir Herbert Emerson, 16 May 1944, JR (44) 12, PRO CAB 95/15.
16. PRO PREM 4/51/10/1394-5 and 3rd meeting of Cabinet Committee, 13 July 1944, PRO CAB 95/15.
17. Eden memorandum, 3 August 1944, JR 44 (21), CAB 95/15; Eden to Churchill, 14 August 1944, in PRO FO 371/42814 WR 682 and PRO CAB 65/43 WM 44 (104), 9 August 1944; R. Braham, *The Politics of Genocide: The Holocaust in Hungary*, vol. 2, New York, Columbia University Press, 1981, pp. 791–7.
18. Rathbone to Eden, 9 August 1944 in PRO FO 371/42815 WR 752 and meeting of National Committee for Rescue from Nazi Terror, 2

August 1944 in Board of Deputies of British Jews archive (BDA), E3/536 F1, Greater London Record Office.

19. Richard Bolchover, *British Jewry and the Holocaust*, Cambridge, Cambridge University Press, 1993; Finger, *American Jewry During the Holocaust*.
20. Mary Sibthorp, 'Half a Million Lives Can Be Saved', *News From Hitler's Europe*, 8 August 1944; Rathbone, speech notes (undelivered) for December 1942, Rathbone papers, XIV/3/85, University of Liverpool archive.
21. For its tiny budget see memorandum, November 1943 in BDA E3/536, GLRO; Chief Rabbi Hertz proudly wrote on 11 June 1944 to Victor Gollancz, a leading figure in the organization, stating that he had 'induced the Federation of Synagogues to contribute £100' to the National Committee. In Chief Rabbi's Emergency Committee Records (CREC), Hertz papers, 137/1, SUA; its threatened demise reported in the minutes of the Anglo-Jewish Association (AJA), 11 October 1944 in AJA records, 37/4/5, SUA.
22. Eleanor Rathbone, *Falsehoods and Facts about the Jews*, London, National Committee for Rescue from Nazi Terror, 1944; for levels of British anti-Semitism in the war see Mass-Observation Archive (M-O A): FR 1948 for 1941 and 1943 and 1944 report summarized in *Sydney Jewish News*, 5 May 1944; PRO INF 1/292, 18–25 July 1944 for the last Home Intelligence report on the subject; Charles Stember et al., *Jews in the Mind of America*, New York, Basic Books, 1966, pp. 79–80, 121 for its rise in the United States. See chapter 5 in this volume by Shlomo Aronson for further documentation about British government paranoia about domestic anti-Semitism.
23. For the response to the Chief Rabbi's request, see Foreign Office memorandum, July 1944 in PRO FO 371/42811 WR 457 and *Hansard* (HC), vol. 402, col. 1008, 28 July 1944.
24. PRO INF 1/292, 18–25 July 1944; Easterman of World Jewish Congress to Hertz, 7 July 1944 outlining action taken to secure publicity on behalf of Hungarian Jewry in CREC, Hertz papers, 139/6, SUA. For American activity see, for example, *JTA Daily News Bulletin*, 24 July; 1, 30 August 1944 outlining public meetings and petitions.
25. Notes of Hertz speech in CREC, Hertz papers, 139/6; see also Foreign Office minutes of this meeting in PRO FO 371/42812 WR 500. For the 'cult of gratitude' concept see Helen Fein, *Accounting for Genocide*, New York, Free Press, 1979, p. 185 and M. Tumin, 'The Cult of Gratitude', in Peter Rose (ed.), *The Ghetto and Beyond: Essays on Jewish Life in America*, New York, Random House, 1969, pp. 69–82.

26. Tony Kushner, *The Persistence of Prejudice: Antisemitism in Britain during the Second World War*, Manchester, Manchester University Press, 1989; Rosette to Ivan Greenberg, 23 February 1944 in Greenberg papers, 110/2, SUA.
27. *JTA Daily News Bulletin*, 3 July and 26 September 1944 and generally Yehuda Bauer, *American Jewry and the Holocaust: The American Jewish Joint Distribution Committee, 1939–1945*, Detroit, Mich., Wayne State University, 1981, ch. 17.
28. Anglo-Jewish Association General Purposes and Foreign Committee, 29 March, 13 April, 17 May and 13 July 1944 in AJA records, 37/4/5, SUA. For a more positive assessment of British Jewry and the Holocaust in the summer of 1944, see the comments of Donald Hurwitz of the Joint Distribution Committee reported in *JTA Daily News Bulletin*, 8 August 1944. Hurwitz commented that 'The terror bombings ha[d] not deterred the Jews of London; on the contrary . . . the added strain merely intensified their wish to aid others.' He added, however, that the major relief organization, the Central British Fund, was having to be reorganized – reflecting the fact that it had almost gone into obeyance in terms of rescue/relief work during the war.
29. *Chronology of Principal Events*, 1944 but see the accumulated and revised *Chronology and Index of the Second World War, 1938–1945*, London, Royal Institute of International Affairs, 1947, p. 276, which mentions Hungarian Jewry in passing – ironically Cordell Hull's declaration on the subject; *Jewish Chronicle*, 30 June 1944.
30. M-O A: D R5176, 29 January 1944; H5331, 31 January 1944; J5344, 29 January 1944; M5376, 28 January 1944; T5443, 28 January 1944; U5447, 29 January 1944; A5004, 1 February 1944 for reactions to the reports of atrocities committed on British prisoners of war by the Japanese. See also the parliamentary debate on the subject in *Hansard* (HC), vol. 396, cols 1029–35, 28 January 1944.
31. For Roosevelt see David Wyman, *The Abandonment of the Jews: America and the Holocaust, 1941–1945*, New York, Pantheon Books, 1985, p. 237; Hull declaration reproduced in WRB, 'Weekly Report', 10–15 July 1944 in Wyman, *America and the Holocaust*, vol. 11, pp. 247–8.
32. *Hansard* (HC), vol. 398, cols 1561–4, 30 March 1944; vol. 401, cols 1160–2, 5 July 1944; vol. 402, col. 1008, 28 July 1944; vol. 402, col. 1410, 2 August 1944; and vol. 404, col. 1380, 8 November 1944.
33. *The Times*, 6 July 1944; *Daily Telegraph*, 6 July 1944; *Daily Herald*, 6 July 1944; *Daily Mail*, 17 July 1944; *Daily Telegraph*, 17 July 1944; *News Chronicle*, 17 July 1944 and, for an overview of British

press coverage, *JTA Daily News Bulletin*, 7 July 1944 and 18 July 1944.

34. *News from Hitler's Europe*, 22 February, 20 June 1944.
35. Ibid., 22 August 1944.
36. Deborah Lipstadt, *Beyond Belief: The American Press & the Coming of the Holocaust 1933–1945*, New York, Free Press, 1986, p. 237 and ch. 10 on reporting of the Hungarian Jewish tragedy in general; *Manchester Guardian*, 25, 31 March; 14, 26 April; 1 May; 16, 23, 25, 27 June; 1, 4, 8 July; 5, 21 August; 12 October 1944; *News Chronicle*, 28 July, 31 August 1944.
37. Koestler's papers are deposited at the University of Edinburgh; Vicky Weisz's at the University of Hull. Count Michael Karolyi, former Premier of Hungary and leader of the exiled Hungarian democrats, did make appeals from London, but he was a figure of little influence in Allied circles – see *JTA Daily News Bulletin*, 19 July and 18 October 1944.
38. *Hansard* (HC), vol. 410, cols 2481–2, 16 May 1945 and vol. 412, p. 162, general index to November 1944–June 1945.
39. The report is reproduced in Wyman, *America and the Holocaust*, New York, Garland, 1990, vol. 12, document 1, pp. 1–64; its impact is covered in WRB 'Weekly Report', 27 November–2 December 1944 in Wyman, *America and the Holocaust*, vol. 11, p. 439 and Lipstadt, *Beyond Belief*, pp. 263–7. In contrast, *The Times* ignored the report and it received the briefest of mentions in *Zionist Review*, 1 December 1944, *Jewish Chronicle*, 1 December 1944 and *Jewish Standard*, 1 December 1944 (which simply reported its massive impact on American public opinion). Throughout the summer of 1944 the weekly *Polish Jewish Observer* (published by the local *City and East London Observer*) produced detailed eye-witness accounts from the death camps. Using contacts from the Polish government and Polish Jewish sources, it produced harrowing documentation from Auschwitz, Treblinka, Majdanek and other death camps. See, for example, the issues of 7 April, 16 June, August and September 1944, 6 October 1944. The national British press published little of this material. For rare exceptions see *The Times*, 8 July and 4 August 1944. It is significant that the latter article – on gas chambers – only appeared in earlier editions and was replaced with news items concerning battles in France and the impact of the flying bombs in London. For the contrasting American reporting, especially the *New York Times*, see Lipstadt, *Beyond Belief*, pp. 233–6.
40. *The Times*, 6 July 1944; George Gallup, *The Gallup Poll: Public*

Opinion 1935–1971, vol. 1: *1935–1948*, New York, Random House, 1972, pp. 472, 504; M-O A: FR 2228, April 1945.

41. 9th meeting of the Cabinet Committee on Refugees, 14 March 1944 in PRO CAB 95/15; Bauer, *American Jewry and the Holocaust*, p. 407.
42. WRB, 'Weekly Report', 26 June–I July 1944, in Wyman, *America and the Holocaust*, vol. 11, p. 228; Wyman, *The Abandonment of the Jews*, ch. 14 for an assessment and an overview of the WRB, including, p. 287, a later self-appraisal by its former leaders.

    The phrase 'Too Little and Too Late' was used by Dr Scherer of the Polish National Council in *News from Hitler's Europe*, 30 May 1944: 'these words are constantly ringing in my ears when I read about the creation of the American War Refugee Board or any other American, English, or even our own action'.
43. For the complex question of the possibility of bombing Auschwitz, see the articles by David Wyman and Martin Gilbert reproduced in Michael Marrus (ed.), *The Nazi Holocaust*, Westport, Conn., Meckler, 1989, vol. 9. Whilst it is true that there was no consistent demand for the bombing of the camp or the railway lines leading up to it from pro-Jewish campaigners, one of the reasons for this was the difficulty they had in reaching, with any urgency, those making decisions within the state bureaucracies in Britain and the United States. It was the marginality of the Jewish voice, rather than the rather nebulous concept of 'bureaucratic indifference' posited by several scholars, that explains the inertia of the state in this area.
44. It is ironic that although the Holocaust in British and American society received an enormous amount of media and popular attention in 1994 because of the success of Steven Spielberg's *Schindler's List*, the *specific* Holocaust in Hungary was almost ignored – especially in Britain where the conference which led to this volume was practically the only exception. Little attempt was made in the commemorations to make any link between the Normandy landings and the precise fate of the Jews in the spring/summer of 1944. There were, however, ahistorical claims that 'D-Day' was for contemporaries part of a 'just war' because of the Nazis' extermination programme – for example, the comments made by John Tusa on BBC1: 'D-Day Remembered', 4 June 1944. See, for a critical response to this approach, Kenan Malik, 'A Britain still at War with Germany', *The Independent*, 6 June 1994.

–10–

19 March to 19 July 1944 – What Did the Yishuv Know?

Dina Porat

One of the most painful issues, still troubling both historians and the public, especially the Jewish one, since World War II is: what did the Yishuv, the Hebrew community in the then Palestine, know, or rather care to know, about the fate awaiting Hungarian Jewry? It is most painful because the war on the Eastern Front was already nearing its end when the Jews of Hungary were being deported to Auschwitz: and because by that late date, German anti-Jewish policies were already known to the last detail, and the Zionist Yishuv, the pride and joy of many in the Jewish people – and not necessarily active Zionists – was expected to react in accordance with the severity of the situation. Hungarian Jewry counted at that time about three-quarters of a million. Together with the Bulgarian and Romanian communities, it remained the last substantial Jewry still living in Europe. Spring 1944 also marked the last chance for large-scale rescue and, perhaps, a last chance to bring a large number of Jews to Palestine, during the last stage of the war or in its aftermath.

Pain and emotional involvement have their impact on the research of the rescue efforts of the Yishuv. This is exactly why two introductory remarks are called for: the first has to do with the real weight the Yishuv carried during the war, and the second with the nature of the relations between Hungarian Jewry and the Yishuv.

After the war, the Yishuv became a state, whose mission it is to rescue Jews and serve as a haven. In retrospect, and only so, the importance of the Yishuv during the war, and its obligation to offer at least an image of a saviour, became central for the Israeli historical research and the general public debate. In reality, the Yishuv, a half-a-million community, lacked any military means and economic or political influence, and could do very little, *vis-à-vis* the German determination to carry out the 'Final Solution' and the Allies' scale of priorities in which winning the war came first. In the larger picture of the war and the Holocaust, the Yishuv could have left only a very small mark.

The second introductory remark concerns the relations between Hungarian Jewry and the Yishuv. Among Hungarian Jewry, very few, about 5 per cent, were Zionists, or involved in Zionist activity as sympathizers. Most others were orthodox, Neolog or assimilated. Similarly, Hungarian Jewry was not central to the life of the Yishuv: the majority of the newcomers to Palestine between the two World Wars, and their leaders, came from Poland and the Soviet Union, the very areas which later became the 'heart of the Holocaust', and were therefore identified in Palestine with the Holocaust. The Jewish Agency Joint Rescue Committee spoke Polish at its meetings; its bulletins dedicated an average of 17 pages to Poland and half a page to each of the other countries. This applied even to Hungary in June and July 1944, in the midst of the deportations from Hungary, which were already common knowledge at that date, and when in fact Polish Jewry did not exist anymore.[1] Soviet and Polish cultural influences were the most dominant in the Yishuv, and Hungarian Jewry was, all in all, something of a stranger to its life and ambience.

And still, since Zionism took upon itself to be the forebearer of the solution for the Jewish people, the question of how much was known in Palestine, and how the information was dealt with, carries a lot of weight, both emotionally and nationally.

Our issue here is the non-classified information which was open to the public, to every individual in Eretz-Israel, regardless of his occupation or political affiliation. Whereas the issue of the information accumulated by the Yishuv leadership has already been dealt with extensively,[2] our issue has not yet been researched and discussed. Before delving into this issue, let us suggest that the definition of information in our case means not only whatever detail became known about Hungarian Jewry during the war, but also the broader scope of knowledge and awareness of the mechanism and the stages of the German anti-Jewish system, which more or less repeated themselves all over occupied Europe.

A major source for our discussion has recently become available with the finding and acquisition of an extensive private collection of about 600 newspaper clippings, gathered between 1940 and 1944. The clippings were cut out of fifteen Hebrew and four Yiddish publications, representing the political spectrum from right to left, secular and religious circles, private and public organizations. Some of these publications are very hard, or even impossible, to come by nowadays. A second important source is the collection of the Joint Rescue Committee news bulletins.[3]

Based on these two main sources, the following questions will be addressed:

- Did the Hebrew community in Palestine and its leaders have ample, immediate, uncensored and uninterrupted information about the unfolding events in Hungary, before and following the German invasion and once the deportations started?
- Did the leaders know more than the public? Is it possible that the press discussed the issue more intensively than the leaders did?
- Did the leadership use the press, to leak or to block information, or to publish formal announcements, concerning Hungarian Jewry?
- Are the bulletins compiled by the Joint Rescue Committee (which was a formal organ of the Jewish Agency) a better source of information than the press?
- The possibility of a German invasion and its expected results were foreseen already in the summer of 1943. Did the press try to alarm public opinion before and after the invasion?

A thorough examination of the press leads to a clear-cut answer to our first question: the press provided the public in Palestine with a full picture of the events in Hungary. Moreover, the flow of information was mostly regular and updated, and came in uninterrupted by the British censor or any other factor. Let us first take a detailed look at the news and its implications.

During 1940 and 1941 there is hardly any mention of the situation in Hungary in the Hebrew press: about 7 entries in 1940 and 9 in 1941. Needless to say, during these years Hungary was still outside the eye of the storm, and was considered a haven for its own Jews and for Jews from outside. On November 1940 Hungary abandoned its neutrality, and joined the Axis. Yet, during the following months there was no discussion by the Hebrew press of the implications of such a major political step. It is only after the German invasion of the Soviet Union that a small number of news items – seven – addresses the grave situation awaiting Hungarian Jews, especially in regard to the threat to deport 120,000 Jews from Transylvania.

In 1942 about 45 news items were published, most of them towards the end of the year, from October to December. The formal announcement by the Jewish Agency Executive, published in all newspapers in late November, that a systematic annihilation of the Jews of Europe was taking place, led to a dramatically intensified awareness of the Holocaust in the

Yishuv, including the press. Most of the news that refers to Hungary at that time discusses the fate of the 200,000 Jews who were forced to join the hard-labour battalions, working close to the Eastern Front. One of the news items is accompanied by an evaluation: the measures exercised by the Hungarians with regard to this hard labour are an extension of the anti-Jewish extermination measures exercised elsewhere (*Davar*, 23.12.1942). This was perhaps the first time that such a gloomy possibility had been considered, and it could indeed be explained by the growing awareness in the Yishuv of the general German plan of extermination and of the idea that it might be adopted by other countries as well.

About 123 pieces of news about Hungary were published in 1943, most of them during the first eight months of the year. This is a perplexing fact, for it is towards the end of the year that the front got closer to Hungary, and the possibility of a German invasion became imminent.[4] A number of reasons could possibly account for this discrepancy between the actual severity of the situation and the intensity of its expression in the press.

First, during the first half of 1943 contradictory news, accompanied by contradictory evaluations, reached the Yishuv. Alongside titles such as 'Persecution of Hungarian Jews' (*Haboker*, 26.1.1943), and 'The Situation of Hungarian Jewry is Getting Worse' (8.3.1943), one could also read titles such as: 'Is the Hungarian anti-Jewish policy weakening?' (*Ha'aretz*, 10.2.1943), or 'Hungarians and Hungarian Nazis express objection to the persecution of the Jews' (*Haboker*, on the same day, 26.1.1943!).

At that stage still no editorials or commentaries on the situation in Hungary were being published, in any of the newspapers, and the views of the editor or the reporter were expressed almost exclusively through the wording of the titles. The only two exceptions – both in April and both full articles written by reporters in Istanbul – enhance the optimistic view: Hungary regrets joining the Axis, and will turn 'to the good side' at the first opportunity. And – the Nuremberg Laws cannot be implemented in Hungary.[5] The following months do not mark a change: 'Hungary will choose immigration as the most desirable solution, and will not deviate from the noble principles of Christianity' (*Davar*, 31.5.1943), The Nazi press complains: 'Hungary does not persecute Jews' (*Ha'aretz*, 25.5.1943), 'Protests in Hungary against anti-Semitism and the deportation of Jews' (ibid. 2 and 4.6.1943), 'The situation of Hungarian Jews is improved' (*Hamashkif*, 16.7.1943), and 'no persecution of Jews in Hungary' (*Haboker*, 3.8.1943).

The contradictory news and the optimistic view regarding Hungarian

Jewish policies prevented a more sober and realistic reading of the map, and the war-map at that given moment included not only the possibility of an invasion, but its consequences to Hungarian Jewry. Two newspapers even went as far as to come up with titles reading 'Hungarian towns convert to Judaism' and 'most of the Hungarian nobility is Jewish'! (*Hatzofe*, 17.6.1943 and *Haboker*, 12.7.1943).

A second reason explaining why the press published more about Hungary until August relates to the Holocaust and the prospects of the ending of the war as perceived by the press in Palestine in 1943. The press published more news about the Holocaust in general, because it started publishing more intensively following the Jewish Agency's announcement in late November 1942, and during the first part of 1943. Then the Holocaust was still a new and painful subject, which shook the community. However, during the second half of 1943 the Yishuv was already looking ahead, to the supposedly approaching end of the war, and to the solution of problems such as mass postwar immigration to Palestine and its absorption. Also, it should be admitted that news, all news, even the most horrible news, may become tiresome and repetitious. This may also account for the decline of interest in the Holocaust in general as well as in the plight of Hungarian Jewry. This dormancy explains the shock in the Yishuv caused by the 1944 events in Hungary. It was as if the Holocaust had already been dealt with and therefore taken off the agenda; and suddenly – such an affliction.

It seems that the reporters of the Yishuv in Istanbul, as well as its emissaries there, grew more sensitive to the changes in Hungary, which is geographically closer to Turkey, because they were caught in the middle: not too far from the Yishuv and its problems, yet closer than the Yishuv to European Jewry and its suffering. These reporters clearly expressed their feelings of concern and compassion, as well as their responsibility, as media professionals, towards all Jews, the Jews of Hungary included. Later in 1943, when warnings and pessimistic views became more frequent, the *Haboker* reporter in Istanbul asks: 'The deportation of Dutch Jews is completed, is it now the turn of Hungarian Jewry?' (12.7.1943). And another reporter, having cited Hungarian Prime Minister Kállay who referred to expulsion [and not to immigration, D.P.], tries to define the unclear impressions and contradictions prevailing in the Yishuv regarding the future fate of Hungarian Jewry: 'Hungary is a riddle . . . a country of contradictions . . . regarding the Jews as well.'[6]

In September 1943, the same pessimistic *Haboker* reporter in Istanbul is not only deeply concerned, he demands actions:

> Why is it that the leaders of the people are not present in the central rescue places [such as Istanbul] . . . the [German] system is the same everywhere . . . Hungarian Jews feel that the catastrophe is nearing, and cannot understand why the wall, all the walls, are not being pulled down . . . all signs show that when the Germans fail, they compensate themselves first and foremost with the killing of Jews . . . the leaders of the people and the Zionist movement should be the first on the scene of rescue.[7]

This was the first time in which the press published a severe criticism of the conduct of Yishuv leaders regarding the rescue of Hungarian Jewry. Also, this is perhaps the first clear mention of the fact that Hungarian Jewry did sense the catastrophe coming, and was aware of the possible consequences of a German invasion of Hungary a long time before it actually happened. It is noteworthy that in spite of such articles the editors of the Hebrew newspapers did not publish any editorials to this effect.

During 1944, 383 news items were published. They may be divided into three parts: January to 19 March (24 items), 19 March to 19 May (134 items), 19 May to the end of July (205).

At the beginning of 1944 the main trends of the end of 1943 continue. The concept that Hungary was a paradise still prevails, but the pendulum continues to swing between hope and pessimism. Newspapers still speak about 'Good new spirits in Hungary'. On the other hand, at least on five different occasions newspapers publish their estimation that the approaching front will change the existing rules of the game in Hungary, and that the change will have an immediate effect on Hungarian Jewry.[8] It should be noted that none of these were published by *Davar*, the organ of the dominant Mapai Labour Party. On the contrary, towards the end of 1943, *Davar* had already made an attempt to calm down its readers. Those who did try to alarm their readers were *Ha'aretz*, then a centre-oriented publication, *Hamizrahi*, issued by the religious Zionists, and *Mishmar*, the leftist opposition organ. Does this fact indicate a possible use of *Davar* by its party? This question requires further elaboration, and will be addressed later in this chapter.

From 19 March to 19 May 1944, between the German invasion of Hungary and the beginning of the deportations, there are many more news items in most of the newspapers, informing the public about every step taken by the Germans and the Hungarians against the Jews, and quite a number of estimations foresee each German step as preceding deportation and then extermination, according to the precedents in the other countries occupied by the Germans. From 19 May on, the newspapers react as if under shock. They publish a lot more, at a rate of 2 to 4 news items a day: 75 items in June, 121 in July, counting the eight major newspapers, and they give accurate details regarding the deportations, such as how many people were packed into one train-wagon, and how many trains left Hungary a day. It should be emphasized that the newspapers in Palestine did not mention the destination of the trains, because they still did not know it. It was only in July that year that the name of Auschwitz became known as a mass-murder location.[9] But they definitely repeated the certainty that deportations, to whatever destination, meant extermination.

A lot more than before was being published during these months. Two to four news items a day in eight newspapers put together makes for an average of more or less one piece of news every three days per newspapers; sometimes more often (*Hazofe* and *Hazeman* in July), and sometimes a lot less (the same *Hazofe* in June), and these were the months when the deportation of Hungarian Jews was a well-known and established fact. Moreover, about ten publications, most of them weeklies, generally serving as an organ of parties and institutes, did not publish during most of the war anything regarding Hungarian Jewry, and, in fact, regarding any other Jewry: they served for other purposes, such as a forum for the discussion of general political and ideological long-term issues, which troubled the parties and fractions in Palestine. Informing the public was a task fulfilled by the dailies.[10]

The number of news items per day or per newspaper is not a full indication of the attitude of the press or the attention of the Yishuv to the plight of other Jews: one should take into account other indications, such as the location of news in the newspaper page, the number of editorials and commentaries that accompany the news, the wording and the contents. Indeed, the contents of the news changed drastically: 'Now Hitler's sword of extermination will be turning over the heads of Hungarian Jews' is the wording of a title two days after the invasion (*Ha'aretz*, 21.3.1944). Three days later all newspapers carry editorials and commentaries (though not front-page titles), for the first time in the war:

> The Yishuv, together with the Jews of all countries, waits with increasing anxiety for news from Hungary . . . the Jews of Hungary could have helped themselves, by leaving Hungary on time, and now the chance is lost. We were too late to rescue Hungarian Jewry. And they know, even the most calm and tranquil among them know, with absolute certainty, and have no illusions this time. (*Davar*, 22.3.1944)

The Zionist reproach (had they left on time they could have been saved) is coupled here with guilt feelings (we were too late to rescue them), and with an acceptance of the coming fate (they know what awaits them). Once again it is publicly asserted that the Jews of Hungary know what is in store for them. Appeals to the leadership to act and grave question marks regarding the future of Hungarian Jewry are frequent as well.

The answer to the first question addressed in this chapter, regarding the availability of adequate current information on Hungarian Jewry during the crucial years of the war, especially 1943 and 1944, is, therefore, clear and unequivocal: the news was made available to the Yishuv. The sources of information were news agencies, radio, the European press, private and community sources, especially those provided by the Hungarian *Landsmannschaft* in Palestine and its activists.[11] Moreover, there is an explicit testimony of the editors of the major newspapers in Palestine that they could publish such news freely following the authorization issued by the British mandate authority and its censor. After the British victory at El-Alamein in October 1942, and certainly after the Allies' announcement in December that year, that a process of extermination of Jewish communities was taking place in Europe, most of the news was authorized for publication through an easy procedure. The editors also state that they were not called upon by the leadership of the Yishuv, or by the parties to which their newspapers belonged, to adopt any specific policy regarding the publication of news. They were given a free hand, to publish as they wished.[12]

Painful as it may be, one must admit that there is no indication that the leadership, regardless of political affiliation, had, or dedicated thought towards having, any kind of policy regarding the publication of news on this issue. The power of the press and its possible uses by leaders was not yet developed or appreciated as it is nowadays, especially not by David Ben-Gurion, then chairman of the Jewish Agency. One may say, then, that the fact that *Davar* tried to calm down the Yishuv towards the end of 1943 and did not publish any alarms at the beginning of 1944, while other newspapers did, has no special significance. Moreover, the number of news items, their wording and the formulation of the titles, their sizes and locations in the newspapers (generally not in a conspicuous spot), and the absence or presence of editorials and commentaries – these do not constitute indications of premeditated policies, but rather of the lack of such policies. In the long run, what counted first were the editors feelings and fears when facing the news from Europe.

Although this is not the main issue here, it should be said that the leadership too had all the necessary information on the situation of Hungarian Jewry. Examining the sources available to the leaders, beside the local press, of course, one sees a large volume of material accumulated in offices in Palestine, originating in four major sources: the European press, especially from the German-occupied countries, systematically collected by a Jewish Agency official in Istanbul, and stored in the Rescue Committee chairman's files.[13] Abundant material was sent by the Zionists in the Rescue Committee in Budapest, and by members of the Zionist youth movements in Hungary, who were all in constant contact with the Yishuv delegates in Istanbul, even after the German invasion. The material was transferred to the Jerusalem Rescue Committee files,[14] and to a central Labour Party office.[15] Additional sources were material from the Polish Government-in-exile in London and its office in Istanbul, transferred to the Jerusalem Rescue Committee by the Polish embassy there: and material decoded by British intelligence in Istanbul, and traded for other material with the Yishuv delegates. In other words, a substantial quantity of detailed information, accompanied by evaluations and commentaries from various sources, was available to the leadership shortly after the events took place: the information-gathering net, established by the Yishuv since the end of 1942, was improved throughout 1943 and could be better utilized in 1944, especially as long as Hungary remained a free country.

Our next question concerns the interrelation between press, public and leadership in Palestine regarding the information on Hungarian Jewry. It seems fair to say that such an interrelation did not exist. The press, representing the public, addressed the leadership, yet the leadership did not express its opinions and positions through the press.

The press, along with the public, on the one hand, and the leaders on the other, went their own ways, in parallel lines that did not meet. Appeals to the leadership to act, to be present 'on the scene of rescue', even severe criticism of the way the leadership handled its rescue policies, were not answered by any of the leaders, as if they did not read the newspapers at all. Not only was the news not censored in any way by the leadership, as mentioned above; no editorials or commentaries were required from the editors, no information was added by the leadership from its own many sources to what the press published. No mobilization of public opinion was exercised. It was only during the Brand affair itself that the leadership did not let any details leak to the press while the negotiations connected to the Brand affair were still in process. There is no written evidence of a specific request made by the leaders to the press to refrain from publishing details that might have come their way, or that the editors knew anything at all. But it is a known fact that two or three editors of the major newspapers such as *Davar* and the *Palestine Post* were frequently consulted on matters of national importance. Even if they were consulted this time as well, and even if they got some independent information on the affair from their own sources, responsibility and respect for the leadership's calculations were displayed in this case, and no leaking occurred between 19 May and 19 July, when the British authorities exposed it all.

One possible explanation for such a disregard of the press and of public opinion on the part of the leadership is that mobilization of public opinion by using the press is a concept that developed fully only after World War II. In the mostly socialist Yishuv, acting according to strict and austere values, a leader did not seek popularity or public attention. Leaders were supposed to do their job, and did so, regardless of what the public might have thought. Ben-Gurion's style of leadership in particular was one that did not take public opinion into consideration. On the contrary, he went on stubbornly with his decisions, even in contradiction of his colleagues' opinions. Also, leadership and public in the small, active and mobilized Yishuv did not form two separate entities: there were numerous second-line activists, mostly in the Kibbutzim, in the Haganah and the Histadrut, who knew each other and worked together in an exceptionally informal way. The fact that the small circle of the Jewish Agency Executive managed to keep the Brand affair secret for two months in such an ambience is all the more a credit to its members and a testimony to the importance they attached to the attempts to rescue at least part of Hungarian Jewry.

Did the leadership, or at least the Jewish Agency Executive, discuss the situation of Hungarian Jewry more than the press did, or earlier? The answer is in the negative: as we have seen, the press increased its interest in the issue and in 1943 and 1944 many more news items were published. From March 1944 on, it also became an issue for editorials and commentaries. On the other hand, the leadership, in its various organs, mentioned the Hungarian issue briefly and sporadically, but did not discuss it until 25 May, when the details of the German proposal Brand brought from Budapest reached Jerusalem via Istanbul. It should be mentioned again that the material and information that accumulated in the files discussed above could offer the leaders not only a detailed picture of the situation, but an insight into the way the Hungarian authorities were robbing the Jews of their rights and paving the way for the Germans. The swift taking over of Hungarian Jewry cannot be explained without what later turned out to be preparations, made before the Germans came, in legislation, confiscation of property, deportations and mass enslaving of the youth in hard-labour camps.

Why was the future fate of Hungarian Jewry not discussed in the meetings, prior to the Brand affair? Perhaps because the leaders assumed that Hungarian Jews were fully aware of their situation. At least, this is what could be clearly understood from the information coming to them from Hungary, information that surpassed by far that in the possession of the press. Yet the press, too, mentioned time and again that Hungarian Jews knew full well what was in store for them. How could they not know, when the year was 1944, when the murder of the Jews was known throughout the world, published by the BBC and the Allies, let alone Jewish institutes and news agencies? When Brand met Moshe Shertok, head of the agency's foreign department, in Haleb, he told him in not so many words: 'Hungarian Jews know today what deportations mean. They know it means extermination.'[16]

Survivors from Hungary vouch even today that they had no idea what the deportations meant and that they had never heard of mass killings. They regard the claim that they knew as an unforgivable insult to their dead, because it is an insinuation that Hungarian Jewry had the information, and still went to the trains passively, in such numbers and speed. Perhaps they did not know in the sense that the information did not become an internalized awareness, because human beings tend to believe that someone else, and not they, is endangered, even when evidence to the contrary is visible; because Hungary was free for so long, and because the quick German invasion was followed by even quicker steps taken against them, with the ruthless help of their neighbours and the authorities of their own country, which they still deemed theirs, so much so that they were taken by surprise and were helpless. Perhaps in Budapest the Jews knew and heard more, but in the more far-flung areas of the country, in the small towns, only the activists knew. This distinction between the Jews in the capital and the Jews in the provinces was not made in far-away Palestine, to which, as has already been mentioned, Hungarian Jewry as a whole was a stranger.

Whatever the answer, the Yishuv leaders did not assume that their task was to notify Hungarian Jews of what was already known to them. Although this issue is not within the scope of our discussion, it should be mentioned here that ten years later, during the Kasztner trial, the former Yishuv leaders, together with Kasztner himself, were accused of concealing the truth from Hungarian Jewry. In its ultimate verdict the Israeli supreme court absolved them completely of the accusation, emphasizing that in previous rulings the reality of the Holocaust period was not taken into account sufficiently or not properly understood. In other words, the supreme court expressed its feeling that the issue of knowledge and awareness during the Holocaust was too complicated to be judged in court in a clear-cut, superficial manner.

The fact that the Yishuv leadership did not discuss the situation in Hungary prior to the German invasion might also be attributed to the date we are reconsidering: the leaders were already preparing themselves for the approaching end of the war. 'The planning Committee' was at the height of its activity, was drawing maps, scenarios and charts, concerning immigration, settlement and allocations of resources, to take place after the war. Also, at that late date, the leaders had no more illusions, if they had had any before, regarding the determination of the Germans to kill, and the unwillingness of the Allies to rescue, especially in large numbers. There is no guarantee as to the amount of time each of them dedicated to reading through the files containing the material coming in from Hungary up until March 1944. Perhaps just a few of them did, and the rest knew the picture from the press and the radio. For instance, the Jewish Agency representative in Cairo warned British intelligence officers that on a radio broadcast the Germans spoke about the killing of a million Jews in Hungary.[17]

It is possible that they did not discuss the issue, not because they did not know enough about it, but, on the contrary, because they knew enough to realize that there was not much they could do. They certainly could not stop the invasion, or the German measures that followed it. They could have warned and raised their own and their public's voice, by using the press, in order to alarm world public opinion, but they doubted the results, given the meagre response of the Allies so far.

Despite all the aforesaid, this same leadership changed its course completely when the details of the Brand affair reached it via an emissary who came from Istanbul. Since then, top leaders such as Moshe Shertok, head of the Agency's foreign department, Haim Weizman, president of the World Zionist Organization, and Ben-Gurion himself, devoted their best efforts to the rescue of Hungarian Jewry. The condition made by Eichmann, that no Jews would be allowed to go to Palestine, and only Spain and Portugal could serve as countries of destination, did not have an effect on the Jewish Agency's readiness to struggle for the rescue of Hungarian Jewry. It is our conclusion, then, that the amount of public expression in the press, or otherwise, and the intensity of prior discussions of an issue are not indications of the readiness to act, even without hope of success, when crises come.

Notes

1. Bulletins of the Jewish Agency Rescue Committee, June 1944, pp. 12–29 are dedicated to Poland, and Hungary is referred to on pp. 2–3. July: pp. 9–25 Poland, and a third of p. 4 – Hungary.

2. On the issue of the Yishuv leadership see the bibliography in D. Porat, *The Blue and the Yellow Stars of David, the Zionist Leadership in Palestine and the Holocaust, 1939–1945*, Cambridge, Mass., 1990; and R. Streitman and S. Aronson, 'The end of the "Final Solution" ?: Nazi Plans to Ransom Jews in 1944', *Central European History*, vol. 25, no. 2 (1993), pp. 177–203.
3. The newspaper clippings collection is now in my possession. The bulletins collection was partly xeroxed in the Central Zionist Archives (C.Z.A.), and partly given to me through the courtesy of Mrs Landau, widow of Menachem Landau, member of the Rescue Committee Council.
4. See for example *Hazeman*, 25.12.1943, and *Haboker*, 12.11.1943.
5. Haimm Balzan of *Ha'aretz*, 9.4.1943, and Assaf Halachmi, of the same newspaper, 27.4.1943.
6. Chaim Dagan, *Ha'aretz*, 27.4.1943, and David Giladi, *Hatzofe*, 23.6.1943.
7. *Haboker*, 19.9.1943.
8. *Ha'aretz*, three warnings; *Hatzofe* and *Mishmar*, one each. Hopes: *Mishmar* and *Hatzofe*, one each.
9. On the question of when the function of Auschwitz became known to the Yishuv see Porat, *The Blue and the Yellow Stars of David*, ch. 9.
10. Six major examples are: *Ha'olam* (World Zionist Organization). *Hapoel Hatzair* (Labour Party), *Bama'ale* (Labour Party youth movement), *Kol Hapoel* (Poalei Zion, leftist section of the Labour movement), *Hadoar* (The Hebrew federation in the United States) and *Hashachar* (affiliation unknown).
11. Dr Avraham Wiessburg was the chairman of the Hungarian Immigrants Association. As such he maintained close contact with Yitzhak Gruenbaum, the Rescue Committee chairman, whose files (especially A127/545,6 in the C.Z.A.), show an extensive correspondence between the two.
12. See Haviv Cna'an, *The War of the Press; The Struggle of the Hebrew Press in Palestine against the British Authorities*, Jerusalem, 1969, pp. 144–52.
13. Files A127/545,6 in the C.Z.A. The official, Eliezer Leder, managed to get a lot of foreign press and information from the British and American intelligence offices in Istanbul, where Jews and Eretz Israelis worked.
14. See files S26/1190aa, ab, ac, in the C.Z.A.
15. Section 101/44 Vol. B, the Labour Party archives in Beit-Berl.

16. For the Brand–Shertok conversation see in 11.6.1944, S26/1251, C.Z.A.
17. M. N. Penkover, *The Jews were Expendable; Free World Diplomacy and the Holocaust*, Urbana and Chicago, Ill., 1984, p. 187. It should be noted that Penkover does not mention the name of the Jewish Agency's emissary in Cairo.

Acknowledgement

I wish to thank my student Haim Feirberg for his help in preparing this chapter.

–11–

Conclusion: The Holocaust in Hungary: Was Rescue Possible?

Yehuda Bauer

In order to examine the question of whether Hungarian Jewry could have been rescued in 1944, it is essential, first of all, to sketch the framework in which the Hungarian Jewish tragedy took place. I would like to start with a paradox. Hungary under the premiership of Miklos Kállay was seeking a way out of the war and had sent representatives to the Anglo-Americans in Italy and Istanbul and elsewhere, and the Germans were aware of this. It has been suggested that possibly the Allies encouraged the Germans in their decision to occupy Hungary on the eve of the Anglo-American invasion of Europe in order to divert German forces from the West. I have seen no documentation to support this claim, but even if the Allies had taken such a line, I doubt whether that would have had any effect on German policy: the Germans had their own very good reasons why they should activate Operation Margarethe, the occupation of Hungary. It would seem, from reading the Klessheim discussions that preceded the occupation, between Horthy and his team, and the Nazi leadership, that the Germans were genuinely worried about the possibility of a Hungarian withdrawal from the war. Defeated and dispirited as the Hungarian army already was, a Hungarian defection would have caused a real disaster for the German forces desperately trying to hold off the Soviet advance. The main reason for the occupation of Hungary on 19 March 1944 was the German desire to prevent the Hungarians from leaving the German alliance.

Was the Jewish issue part of the Nazi motivation? Again, that depends on one's reading of the Klessheim discussions.[1] I would suggest that the Jewish issue did play a part, and the Nazi leadership really thought that the presence of a Jewish influence in Hungary was at the back of the Hungarian attempt to surrender to the Western Allies. That thought was of course the result of a Nazi ideology that had led to the so-called 'Final Solution'. But it was a secondary motive, and it is doubtful whether the

Germans would have occupied Hungary if their obsession with the Jews had been the only or even chief motivation. What, then, is the paradox? The paradox lies in the fact that had Hungary remained a loyal ally of Germany, on the Romanian model, there may not have been a German occupation and the chances of Jewish survival would have been greatly enhanced. Not that there could not have been other developments that might have endangered the Jewish population, but in Romania at least it was Antonescu's continued, desperate, support of Germany that ensured the survival of the Jews of the Romanian Regat until the palace revolution there took place in August 1944. It was Kállay's policy of extricating Hungary from the war that brought disaster on the Jews.

The central question we have to deal with, I believe, is that of the options that the Jews had in a situation in which two main factors became operative. One was the presence of the German forces, mainly SS units, weak though they may have been, that occupied Budapest.[2] The second was the establishment of the Sztojay government, representing the most right-wing, pro-German elements of the ruling caste in Hungary outside of the outright Nazi Arrow Cross movement. It is perfectly clear, as Randolph L. Braham's monumental work has shown, that without the active and initiatory participation of the Hungarians, the deportation of the 437,000 Jews from the provinces to Auschwitz could never have taken place. But it was not only the gendarmerie under Laszlo Ferenczy that played a crucial part in the deportations of May–July 1944. The whole government machinery, led by the Ministry of the Interior and the two secretaries Laszlo Baky and Laszlo Endre, was mobilized to mark the Jews, despoil their property, prevent them from escaping, and prepare them for deportation and death by a system of concentration that was initiated by the Germans, but that was enthusiastically adopted by their Hungarian allies. There was, of course, a background to this. As we all know, the Hungarian governments of Bardossy and Kállay were not exactly Jew-loving. In August 1941, there took place the massacre of between 14,000 and 16,000 Jews at Kamenets-Podolsk (there was also the much smaller massacre of Serbs and Jews at Novi Sad). These were the results of Hungarian initiatives, to which the Germans agreed. Another Hungarian initiative, by General Jozsef Heszlenyi, in 1942, to deport 100,000 Jews from Hungary to Poland or the Ukraine was rejected by Eichmann, and the rejection confirmed by Himmler, because the SS wanted *all* Hungarian Jews, and refused to deal with them piecemeal. The question whether Heszlenyi's initiative was approved by Kállay or not puzzled the Germans at the time – Kállay's secretary at the Ministry of Defence, Gedeon Fay-Halasz, supported it – and I have not seen any convincing solution to the problem to this day.[3]

Another background element for the deportations was the issue of the labour battalions attached to the Hungarian army in which Hungarian Jewish men were forced to serve in lieu of regular army service. In effect, most young Jewish males served in these units, and that in itself made the option of resistance a near-impossibility. There were tremendous losses – probably about 40,000 men died in the Soviet Union in 1942–3, from starvation, disease, in minefields and through war action, in the most humiliating and inhuman conditions. This was not only a most severe blow to Hungarian Jewry before 19 March, but conditioned, it seems, Hungarian soldiers and officers, and one must suppose the general public as well, for a stand of indifference or worse when the whole Jewish population was threatened.

There was another, very major element in the situation, from the Hungarian side: the attitude towards the Jews of the overwhelming part of the Catholic hierarchy, and to a lesser extent of the Calvinists and the Lutherans, was one of radical theological anti-Semitism. The Catholic Primate, Justinian Szeredi, supported by most of the hierarchy, persevered in his anti-Semitic stance even against the interventions of the nuntius, the Italian Angelo Rotta, who may be recognized by Yad Vashem as a righteous person. The Calvinists attempted to persuade the Catholics to join them in a protest against the treatment of the Jews, but to no avail. They apparently did not dare to act alone.

The psychological preparation of the victim followed the precedent set in other European countries: the Jews were humiliated, cowed, terrorized, deprived of citizenship, of property, of status in the community. In Hungary these blows had a number of crucial aspects: first, they were sudden and dramatic, and left no time for adjustments or organization of any kind of resistance; second, and paradoxically, while the blows were sudden, they were not the first, and the previous attacks on Hungarian Jewry had prepared the ground for the final denouement. The Kamenets-Podolsk and Novi Sad massacres especially had made a deep impact on the helpless Hungarian Jews.

It is in this context that I would like to address, again, the crucial question of prior information about the mass murder of European Jews that had been going on for two and a half years before the German occupation of Hungary. The problem was raised first, I think, by many survivors who argued that had they known where they were being sent, they would have resisted or fled or hid. They accused the then leaders of having hidden the bitter truth from them, and the accusation was directed, again paradoxically, less against the *Judenrat* in Budapest, which in its make-up really represented Hungarian Jewry, but against the small group of Zionist activists, the Va'adah, led by Otto Komoly and Reszö Kasztner, whom no one had elected, who were really quite unknown, and who did not even represent all of the 5 per cent or so Zionists among the mass of Jews. That mass remained pathetically loyal to the Hungarian homeland and nation, whether they were neologue or orthodox. The accusation was picked up after the war in Israel by the right-wing intelligentsia opposed to the Labour government of the early 1950s, which was seen as the heir of the Left–Centre group that had stood at the head of the Va'adah. At that time, during the so-called Kasztner trial, the lawyer Shmuel Tamir, later a Minister of Justice in a rightist Israeli government, repeated these accusations and convinced a very large number of people of their truth.[4]

It is a fact, however, that a very large number of Hungarian citizens owned radios with which they could and did listen to BBC broadcasts in Hungarian.[5] The Jewish issue was certainly not at the centre of these propaganda broadcasts, but it was mentioned, in no unmistakable terms, several times during that period. It seems very unlikely that only non-Jews listened in, or that what was said in the broadcasts about Jews did not spread from non-Jews to Jews. Hungarian soldiers and officers returned for leave from the front, and the wounded were repatriated. They told their stories about what they had seen and heard in the Ukraine. In the summer of 1943, some 6,000–7,000 survivors of the Jewish labour battalions also returned, and they had seen and heard. The Kamenets-Podolsk massacres had become common knowledge among Jews. Between 1942 and early 1944, some 2,500 Polish Jews had managed to flee to Hungary from Galicia, via Subcarpathian Russia (PKR, Karpatalja) occupied by Hungary.[6] They told their story to people who were prepared to listen. Some 7,000 Slovak Jews had fled to Hungary in 1942, including a few hundred Polish Jews who had arrived in Slovakia in late 1941 and early 1942. They did not run away because they did not like the climate of the Slovak mountains, but because they had had information about the fate awaiting Jews in Poland. By the summer and early autumn of 1942, Slovak Jewry had received the information about the mass murders that were going on in Poland, and those who fled then came to Hungary with that information.

There may have been isolated villages or population groups who were really quite innocent of any possibility of information. But the evidence appears to be overwhelming that the information was available, not about Auschwitz and not about the details of the killings, but about the mortal danger that any deportation by Germans generally, and to Poland specifically, entailed. Information was, in other words, available about the murderous policy of the Germans. The problem was that people refused to listen, refused to believe that what they did not want to hear was the truth, refused to admit that it could happen in Hungary even if they admitted that it was happening in Poland – in short, they rejected the information, by and large. They then became easy prey to rather simple German tactics. When the Germans told them that they were being sent to labour camps, they believed it, in many cases one can say that they believed it eagerly, because it saved them from facing a life-endangering truth. Many Hungarian Jews had, or could easily have had, the information; but they did not have the knowledge, that is, the realization, that the information was correct, and that they should act accordingly. They behaved, as a group, and *grosso modo*, not unlike a patient with a terminal illness who refuses to admit his or her condition.

Part of this gap between information and knowledge, as I have repeatedly called it, was due, I believe, to the fact that if they had admitted that the information was true, they could have done very little to save themselves. By and large, there was nowhere to hide. By and large, there was no one to help them, from among the surrounding population. By and large, there was nowhere to run. And it is this that makes the mass reaction of Hungarian Jews so tragically understandable, almost inevitable. And when the end of the war came, and the poor traumatized remnants returned, first, to Hungary and then emigrated, most of them, to other countries, they refused to remember that they had heard about Poland, about Kamenets-Podolsk, and many, though by no means all, began looking for scapegoats.

All this brings me back to the problem of the options that Hungarian Jews had in this trap situation. I have just said that there was nowhere to run. Actually, this is not 100 per cent accurate. Attempts to reach the areas of Yugoslavia controlled by Tito's partisans indeed failed completely. But several thousands managed to flee to Slovakia in what was known among the Zionist youth movements as the *re-tiyul* (return excursion), almost all of them of course Slovak Jews who had fled to Hungary earlier on. 4,500 to 5,000 Jews, largely ultra-orthodox and Zionist youth, managed to flee to Romania, though many others were caught and shipped to Auschwitz – the Germans and Hungarians guarded the frontier very carefully.[7] For the 800,000 or so Hungarian Jews these were not realistic options.

The other option was armed resistance. In Poland and the Soviet territories, armed resistance was motivated by the desire for revenge, by the refusal to be killed without resistance, and was engaged in against the most awful odds. Ultimately, it was a form of protest engaged in by the few who could gain access to arms, for moral reasons. It usually led to or was accompanied by the mass slaughter of the population. The heroes of this fight, if they succeeded, fled into the forests. There, if they were not killed by Soviet or Polish partisans, they continued to fight the Germans. In Hungary, all this was an impossible scenario. There were no arms, and there could be no arms, because Jews had no access to them. There was no period of preparation because of the suddenness of the Nazi onslaught. The Jews were not concentrated, there was no support for such a course of action among the general population, and the Jews themselves, having been brought up as loyal citizens of a well-ordered society, were psychologically quite incapable of engaging in armed action against their Hungarian state that had become an accomplice in their murder. In addition, as I have already mentioned, most of the young men were in forced labour battalions.

Shlomo Aronson has termed this situation a trap, and I agree that this is a good way to describe the Hungarian situation especially. But the notion of a trap, like all such attempts at describing complicated situations in supposedly exact terms, may be misleading. The trap was not complete, not absolute.[8] And there was an option, which I think was realistic in part and illusionary in part, namely the option of negotiations. It was the partial success of the negotiations that enabled another option to become realistic, namely the option of partial rescue, in Budapest, in late 1944, by the neutrals and the Zionist youth movements.

By early 1944, Heinrich Himmler was prevaricating. He saw that the war was going badly for Germany. He knew that the conservative opposition to Hitler was engaged in some sort of anti-regime conspiracy, though he did not know the details of the actual planned assassination attempt against Hitler, and I suspect he didn't want to know too much. But if the Führer was to order, at some point, the exploration of possibilities for a separate peace with the West, or if the Führer was removed by the conservative opposition he, Himmler, would move in. In February 1944, Hitler had dissolved the Abwehr as the strategic intelligence service of Germany, and had handed over its functions to the SS, and its intelligence service, the SD, under Walter Schellenberg. The Jews, in Himmler's eyes, were obviously behind the Allied Powers, and it was quite logical for him to use the Jews who were in German hands as a means to reach the Jews of the West, and ultimately the Western Powers themselves, especially the United States. It was not the only venue he tried, we must remember. He agreed for Schellenberg to meet with an important American go-between, Abraham Hewitt, not a Jew, in Sweden, in late 1943. He was even trying, very tentatively, to use a Jewish Abwehr agent in Sweden,

Edgar Klaus, in an attempt to see what the Soviets were demanding in return for a ceasefire. In the spring and summer of 1943 he had tried, equally cautiously and non-committally, to see whether Jews could not be exchanged for German POWs in Allied hands, through the negotiations conducted by the British via the Swiss representatives in Berlin, the so-called Feldscher contacts. He was scared of his beloved Führer, but he was preparing the ground. Crucial in this was the agreement of Hitler on 20 December 1942 to exchange Jews for foreign currency, if such payment was really significant. All this, while the mass murder was continuing, and without losing sight of the ultimate aim of the Nazi ideology versus the Jews, namely their complete annihilation. But this aim was the *final* aim, and if Germany was in danger, then temporary compromises and zigzags in the implementation of what they called the 'Final Solution' were perfectly alright.[9]

The negotiations in Slovakia preceded the ones in Hungary. They had been even more tentative, from the German side, than the others I have mentioned. The Jewish leadership then, and in their wake Jewish historiography – I have to include myself in this criticism – have allowed themselves to be misled into thinking that the Nazi negotiator in Slovakia, Dieter Wisliceny, had offered serious proposals to the Jewish leaders, Gizi Fleischmann, Rabbi Michael Weissmandel, Andre Steiner and the others. In fact, all he had was the indirect agreement of Himmler, through one of his secretaries, that he should see what could be got out of the Jews in terms of money and contacts with the West. Eichmann, who one must assume was not very happy about this, was in the know. There were the details – the Jews should pay $2 million, with a first down payment of $200,000, and then the deportations from the West and the South-east would cease. These details were the product of Wisliceny's own fertile mind. He had received no instructions to offer and demand conditions from Himmler. But there *was* an agreement of Himmler to keep in touch with the Jews, and he would then see what should become of it, until he gave the order, in late August 1943, to stop all contacts. It is typical for the way Jews deal with the Holocaust that out of this there arose the well-known accusations that huge numbers of Jews could have been saved, if only $200,000 had been paid to the Nazis in 1943. By the way, almost all the money *was* transferred to Bratislava, in the summer of 1943.[10]

The Himmler initiative, via Eichmann, to Joel Brand to go to the Allies and offer Jews for trucks and other material, was a continuation of these Slovak contacts. This was in April 1944, as Himmler's awareness of some kind of a conservative plot was growing, and as the Allied invasion of the West became just a matter of time, as the Germans well knew. There is evidence to prove Himmler's direct involvement.[11] What I am equally convinced of is that the main mission, to Istanbul as it turned out, was not that of Brand. The main mission was that of his companion, Antal (Bandi) Grosz, a petty criminal and multiple agent of German, American, British, Hungarian, Polish, Japanese and Zionist intelligence services and groups. The SD had no contacts leading to the Americans, and would not dare to use a more respectable figure who could not be disavowed if the mission was prematurely discovered by rival German agencies. Grosz had all the ideal contacts and, yes, he could be disavowed easily, as Randolph Braham has pointed out a long time ago. His task was to arrange for a meeting between SD representatives and American OSS and/or British intelligence officers, in Switzerland. The purpose would be to discuss the possibilities for a separate peace. It seems that the idea was that if the direct approach through Grosz did not work, the Brand proposals might also lead to contacts with the West.

Ben-Gurion and Sharett (Shertok) in Palestine were quite clear about the import of the mission by 11 June 1944, that is, after a meeting between Brand and Shertok in Aleppo. I also think that they were fairly well aware of what we now call the trap. Their policy was to convince the Allies to conduct negotiations for the sake of negotiations, in order to gain time, providing the Germans stopped the murder while the negotiations were going on. If the Allies were not prepared to do this themselves, they suggested that Gustav Kuhlmann, the deputy director of the Intergovernmental Committee on Refugees headed by Sir Herbert Emerson, should do it, as this was not an official Allied agency; neutrals were also members, and Kuhlmann was a Swiss. If that did not work, the Jewish Agency was prepared to send a representative of its own to Hungary. And in order to avoid talking about trucks or other goods, which of course would be out of the question for the Allies, money would be offered, as my colleague Tuvia Friling has pointed out. Practical steps to this end were taken by the Agency and the JDC ('Joint'). I have here summarized policies that need a much greater elaboration, but this was the gist of the approach.[12]

Of course, there was a trap. Any independent Jewish attempt to rescue Jews by negotiations would run counter to declared Allied policy that demanded unconditional surrender and no separate negotiations about anything. Jews could be accused of betraying the Allies. Special Allied efforts on behalf of the Jews would be grist on the German propaganda mill which would present the war of the Allies as a Jewish war and possibly exacerbate already existing anti-Semitic feelings in Allied countries. A mass exodus of Jews from Europe, if offered by the Germans, could hardly be refused by the Allies, but it would in practice mean stopping the war, or at least Allied air attacks, as Allied aircraft could not attack railways while trains with Jewish emigrees–expellees–survivors were travelling through Europe.

The Jewish leaders also asked for the bombing of Auschwitz and the railways leading to it. That, as we know, was first sabotaged by British Air Ministry officials, and then referred to the Allied Chiefs of Staff in Washington, who had decided in January 1944 not to use military means for what they called 'civilian' purposes. The decision originally had nothing to do with the Jews, but it was now used to deny the Jewish requests.[13]

Yet, the trap was not as completely sprung as it seemed. The Americans were hesitant, and I at least have never found evidence that they received the full interrogation of Bandi Grosz from the British, so that they may not have been aware of the full import of his role in the Istanbul mission. It was the British Cabinet that on 13 July 1944 discussed the separate peace feelers of the SS, and it may be, subject to further research, that they did not want to let the Americans know what they had got out of Grosz. From 19 July, when the information about the Brand mission was leaked to the press in order to put an end to these German feelers, the policies of the two Western Powers diverged. The British would not have anything more to do with the Brand–Grosz mission, whereas the Americans were willing, in principle, to permit negotiations by non-Allied subjects that would be conducted to gain time.

What of all this was known in Budapest? Kasztner and Hansi Brand, Brand's wife who was actually the main motor of the Va'adah, tried to carry on the negotiations with the Nazis, obviously in order to save whatever they could from the disaster. What followed has all the marks of Heinrich Himmler on it. There were three competing SS agencies in Budapest, headed by men with the same rank of *Obersturmbannführer*, that are relevant to our story: Eichmann's *Sonderkommando*, charged with deporting the Jews to be killed; Gerhard Clages's SD command in Hungary, charged with intelligence work towards the Balkans and Turkey; and Kurt A. Becher's economic section, charged with despoiling Hungarian Jewish property in favour of the SS and economic policy generally. As Kasztner put it himself, the Germans were brilliantly organized: Becher robbed and Eichmann killed. It had been Clages who had sent Grosz; and Becher had been involved in sending Brand. In principle, Kasztner had little to offer to Clages, though contact was maintained. But Becher, who had the ear of Himmler, was approached for a continuation of the negotiations on an economic basis, despite the fact that Brand did not return.

Brand and Grosz had arrived in Istanbul on 19 May 1944. From the very start of the contacts between the Va'adah and the SS, emigration to Palestine was discussed. This developed, parallel to the Eichmann–Brand meetings, and continuing throughout June, into a German agreement to send a trainload of Jews to Spain, no longer to Palestine; that was, as we know, the origin of the famous Kasztner train. I think the testimony of Kasztner and Hansi Brand need not be doubted – what they wanted to achieve was, first, to break the finality, so to speak, of the 'Final Solution'; that is, by having a significant number of Jews escape to a neutral country to make it conceivable that the Germans might not kill all the Jews. Second, they hoped for a continuation of the process, and the escape of further trains, in exchange for money, goods or contacts. Kasztner had no inkling of the Hitler–Himmler conversation of 20 December 1942. But his talks with Becher were, to him, revealing, and he knew he was talking to someone who had a direct line to Himmler. The train, as we know, went to Bergen-Belsen, not to Spain, which was impossible in any case because of the Normandy landings. But the passengers ultimately were rescued into Switzerland, though no further trains were sent.[14]

The argument has been advanced, against Kasztner, that the price for the train, on which he also sent his closest relatives and friends from his hometown Cluj, was his agreement not to cause trouble for the Germans in their plans to deport Hungarian Jewry. Eichmann himself said so, postwar. I would not suggest that we rely too much on a fugitive Eichmann's rationalizations after the German defeat. Kasztner was a Zionist journalist, who had become a Hungarian citizen only after the annexation of Northern Transylvania by Hungary from Romania in 1940. He was completely unknown among Hungarian Jews, except for a small circle of people in the capital, and except for his hometown of Cluj. His impact, had he gone out to warn the provincial Jews, would have been nil. I have already discussed the refusal of many, or most, Hungarian Jews to admit the reality. But one has to add that such an effort to warn the Jews in the provinces *was* in fact made, by members of the Zionist movements, who were attached to the Va'adah, albeit in a somewhat problematic relationship. Some of these emissaries are still alive in Israel. Without a single exception, they were not listened to, and in some cases they were kicked out of their communities as *agents provocateurs*. In fact, according to Hansi Brand, she and Kasztner put their relatives on the train in order to convince the Jews that the train was not going to Auschwitz, as many feared. Some credence must be given to this argument, and as we know some people refused places on the train because of that fear. Indeed, when the train stopped on the Slovak border, the ultra-orthodox element on the train tried to reach a separate deal with the Nazis through pressure from abroad, because they thought the train would go to the gas chambers.

In late April, the first report on what was really happening at Auschwitz, by two Jewish escapees from the camp, Rudolf Vrba and Alfred Wetzler, was drawn up in Slovakia (they had escaped earlier in the month). In late May, this was supplemented by another report by two other escapees, Czeslaw Mordowicz and Arnost Rosin. The exact path of these reports has not been satisfactorily reconstructed. It appears that only in early June did the combined Auschwitz report reach the Horthy clique, via Hungarian underground circles and a member of the *Judenrat*, though the general content of the report had reached them earlier. It most probably had some impact on Horthy and his people; but what is clear is that it achieved a much greater impact in neutral Switzerland, which it reached about mid-June from at least two sources. Somehow it also reached Sweden, apparently in a shortened version.

This was the first time the free world had heard about the mass killings at Auschwitz (the information had been available from mainly Polish sources before, but was ignored as being basically unreliable. The fact that it was a camp where mass killings were taking place had been broadcast, in just one sentence apparently, in the spring of 1943.) Until then it had been, in Allied and neutral eyes, a huge labour and concentration camp, mainly for Poles. The Swiss press especially reported and commented on what the Germans were doing, despite Swiss neutrality. There was a parallel effect, though much weaker, in Sweden. The Vatican had received the information directly from its representatives in Slovakia. The intervention of the neutrals, the Swedes, the Swiss, the Vatican, the International Red Cross, and the American warnings transmitted to Horthy, in the latter part of June, against the deportations of Jews, were some of the factors that made Horthy intervene, from 26 June on, and that finally stopped the deportations in early July. There were other factors as well. The extreme right wing, represented in the government by Baky and Endre, and the gendarmerie, were planning an anti-Horthy and pro-Nazi coup. Horthy got wind of it and concentrated loyal army units in the capital. He was now ready to return to the Kállay line, and the continued deportations of Jews were no longer in his interest. In addition, however, the Hungarian counter-intelligence obtained a copy of a cable sent on 24 June, by Roswell D. McClelland at the American Legation in Berne to Washington, in which he repeated a request of 16 May by Rabbi Weissmandel of Slovakia to bomb the railways leading to Auschwitz. When, on 2 July, American aircraft bombed the Budapest railway station, Horthy saw in it a Jewish act of revenge. It was, as he himself said to the Germans, a factor in his decision to stop the deportations.[15]

Clearly, if Horthy stopped the deportations in early July, he could have stopped them earlier as well. There were no German troops of consequence in Budapest, and the Germans were otherwise occupied. Rescue was possible, and it seems that had information about Auschwitz arrived in Switzerland and elsewhere earlier and made the impression it did when it finally arrived, perhaps more people could have been saved. However, the Va'adah and Kasztner had really no influence on these events, with the exception perhaps of their problematic role in transmitting the Auschwitz protocols to the Hungarian authorities and the Swiss. Kasztner's opponent in the original Va'adah, Moshe Krausz, who by that time was living in the Swiss diplomatic compound, was a major figure in the story of transmitting the protocols to Switzerland.

The negotiations of Kasztner with Becher threatened to fizzle out, because Kasztner could not come up with a contact line to the West, after the failure of the Brand mission. Finally, it was his idea to involve a Swiss citizen, the representative of the JDC in Switzerland, Saly Mayer. The negotiations that started on the Swiss border between Mayer, and Becher, who represented Himmler, did rescue some Jews. It was due to these talks that the Kasztner train people were brought to Switzerland, in two batches, in August and December 1944. I have written extensively on these negotiations, and I believe that there is proof that they contributed to the fact that the Jews of Budapest were saved from imminent deportation to Auschwitz, in August 1944. If this is so, and I think it is, then the question no longer is whether rescue was possible at all, but whether more Jews could not have been rescued. Kasztner's role in all this, and the role of Hansi Brand who was advising, pushing and encouraging him, is crucial.[16]

The final stage of the Hungarian Jewish tragedy, the period of the Szalasi regime, from 15 October 1944 on, in a way presents the culmination of these developments. The Arrow Cross movement was a Nazi movement, aspiring to the total annihilation of the Jewish population. Eichmann, too, who had returned to Budapest, wanted to get rid of as many Jews as possible, and he eagerly seized on the need expressed by German military authorities in Austria to build fortifications on the Austro-Hungarian border. The November death marches of Budapest Jews, mostly women, the very young and the older men, were the result. In addition, men of the forced labour battalions were also directed to the border. There was a difference, however, between these marches and the completely senseless death marches that were to start in January 1945, and were designed to kill off as many people as possible: the Germans really needed a working force on the border, and when the completely exhausted Jewish men and women arrived there from Budapest, a few commanders, including some of the worst SS figures such as Rudolf Höss and Hans Jüttner, wanted to send them back because they were utterly useless.

At Himmler's orders the death marches were stopped around 27 November, and Becher was to claim credit for this after the war. There may have been some influence of the Kasztner–Becher team on this, because by that time Himmler was already openly and desperately looking for contacts with the West and the neutrals. A continued deportation from Budapest, in full view of the neutral representatives there, was hardly in his interest.

What is interesting is the domino effect of the situation in the Hungarian capital on the neutral diplomats. It started with the Swiss deputy consul Charles Lutz, whose activity in providing Jews with protection papers showed the way to the others. Also, more people were saved by Swiss papers than by the Swedish papers produced at the behest of Raoul Wallenberg. But it was Wallenberg, the dashing and courageous Swede, who captured people's imagination, and rightly so, because he went out himself and intervened personally on many occasions to save Jews. Lutz did so only a few times. Others, like the Italian Fascist, Georgio Perlasca, who pretended he was the Spanish consul, and Frederick Born of the Red Cross and others followed suit. A special role was played by the papal nunciature under Angelo Rotta, who stood at the head of the neutrals and negotiated with the Szalasi regime regarding the Jews, quite apart from playing his part in providing protection papers and protecting children's homes. It is interesting to see how the neutrals copied each other, not wanting to fall behind in the rescue operations. The reason for this is part political, part psychological, I believe. The war was nearing its end and the neutrals were increasingly motivated to take a stand against the losing Germans. The protection of Jews was a relatively easy way of showing identification with the Allied war aims as the neutrals understood them, and what I would call positive anti-Semitism also played a part: they really believed that the Jews in America were powerful, and that they had an impact on the American government, so help to Jews in Budapest would be a good idea. Undoubtedly, Rotta and Wallenberg and Lutz and Born and Perlasca were, as individuals, motivated primarily by a revulsion against Nazis, German or Hungarian. But they happened to fit into a political framework that became possible at the end of 1944.

All the work the neutrals did, however, would have been much diminished had it not been for the Zionist youth movements. It was they, Hashomer Hatzair and Noar Zioni and Dror and Maccabi Hatzair and

Bnei Akiva, who buried their factional differences, and organized to produce, first of all, massive forgeries of genuine protection papers. In addition, they forged large numbers of other essential documents such as identity papers, releases from forced labour, ration cards and so on. They supplied such papers also to the rather pathetic Hungarian resistance movement that sprang up at the time. When the ghetto of Budapest was established, they in fact took over the children's houses, and supplied them, as much as they could, with food, medicines and other supplies. They put their youth leaders in them to keep the children occupied – other youth leaders and counsellors came from other groups or volunteered as individuals – and they sent their young adult members, in Fascist uniforms, to rescue children from certain death at the hands of the Arrow Cross murder gangs. The Jews of Budapest faced several weeks of the most horrid starvation, disease and murder, before they were finally liberated by the Soviet army. Many of them died, and no neutrals and no Zionist youth could save them. But there is no doubt that without the Zionists and the neutrals many more would have fallen victim to Hungarians, Germans and the lack of food and warmth in the freezing houses.[17]

Finally, then, let me return to the question whether rescue was possible. The question, as I have indicated, is the wrong question, because the trap was not completely closed. Rescue, tragically partial as it was, did actually take place, and the major Jewish figures responsible for that inside Hungary were Kasztner and his group. The fact that Kasztner intervened in favour of Becher, Jüttner and other Nazis after the war to save them from Allied prosecution because they had helped him, for their own, very Nazi, reasons, will forever remain a very black mark on his record. Some of his other actions were also very problematic. His postwar claims, for instance his argument that he had been instrumental in rescuing a group of some 15,000 Jews, by having them transported for work to camps at Strasshof near Vienna, may be doubtful. Yet it is clear that he was involved in handing over the camp at Bergen-Belsen to the British without the Germans putting up a fight or destroying the camp, and that he tried his best to save other Jewish camp inmates in the last stages of the war. He did that in total disregard of his personal safety, at a time when he could easily have stayed with his family in Switzerland. He is, I think, a real-life hero, not your picture postcard one: not a person, perhaps, you would have wanted to spend five years on a lonely island with, a man with many faults, but – he tried to rescue Jews. How many of his critics saved the numbers that he was involved in saving?

The Germans may have been willing to sell Jews, but the Allies could not pay the price the Germans demanded. Yet, in that trap situation, negotiations were a way out, not for the rescue of the majority, to be sure, but for the rescue of some, maybe more than were actually saved. The key, however, was hardly in Jewish hands.

I must admit that I am deeply disturbed by much of the Jewish, especially Israeli, historiography on all that. There is a clear tendency to accuse the leadership of those days of responsibility for not rescuing more, and it is in many ways an accusation against the Jews for being responsible for their own murder. The religious interpretations tend towards this kind of self-accusation, claiming that the sins of the Jews caused God to send Hitler to kill us. They, and secular and liberal commentators, accuse Ben-Gurion, Weizmann, Sharett, Kasztner – the Jewish leaders of that time – of not having rescued their people from the Holocaust. This self-accusation is, I believe, the result of a trauma that is far from having been overcome, and is really quite unparalleled in contemporary history. I know of no other nation where similar self-accusations have arisen. Yet it is not really surprising; after all, the Jewish people lost one third of its numbers in the Holocaust. The attitude seems to be that we know that the Nazis murdered the Jews – but who really was responsible? In Hungary, it is Kasztner, or the pitiful group of traditional leaders under Samu Stern and Filip Freudiger called the *Judenrat*. They could have saved, but didn't, these historians or quasi-historians say. The terrible truth is that the masses were inevitably lost because the Germans and their Hungarian allies had total power in their hands, and no American, British, Russian or Jewish rescue team, no bombing of Auschwitz even, could have changed the overall picture.

Was rescue, then, possible? On a large scale, no. Did rescue occur? Yes, and in Hungary it actually achieved some limited results, due to the convergence of Nazi interests, Jewish persistence and some help by the bystanders. Could more have been rescued? I cannot be sure, but it may be possible. How? By utilizing the cracks in the trap the way they were actually utilized, only perhaps more so. It is time, I think, to desist from accusations, and to concentrate on explaining motivations, options, possibilities. That way we may be able to face the reality of the Holocaust, which is essential if we want to overcome the trauma.

Much too little has been said about Hungarian Jewry. Only my good friend and teacher in all this, Randolph Braham, and now, recently, a few others, have joined the fray. It was a great Jewry, it produced great minds and action-minded people. Most of them were murdered with the active help or through the passivity of their non-Jewish neighbours. Some were rescued. Let us remember them, and let us remember the Kasztners, the Krauszes, the Brands, the Komolys, and leave a bit of compassion also for the Sterns, Freudigers, Wilhelms and Petos. They hated each other's guts, by and large, as Jewish leaders mostly do, but most of them tried their best.

Notes

1. Randolph L. Braham, *The Politics of Genocide*, New York, Columbia University Press, 1981, pp. 369–70.
2. Eleven German divisions occupied Hungary, but most of them were removed very soon to participate in the fighting on the Eastern Front.
3. Randolph L. Braham (ed.), *The Destruction of Hungarian Jewry, A Documentary Account*, New York, World Federation of Hungarian Jews, 1963, vol. I, Docs 46–51, 74.
4. Shalom Rosenfeld, *Tik Plili 124*, Tel-Aviv, Karni, 1956 (Hebrew).
5. Donovan Files at the Military History archive, Carlisle Barracks, US, Box 90c, March 1943 report: there were, at that time, 822,000 licensed radios in Hungary, 88 per cent of which were capable of picking up Allied broadcasts. According to a Hungarian government survey of that month, 43.7 per cent of listeners in Hungary did listen to foreign broadcasts.
6. Braham, *Politics*, pp. 307–30, 700–8; Yehuda Bauer, *American Jewry and the Holocaust*, Detroit, Wayne State University Press, 1981, pp. 388–9; Braham, *The Kamenets-Podolsk and Delvidek Massacres*, Yad Vashem Studies 9, Jerusalem, 1973, pp. 133–56; Gila Fatran, *Haim Ma'avak al Hissardut*, Tel-Aviv, Moreshet, 1992, *passim*.
7. Raffi Ben-Shalom, *Ne'evaknu Lema'an Hachaim*, Tel-Aviv, Moreshet, 1977, pp. 49–73.
8. Shlomo Aronson, 'Die dreifache Falle', *Vierteljahreshefte für Zeitgeschichte*, vol. 32, no. 1 (1984), pp. 29–65.
9. Yehuda Bauer, *Jews for Sale?*, New Haven, Yale University Press, 1994, chs 7, 9–12.
10. Akiva Nir, *Va'adat Hahatzalah beKushta – Hakesher im Slovakia*, Paper at the Institute of Contemporary Jewry, 1989; and Bauer, *Jews for Sale?*, ch. 5. The total actually was \$184,000: \$131,000 from Palestine via Istanbul, and \$53,000 from Switzerland.
11. Braham, *The Destruction*, vol. II, doc. no. 291, Veesenmayer to Ribbentrop via Ritter, 7/22/44: 'Die Angelegenheit erfolgte auf geheimen Auftrag des Reichsführers SS.'

12. See my *Holocaust in Historical Perspective*, Seattle, University of Washington Press, 1978, pp. 94–155; and now, *Jews for Sale?*, chs 10–12. Tuvia Friling, *Istanbul, Juni 1944*, Iyunim Bitkumat Yisrael no. 4, June 1994, Beer-Sheva, Ben Gurion University.
13. Bernard Wasserstein, *Britain and the Jews of Europe*, Oxford, Clarendon Press, 1979, pp. 307–20, 349–50; David S. Wyman, *Why Auschwitz Was Never Bombed*, in: Michael R. Marrus, *The Nazi Holocaust*, vol. 9, Westport, Conn., Meckler, 1989, pp. 306–31.
14. See above, notes 9 and 12.
15. Bauer, *American Jewry*, p. 397; Braham, *The Destruction*, vol. II, doc. no. 187, Veesenmayer to Ribbentrop, 7/6/44.
16. Bauer, *American Jewry*, pp. 408–34.
17. Ben-Shalom, op. cit. (n. 7); Avihu Ronen, *Hakrav al hahayim*, Girat Haviva, Yad Yaari, 1994, *passim*. On Lutz, see Alexander Grossman, *Nur das Gewissen*, Wald (Switzerland), Im Waldgut, 1986, *passim*; and Braham, *Politics of Genocide*, pp. 1057–123.

Notes on Contributors

Shlomo Aronson is Professor of Political Science at Hebrew University, Jerusalem, Israel. His most recent publication is *The Quadruple Trap – Hitler, the Allies, Arabs and Jews.*

Jehuda Bauer is currently Chair of Yad Vashem's International Center for Holocaust Studies and Professor of Holocaust Studies at Hebrew University, Jerusalem, Israel.

Randolph Braham is Distinguished Professor Emeritus of Political Science and head of the Rosenthal Institute for Holocaust Studies, City University, New York, United States of America.

Richard Breitman is a professor in the History Department, American University, Washington, United States of America.

David Cesarani is Parkes-Wiener Professor of 20th Century European Jewish History and Culture, Department of History, Southampton University, and Director of the Wiener Library and Institute of Contemporary History, London, England.

Asher Cohen was Professor of History and head of the Strochlitz Institute of Holocaust Studies, Haifa University, Israel.

Yehuda Don is a professor in the Department of Economics and Director of the Institute for the Research of the Economics of Jewish Communities, Bar Illan University, Ramat Gan, Israel.

Tony Kushner is Marcus Sieff Senior Lecturer in the Department of History and Director of the Parkes Centre for the Study of Jewish/Non-Jewish Relations, Southampton University, England.

Dina Porat teaches in the Department of Jewish History and is Director of the Project for the Study of Anti-Semitism, Tel Aviv University, Israel.

Attila Pók is Deputy Director of the Institute of History of the Hungarian Academy of Sciences.

Robert Rozett is Director of the Library, Yad Vashem, Jerusalem, Israel.

Index